# FOUNDATION

# FOUNDATION

## B-Boys, B-Girls, and Hip-Hop Culture in New York

JOSEPH G. SCHLOSS

OXFORD
UNIVERSITY PRESS
2009

# OXFORD

UNIVERSITY PRESS

Oxford University Press, Inc., publishes works that further
Oxford University's objective of excellence
in research, scholarship, and education.

Oxford   New York
Auckland   Cape Town   Dar es Salaam   Hong Kong   Karachi
Kuala Lumpur   Madrid   Melbourne   Mexico City   Nairobi
New Delhi   Shanghai   Taipei   Toronto

With offices in
Argentina   Austria   Brazil   Chile   Czech Republic   France   Greece
Guatemala   Hungary   Italy   Japan   Poland   Portugal   Singapore
South Korea   Switzerland   Thailand   Turkey   Ukraine   Vietnam

Published by Oxford University Press, Inc.
198 Madison Avenue, New York, New York 10016

www.oup.com

Oxford is a registered trademark of Oxford University Press

Library of Congress Cataloging-in-Publication Data

Schloss, Joseph Glenn.
Foundation : b-boys, b-girls, and hip-hop culture in New York / Joseph G. Schloss.
    p.   cm.
Includes bibliographical references and index.
ISBN 978-0-19-533405-0; 978-0-19-533406-7 (pbk.)
1. Hip-hop dance–New York (State)–New York.   2. Hip-hop–New York (State)–New York.   I. Title.
GV1796.H57S34 2008
793.309747'1–dc22      2008029439

Visit the companion Web site at www.oup.com/us/foundation

9   8   7   6   5   4   3   2   1

Printed in the United States of America
on acid-free paper

# Contents

# Acknowledgments

This book is based primarily on my experiences in the New York City b-boy scene between 2003 and 2008. That community, like all communities, is built on relationships. This book, on every level, is a product of these relationships and the individuals who work to maintain them, and I would like to take a moment to offer my thanks.

One of the running themes of my work is that hip-hop did not "just happen," that it was the result of specific innovations and choices made by specific people in specific times and places. And even if we do not know—and may never know—all of their names and the exact nature of their contributions, we do know that they existed. So I would first like to thank all of the pioneers of hip-hop, both known and unknown, who created this remarkably complex and vital series of art forms.

Second, I would like to thank all of the b-boys, b-girls, rockers, deejays, and others who have spoken with me, on and off the record, about hip-hop dance. The individuals who are quoted here represent neither a statistical cross-section of dancers in New York, nor an exclusive list of the most significant b-boys and b-girls (though the list includes many I am honored to know). They are the people I have met as part of my experience. My relationship to each of them is slightly different from all of the others, and while everyone I spoke with was extraordinarily supportive and gracious, I would like specifically to acknowledge several of them.

MiRi Park, aka Seoulsonyk, has had a profound influence on this book as a friend, sounding board, reader, and consultant. While I accept full responsibility for any factual errors or general foolishness to be found in the pages that follow, her insight and critique has allowed me to substantially reduce both, and for that I will always be thankful.

Ralph "King Uprock" Casanova ran a free, open b-boying practice every Thursday afternoon in the gymnasium of P.S. 93 in Ridgewood, Queens, for much of the time I was researching this work. He also sponsored monthly battles in the same venue. These events provided a kind of home base for my research, offering me not only opportunities to meet people, but also a chance to establish continuity in my relationships with them. I am clearly not the only person who owes him a debt of gratitude, as there are very few contemporary b-boys and b-girls in New York who did not spend some time there at one point or another, benefitting from both his knowledge about rocking and his organizational skills.

One of the people I was honored to meet at one of Casanova's battles was the photographer Martha Cooper, who was one of the first outside documenters of hip-hop (the book that she coproduced with Henry Chalfant, *Subway Art* [1984], is considered not only a classic study of early graffiti but also a significant influence on the subsequent development of hip-hop culture). She soon became a friend, valuable critic, and connection to many of the more senior b-boys whom I was able to interview, including Alien Ness and Ken Swift. She also provided several of the photos for this book. Thanks, Marty!

The b-boys, b-girls, and others whose voices appear here are, of course, the heart of the book, and my appreciation for their help is boundless. My thanks go to Character, Phantom, Rob Betancourt, BOM5, Buz, Anthony Colon, DJ DV-One, DJ E-Rok, KaoticBlaze, Ken Swift, Kevski, GeoMatrix, Michael Holman, Eddie Luna, Mr. Supreme, Pedro "Pjay71" Martinez, Amigo Rock, Ru, Richard Santiago, Emiko Sugiyama, Tiny Love, Trac 2, and Waaak One. I would particularly like to thank PopMaster Fabel and Alien Ness, who have served as older brothers/gurus (a rare and underappreciated combination to be sure), helping me to understand the culture, challenging me when necessary, and keeping me going when my energy flagged.

In this project, there were a huge number of b-boys and b-girls whom I spoke with informally or briefly, but whom I was not able to formally interview due to time limitations. I would specifically like to thank Kwikstep and Too Sweet in this regard, and I apologize to any others who may fall into this category.

Beyond that, there have been a number of people whose advice, critique, and support have been essential to this manuscript. My editor at Oxford University Press, Suzanne Ryan, has been an ongoing source of energy, inspiration, and valuable advice, and I am deeply thankful. I would also like to thank Oxford's anonymous reviewer, whose thoughtful critique contributed substantially to both the tone and nature of this work.

Other individuals whose valuable insight have affected the specific content of this book include Lynne Fredricksen, Kyra Gaunt, Jocelyne Guilbault, Benson Lee, Benjy Melendez, Wanda Melendez, Elizabeth Mendez-Berry, T. J. Desch

Obi, Marc Perlman, Raquel Rivera, Francis Rodriguez, Grete Viddal, Oliver Wang, and Christie Z-Pabon.

People who have provided less specific, but no less important, insight into hip-hop culture and/or life in general include Bill Adler, Harry Allen, Adisa Banjoko, Howie Becker, Mike Beckerman, Jane Bernstein, Andy Brown, Jalylah Burrell, Garnette Cadogan, Dan Charnas, Lisa Coleman, Njeri Cruse, John Elstad, Sujatha Fernandes, Marcella Runell Hall, Mae Jackson, Imani Johnson, David Locke, Wayne Marshall, Ivor Miller, Ingrid Monson, Sarah Montgomery-Glinski, Matt Morin, Mark Anthony Neal, Dawn Norfleet, Deborah Pacini Hernandez, Lara Pellegrinelli, Holly Beth Plowman, Guthrie Ramsey, David Sanjek, Jay Smooth, Jason Stanyek, Chinua Thelwell, and Jessamyn West. I would particularly like to thank Jeff Chang, who has helped me to sift through many of the ideas in the following pages, and Joe Conzo, who provided an excellent photo of PopMaster Fabel.

Institutional support of both a material and spiritual nature has been provided by Tufts University, New York University, Baruch College of the City University of New York, the Experience Music Project, the Society for Ethnomusicology, and All-City Thinkers. And a special shout to all *Flavor* magazine alums.

Finally, my deepest thanks to my family tree: John and Suzanne Schloss, Sara Schloss Stave, Channing M.-L. Stave, and Stratton Stave, the b-boy of the future.

# FOUNDATION

# 1

# Introduction

Hip-hop is a problem. It is the cultural embodiment of violence, degradation, and materialism. Hip-hop is rappers exploiting women in videos and shooting each other in front of radio stations. Hip-hop is parties on $20 million yachts and Cam'ron claiming that he would never "snitch" to the police, even if he knew that a serial killer was living next door. It is a multibillion-dollar industry based on debauchery, disrespect, and self-destruction.

Yet, when I think of hip-hop, I think of shopping for rare funk records on a Saturday afternoon. I think of a 12-year-old girl defeating two older boys in a dance battle as her mother proudly videotapes her. I think of people from all over the world popping and locking in Manhattan's Union Square as the sun sets on a hot summer evening. I think of Zulu Nation founder and deejay pioneer Afrika Bambaataa wandering around a jam, happily taking pictures of random strangers—including me—as if we were his nieces and nephews.

That, to me, is hip-hop.

So why is the hip-hop I've been experiencing so different from the hip-hop that I see on television and read about in books? After all, it's not as if the hip-hop portrayed in the media doesn't really exist; it does. But hip-hop, as both a community and an art form, is far more heterogeneous than it is given credit for. Should that make its more troubling aspects immune to criticism? Not at all. If anything, hip-hop's conceptual diversity actually *encourages* criticism: that's what battling is all about. And just as it would be an insult to refuse to battle someone, it would be an insult to refuse to critique them. It would mean that you didn't take them—or their point of view—seriously. When it comes right down to it, the most sincere, most effective, most passionate critic of hip-hop has always been hip-hop itself.

But to understand hip-hop's powerful self-critique, we need to understand hip-hop *on its own terms*. Not only because it has interesting symbolic, political, and social implications (although they are important), not only because it confirms our theories about the work of art in the age of electronic reproduction (although that's valuable, too), but simply because the way hip-hop sees the world is itself a legitimate and consistent and fascinating intellectual system. And dance is a crucial part of that system.

For most people, "breakdancing" belongs somewhere between parachute pants and Rubik's cubes, a Reagan era fad that lingers only as a punch line, if it lingers at all. From that perspective, the idea that the dance could have a serious contribution to make to the discussion of hip-hop's influence in American culture may seem laughable. But to its adherents, b-boying (its correct name) is no joke. It is a profoundly spiritual discipline, as much a martial art as a dance, as much a vehicle for self-realization as a series of movements. "Ultimately, in so many ways, I just feel like b-boying is . . . a metaphor for life," says MiRi Park, also known as b-girl Seoulsonyk, a dancer and writer in her late 20s. "And the culture . . . is a culture that the world should aspire to be. . . . Hip-hop, just its ideology, allows you to be the best person that you can possibly be, which is not what I get from mainstream culture" (Seoulsonyk, interview). Even hip-hop's staunchest defenders may have to take a moment to digest such a statement. It is relatively easy to rationalize hip-hop as a necessary evil whose value lies primarily in its role as a diagnostic tool for the ills of America. But few would go so far as to say that hip-hop in and of itself can actually make you a better person. Few would say that America should not only accept hip-hop grudgingly as bitter medicine, but actually embrace and support it as something valuable for its own sake. So how can we explain this discrepancy?

A large part of the confusion is semantic. The term *hip-hop* is used to refer to three different concepts, which—although they do overlap—are distinguishable from each other. In the first sense of the term, hip-hop refers collectively to a group of related art forms in different media (visual, sound, movement) that were practiced in Afro-Caribbean, African American, and Latino neighborhoods in New York City in the 1970s. The term, when used in this sense, also refers to the events at which these forms were practiced, the people who practiced them, their shared aesthetic sensibility, and contemporary activities that maintain those traditions.

Perhaps the most important aspect of this variety of hip-hop is that it is unmediated, in the sense that most of the practices associated with it are both taught and performed in the context of face-to-face interactions between human beings. To some degree, this constitutes an intentional rejection of the mass media by its practitioners, but to a great extent it is just the natural result of the practices themselves. Activities like b-boying and graffiti writing are simply not well suited to the mass media. Although in both cases, brief attempts were made to bring these forms of expression into mainstream contexts (b-boying in a series of low-budget "breaksploitation" movies in the early 1980s and graffiti as part of a short-lived gallery trend around the same time), neither developed substantially in those environments. This, it has been suggested, was not so much because the forms lacked appeal, but because—on an economic level—b-boying was an advertisement with no product.[1] This reality is reflected in the phrase that is often used to refer to this branch of hip-hop: "hip-hop culture," which suggests something that is lived rather than bought and sold.

The second sense of the term *hip-hop* refers to a form of popular music that developed, or was developed, out of hip-hop culture. This hip-hop, also known as "rap music," resulted from the interaction between hip-hop culture and the preexisting music industry. As we would expect, this hip-hop features elements of both sensibilities. My students are often surprised when I point out that, even when hip-hop lyrics seem to reject every aspect of mainstream culture and morality, the one thing they almost never reject is a strict 16-bar verse structure derived from Tin Pan Alley pop music. But this should not be surprising. This hip-hop, in contrast to hip-hop culture, is deeply intertwined with the mass media and its needs, largely because it *does* have a product: records, CDs, MP3s, and ringtones.

Although the concept of hip-hop as popular music is commonplace now, it was far from self-evident that such a thing would emerge. It is often forgotten that hip-hop existed as a culture and performance context for at least five years (1974–1979) before it became a genre of popular music. For many in that era, the idea of hip-hop as a product was literally unthinkable. "I did not think that it was conceivable that there would be such thing as a hip-hop record," Chuck D of Public Enemy told writer Jeff Chang. "I could not see it.... I'm like, record? Fuck, how you gon' put hip-hop onto a record? Cause it was a whole gig, you know? How you gon' put *three hours* on a record?" (Chang 2005:130). Chuck D's comments point up the broad chasm between hip-hop as an experience (hip-hop culture) and hip-hop as product (rap music). It is worth emphasizing that I am making the distinction between "hip-hop culture" and "rap music" on practical grounds, not moral or aesthetic ones. The "rap music" category includes *all* commercially recorded hip-hop, both "mainstream" and "underground," from the most culturally uplifting to the most destructive.

Finally, the term *hip-hop* is increasingly used as a kind of loose demographic designation for contemporary African American youth, regardless of whether or not they have any overt connection to rap music or to other hip-hop arts. This is the sense of hip-hop that is evoked by such phrases as "hip-hop attitude" and "the hip-hop generation." Hip-hop, in this sense, is usually invoked to emphasize age and class over race when singling out young African Americans, either for praise or criticism. At its best, this makes social distinctions more precise without sacrificing their relevance to readers. Used more opportunistically, the term allows writers the freedom to generalize broadly without appearing to traffick in racial stereotypes.

The demographic sense of the term can be seen in a *Chicago Sun-Times* op-ed piece titled "Hip-hop Attitude Leads to Mayor's Downfall," in which hip-hop is blamed for the misbehavior of Detroit mayor Kwame Kilpatrick:

> Kilpatrick's real mistake was in believing the hype that is hip-hop. It's a culture stuck in perpetual teendom, where artists, trends and music constantly morph into new states of hipness to maintain credibility. To the extent to which this evolution creates better art, great. But the pressure, for example, for young girls to eschew their natural beauty in favor of the Lee-Press-On-Hair good looks of the newest video 'ho, well, there's something morally corrupt in that. That young men know droopy jeans originated in prison culture yet still embrace that look in the name of coolness is corrupt.
>
> Hip-hop has a jewel-encrusted veneer that covers some pretty rotten values. We see rappers surrounded by scantily clad women sipping Cristal by their pools, as flaunted on TV reality shows. We see a generation of young women determined to use their feminine wiles to get ahead instead of valuing the education they can put in their heads. (Oh, why is Flava Flav even a phenomenon?) We've even embraced a woman who once called herself SupaHead. Illegal drug use, marijuana, is encouraged. (Douglas 2008)

Similarly, in an online column, Jason Whitlock blames hip-hop for the lack of discipline among contemporary football players:

> Hip hop is the dominant culture for black youth. In general, music, especially hip hop music, is rebellious for no good reason other than to make money. Rappers and rockers are not trying to fix problems. They create problems for attention.
>
> That philosophy, attitude and behavior go against everything football coaches stand for. They're in a constant battle to squash rebellion, dissent and second opinions from their players.... What we're witnessing today are purposeless, selfish acts of buffoonery. Sensible people have grown tired of it. Football people are recognizing it doesn't contribute to a winning environment. (Whitlock 2007)

More positive versions of the demographic sense of the term *hip-hop* have been produced by Bakari Kitwana, who coined the term "hip hop generation" (Kitwana 2002), and Jeff Chang, who writes:

> Kitwana grappled with the implications of the gap between Blacks who came of age during the Civil Rights and Black Power movements and those who came of age with hip-hop. His point was simple: a community cannot have a useful discussion about racial progress without first taking account of the facts of change.... My own feeling is that the idea of the Hip-Hop generation brings together time and race, place and polyculturalism, hot beats and hybridity. It describes the turn from politics to culture, the process of entropy and reconstruction. It captures the collective hopes and nightmares, ambitions and failures of those who would otherwise be described as "post-this" or "post-that." (Chang 2005:2)

It is clear, then, that many misunderstandings about hip-hop stem from a confusion of terms, or perhaps a deeper confusion between the concepts that those terms represent. The three kinds of hip-hop—hip-hop culture, rap music, and hip-hop attitude/generation—are closely related to each other, but they are not the same thing. If, for example, one were to apply Douglas's sense of the term hip-hop ("scantily clad women sipping Cristal by their pools") to Seoulsonyk's comment above ("Hip-hop...allows you to be the best person that you can possibly be"), Seoulsonyk would appear misguided to the point of psychosis. In reality, however, Seoulsonyk (who holds an Ivy League graduate degree) is using the term *hip-hop* to refer not to a world of poolside debauchery, but to the discipline and aesthetic principles associated with a traditional form of Afro-diasporic competitive dance that she learned directly from one of its early practitioners, Richard Santiago. Taken in that context, her words seem entirely sensible.

I am *not* suggesting that any one of the three senses of hip-hop is inherently more legitimate than the others. Quite the opposite: hip-hop's strength lies precisely in the diversity of its concepts and practices. Trying to weed out the good hip-hop from the bad (or, more commonly, the "authentic" from the "commercial") sets up a loaded and almost completely useless distinction. And when that distinction is applied to scholarship, it can distort the work in any number of ways. The most obvious of these is the romanticism that so often accompanies the campaign for moral legitimacy in hip-hop. Academic scholars' tendency to ascribe the loftiest motives to the most mundane choices made by hip-hop practitioners is the main reason that most hip-hop scholarship is considered laughable by the hip-hop community. At the same time, this tendency has also created a kind of backlash. The fact that many academics have overstated hip-hop's profundity may tempt others to actually *understate* profundity where it really does exist, just to avoid being associated with academic romanticism. This tendency exerts a particular influence on works, such as this one, that attempt to address the unmediated, cultural aspects of hip-hop. Finally, the overemphasis on morality positions the good-versus-bad question as the defining factor in any individual or group's attraction to any given aspect of hip-hop. This, in turn, presumes that interest in certain aspects of hip-hop, and not others, is based primarily on moral grounds. Other possible motivations, such as personal aptitude or pure aesthetic appreciation, recede into the background.

As I have discussed elsewhere with regard to sampling, the disproportionate emphasis on questions of morality—positive or negative—in hip-hop has tended to distort its portrayal in both scholarly and popular writing:

> I believe that the main reason that the indigenous discourse is overlooked is that it is not primarily concerned with the issue that most sympathetic researchers are interested in: justifying the use of sampling. By this I mean that most scholars seem

concerned with demonstrating ways in which sampling, despite its rejection of live instrumentation, is consistent with more conventional value systems, whether those be social, political, musical, or otherwise. Hip-hop producers, by contrast, are rarely interested in such moves because for them sampling doesn't require justification on any grounds; it is the foundation of the musical form. (Schloss 2004:66–67)

Academic writers are often consumed with hip-hop's moral or artistic legitimacy, a pursuit that necessarily focuses on the relationship between the subject of their study and the standards of whatever outside authority the argument is appealing to. This naturally tends to downplay the artistic discourse going on *within* the community. While this is true for discussions of all varieties of hip-hop, it takes specific forms when it comes to b-boying.

Perhaps the most obvious of these is a hesitancy to focus on the body in discussions of the arts of the African diaspora, for fear of implying that the activity is not intellectual. While that fear is based on Eurocentric mind-body distinctions that have long since been debunked, the issue remains sensitive. As Kyra Gaunt has written:

The tendency to accentuate the "positive" (the *artistic*) and diminish the negative (*embodiment, sexualized dancing, unequal gender relations within black culture*) has led to fixations on the analysis of musical sounds and textures at the expense of the embodied and gendered social relations expressed in black music practices. (Gaunt 2006:7; emphases in original)

Another reason that the internal discourse of b-boying has been overlooked is that most academic hip-hop scholarship still operates within the framework of literary analysis and culture studies. Literary analysis naturally tends to emphasize forms of expression that are specifically concerned with the artistry of language, while culture studies tends to emphasize forms of expression that are deeply engaged with the mass media. Both naturally make use of modes of inquiry that are well suited to those areas of study, in particular the abstraction of processes into texts and their subsequent analysis as such. But this approach has two negative effects when it comes to studying the practice of b-boying. First, it puts the theory in the hands of the scholar, thus implying that b-boys and b-girls do not have their own theories about what they do, which is clearly not true. And second, in doing so, it relieves the scholar of the obligation to actually engage with the community. In the case of something like rap music, which is intended to be experienced by people who have no personal relationship with the artist, this may not be a substantial liability. But in the case of b-boying, which is intended to be experienced in person, such an approach can distort its subject to the point of invisibility. Unmediated hip-hop, by definition, cannot be understood without becoming personally involved in it.

In retrospect, it seems strange that I didn't become interested in b-boying until almost 20 years into my relationship with hip-hop. But then, on the other hand, why would I have? B-boying doesn't really exist in the mass media. Like most b-boys and b-girls, I was introduced to it by people I met along the way, and if I had never met them, I would probably still be largely unfamiliar with it. In fact, b-boying's unmediated character has profoundly affected its relationship to other aspects of hip-hop, in several ways.

Foremost among these, as I mentioned earlier, is its connection to the role of the body in the experience of other aspects of hip-hop. While many hip-hop scholars acknowledge the significance of dance and physicality, very few actually address the body in any depth (one notable exception, very influential on the present work, is Gaunt 2006). In reality, dance and movement are indispensable to the understanding of hip-hop culture, since physical movement underlies virtually every element of its expression. As I mentioned, this is part of a larger tendency among writers—scholarly and popular alike—to focus on the product of hip-hop over the process. This is primarily due to hip-hop's collision with the popular music industry in 1979. That interaction resulted in a mass-produced physical product, the rap record, becoming the most widely known aspect of hip-hop culture. In response, writers, critics, and scholars developed ways of looking at hip-hop that were designed to analyze a mass-media object. But those approaches tend to focus on the result, the recording, rather than the process that created it. The physicality inherent in that process—the way a producer moves as he hits the sample pads or nods his head when trying to "lock up" a beat; the way an emcee shifts her weight back and forth to the rhythm, emphasizing her words with broad slashes of her hands—receded into the background. But a more inclusive view of hip-hop shows the mind-body connection to be at the very core of its aesthetic.

An introduction to the practice of graffiti writing, for example, actually presents a series of yoga-like training exercises that students are expected to complete before even picking up a spray can:

> These exercises are suggested to all writers as a way of maintaining the body's painting abilities, and of keeping the essential painting body actively engaged in physical and kinesthetic activities related to spray-can use.... One must learn how to use the entire body for painting. The painting stance has often been compared with fencing. The body must be able to bend low, reach high, and make adjustments, all within the frame of its physical ability to do so. (Raven 2007:232)

And in his discussion of deejay battles, Mark Katz devotes a substantial amount of space to the deejays' movements:

> In addition to the verbal and instrumental aspects of a routine, the physical element can be just as crucial. Part of the appeal of a successful routine is the sight of the

swift and intricate motion of the DJ's hands; in fact, it is sometimes hard to appreciate the difficulty of a routine without seeing it.... To make their virtuosity clear to audiences and judges—and in fact, to make their routines even more demanding—DJs often employ what are called "body tricks." These moves do not—or should not—affect the sound of the routine, but add to its visual appeal and level of difficulty. This may involve spinning in place between beats, or scratching or juggling the records with the hands under the legs or behind the back. Sometimes DJs will use any part of the body other than the hands (which can lead to rather lewd gestures). Body tricks often act as self-imposed hurdles for the performer to overcome, though sometimes they're purely for show. (Katz 2004:126)

Since dance, quite naturally, is the aspect of the culture in which physical movement is the most thoroughly abstracted, analyzed, and realized, its principles in many cases can be productively applied to the physical aspects of other hip-hop arts. In fact, since beginning this project, I have started to make students in my hip-hop classes dance at the beginning of each meeting to the music we will be discussing that day. I have found that there are things that one can learn about a song instantly by dancing to it, which might take hours to articulate verbally. When you discover what kinds of movement can be performed to a song—and what kinds cannot—you discover a wealth of information about the social and physical environments in which it was intended to be heard, how the musicians viewed those environments, what their priorities were, and so forth. One of the most profound experiences I've had as an educator was when students in my spring 2007 Hip-Hop and American Culture class at Tufts University insisted on ending the semester by dancing together. I plugged in my iPod and dropped the sureshot "Scenario" by A Tribe Called Quest, as the entire class spontaneously formed a circle and students took turns in the middle showing off their best moves. The fact that, to this day, I am unable to articulate the power of that moment in words only proves my point.

Another area of hip-hop into which b-boying can provide deep insight is the role of competition and the specific ways it can affect one's outlook toward cultural production. This is an important factor in any discussion of hip-hop culture and one for which b-boys and b-girls have developed a highly sophisticated analysis. Battling is foundational to all forms of hip-hop, and the articulation of strategy—"battle tactics"—is the backbone of its philosophy of aesthetics. And, again, since these tactics are part of the process, and thus largely invisible in the final product, they are frequently overlooked. This is particularly the case as many battle tactics address the things one *shouldn't* do, strategies that leave one open to attack. But of course the casual observer can't see the things that an artist *doesn't* do, so those things—crucial as they may be—often go unnoticed. When Eminem first came to prominence, for example, several emcees told me that the most surprising thing about him was that he insulted his own mother, a move that was not only morally suspect but also the battle equivalent of forfeiting. The strategic avoidance of this subject on the part of other emcees, to my knowledge, had never been noted by any writers. B-boying, since its primary expressive environment is the battle, is more explicit than most other elements in articulating its battle strategy, at least if one is inclined to ask. Like its articulation of physicality, b-boying's articulation of competition can also provide a valuable perspective for other elements of hip-hop.

B-boying also illuminates another of hip-hop culture's most distinctive features: it was designed not only *for* teenagers, but *by* teenagers. The original hip-hop culture, taken as a whole, includes almost everything an adolescent could be interested in: music, dancing, sports, vandalism, fashion, various games and pastimes, art, sexuality, the definition of individual and collective identities, and numerous other activities. But what's even more striking is that, rather than leave these pursuits behind as they entered adulthood, many of these teens simply made them more elaborate and sophisticated as their mentality matured. The result is that the pioneers of this art form have been refining their aesthetic for upward of three decades, are still a vital part of the community, and are barely even in their 40s. During the course of my research in New York City, I regularly saw DJ Kool Herc at hip-hop events and enjoyed pointing him out to friends: "See that guy sitting on the picnic table over there? He invented hip-hop. No, seriously." The result is that young adherents who live in New York cannot help but have a deep sense of history, even if they don't consciously realize it. The vast majority of serious b-boys and b-girls in New York have studied directly with the elders of the art form, and even those who haven't are still affected by the presence of these individuals in their environment.

Waaak, a b-boy and graffiti writer in his mid-20s, for example, notes that one of his influences in rocking—a hip-hop dance form closely related to b-boying—was a mysterious, possibly homeless, man that he met one night while writing graffiti in Bushwick, Brooklyn:

So we're walking with the guy. We're drinking 40s.[2]...And we're talking. And we're walking down Knickerbocker Avenue, and he's like a old Spanish guy....And he's just blessing me with history on Bushwick, you know? He's blessing me with some stuff *I* didn't know.

And...he said something about dancing and we made some comment about rocking....So the guy hands my boy the 40, and he starts [dancing]. Next thing you know...the sun is coming up. We stop painting. And I stood on the corner with this guy, rocking with him for like a *hour*. You know what I'm saying? Like, some random drunk dude...I've never seen him in my life! But he was, like, doing some shit I'd never seen....I was seeing shit from this guy that was: "Oooooh, *shit!*" Like, "*What?*"

And the guy was being a little vague, and he wasn't giving too much [information]....He really didn't understand why or how important it was to me. But...[just] seeing him getting down. And seeing such a different rocking style from what I had been knowing the last three or four years, was incredible.

So, yo: New York. I'm fortunate enough to be in the right places and in the right time, and just, like, take these opportunities to build with these dudes. So I always tell the young kids nowadays, "Yo, talk to those elders. One day they're not gonna be there." Get that information. Get those jewels. You know what I'm saying? That's why they're there. (Waaak One, interview)

These kinds of experiences have, in turn, deeply affected the stylistic concerns of the New York b-boy community. The self-policing inherent in having the elders present has led to New York b-boying taking on a noticeably traditionalist approach, as compared to other b-boying communities around the world. Since the '90s, in fact, there has been an ideological split in the b-boy world between those who favor more acrobatic "power moves" and "air moves" and those who favor the more traditional, intricate, and rhythmic style. As a community, New York comes down firmly on the finesse side of the debate.

Of course, to even have such a debate in the first place, both sides must be in conversation with each other. In reality, New York is only one node of a community that is truly international. Dancers from around the world visit New York regularly, while b-boys and b-girls from New York routinely travel to other states and countries to compete, teach workshops, and judge competitions. Yet there remains a unique sense of history in the New York b-boy scene—a mixture of the past with the present—that does not exist in other places. For better or worse, this book is deeply informed by that perspective, starting with its title.

*Foundation* is a term used by b-boys and b-girls to refer to an almost mystical set of notions about b-boying that is passed from teacher to student. In addition to the actual physical movements, it includes the history of the movements and the form in general, strategies for how to improvise, philosophy about dance in general, musical associations, and a variety of other subjects. The idea that a core b-boy philosophy should be so important that it requires a special term says a great deal about the dance and why it is so significant in the lives of its practitioners.

In "'The Original Essence of the Dance': History, Community, and Classic B-Boy Records," I look at the role of music in preserving the dance's cultural traditions. Specifically, the chapter addresses what I have termed the "b-boy canon," a recognized repertoire of songs that b-boys and b-girls are expected to be able to dance to. I look at the many ways that the negotiation of such a canon—which songs are included and why, how specific musical figures encourage certain kinds of movement and discourage others, etc.—can create and define a community.

In the following chapter, "'Getting Your Foundation': Pedagogy," I address the relationship between the teaching philosophy expressed by b-boys and b-girls and the content that they transmit. Again, "foundation," a concept that combines the physical knowledge of specific movements with a profound historical and philosophical context in which to place those moves, is essential to the process. This chapter also explores the ways that gender is implicated in the teaching process and thus in dancers' identities. Finally, I briefly discuss the term *b-boying* itself along with some of the discourse in the community regarding the use of that term.

In the next chapter, "'We Have to Be Exaggerated': Aesthetics," I discuss the artistic principles of b-boying. Specifically, I look into the many ways in which the dance provides an opportunity to engage with social issues on a more abstract level than might otherwise be available. These include such areas as the choice of a b-boy or b-girl name, the way individual and group identities are expressed through clothing choices, and the aesthetic values and formal structures of the dance itself. The form of b-boying, in particular, provides a narrative structure that gives meaning to the specific moves. Each performer begins with toprock (rhythmic upright dancing that introduces a dancer's style and character) before dropping to the ground and engaging in footwork (disciplined, flowing moves that display rhythm, finesse, and creativity), power moves (displaying strength), and air moves (acrobatics). Each dancer's turn ends with a freeze, a concluding pose that summarizes his or her statement. Every time b-boys or b-girls return to their feet, they have made an assertion about who they are, and the group has accepted or rejected that assertion.

In the fifth chapter, "'In the Cypher': B-Boy Spaces," I address these issues with specific regard to the spaces in which b-boying has developed and takes place. This discussion includes exploration of the physical surfaces on which the dance has developed, the musical and spiritual environment in which it is performed, and the socially constructed dance space known as the "cypher." This term, drawn from the lexicon of the Nation of Gods and Earths (also known as the Five Percenters, an African American spiritual movement that developed in Harlem in the 1960s), refers to the circle of onlookers in which the dance is performed. While the concept of a circular, more or less participatory audience is found in many traditions of the African diaspora (and elsewhere), it has developed a unique character and set of associations in the context of b-boying.

The sixth chapter, "'I Hate B-Boys—That's Why I Break': Battling," concerns the most fundamental context for the dance. In looking at the ways that both the idea and reality of competition affects the lives of b-boys and b-girls, we can see the way that b-boying teaches specific skills for dealing with conflict in other contexts. In this chapter, I also take some preliminary steps toward looking at b-boying through the lens of recent work on the martial arts traditions of the African diaspora.

"From Rocking to B-Boying: History and Mystery" attempts to forge a critical engagement with b-boy epistemology by exploring the ways that b-boys and b-girls think about the history of their dance. In this chapter, I suggest that the b-boy community's model of historical inquiry is itself a kind of battle, based on the same principles as the actual dance battle: respect, personal honor, and giving credit where credit is due (as opposed to the kind of broad social analysis that one might find in an academic study). In order to explore this issue, the chapter focuses on a specific debate within the hip-hop community: the historical relationship between "rocking," a battle dance associated with Latinos in Brooklyn, and b-boying, whose origins are associated with African Americans in the Bronx. In so doing, I attempt to find ways to reconcile an academic approach with that of the community, as opposed to simply replacing one with the other.

Such reconciliations have implications for the study of hip-hop that go far beyond b-boying. Frankly, it is rare to see academic scholarship that takes hip-hop's own intellectual principles seriously (as opposed to taking hip-hop seriously as an *object* of intellectual inquiry). As I suggested earlier, this is primarily due to the fact that the vast majority of academic hip-hop scholarship has focused on commercial recordings of hip-hop music, a subject which does not necessarily require a substantial engagement with the intellectual principles of its creation. But for aspects of hip-hop culture where appreciation is bound up in face-to-face relationships, it is far more likely that the conceptual principles of the art will be articulated at some point. That has certainly been the case with my research.

Ethnography—participant observation—is the foundation of this study, and it has deeply affected the nature of my approach. I attended virtually every major b-boy event in New York City between 2003 and 2008, studying the dance both formally and informally. As in any fieldwork situation, the personal nature of my relationship to this community means that my quest for knowledge about its ways has also been very personal.[3] In other words, in addition to the general commitment to objective inquiry and self-criticism that should be part of any ethnographer's approach, I am particularly devoted to accuracy because the information is also important to me for its own sake. B-boying (to the limited extent that it can be practiced by a relatively sedentary, 40-year-old college professor) is a part of my life.

This book is based primarily on my experiences in a specific time and place, New York City in the early and mid-2000s. The people who are quoted here represent neither a statistical cross-section of dancers, nor a list of the most significant b-boys and b-girls. They are the people I have met as part of my experience. The nature of the way they are quoted, I hope, reflects this. Some are elders and teachers, some are contemporaries, some are friends. My personal relationship to the New York b-boy scene is also manifested in choices I've made about how to write about what I've learned. I have dealt elsewhere with many of the issues involved in writing about hip-hop, particularly the potentially jarring juxtaposition between my academic writing style and the transcriptions of my consultants' comments, which were delivered improvisationally and without preparation (Schloss 2004:11–12). I feel that the best way to address this issue is simply to point it out and to ask the reader to keep in mind that the differences that appear are primarily differences of style and expressive context. One thing that I especially love about b-boy discourse is the way it uses aggressive, raw, and often profane language to talk about the most abstract issues of aesthetic philosophy. This juxtaposition, as exemplified by Ken Swift in particular, is itself an important part of the b-boy aesthetic.

Perhaps the most daunting obstacles I've encountered in terms of writing are also the simplest: the terms *b-boy* and *b-boying*. As I discuss more extensively in the third chapter, the term is clearly gendered, which leaves a writer who wishes to refer to dancers of both genders with a substantial stylistic challenge. One option is to refer to "b-boys and b-girls" in each case, which can become unwieldy. Although I actually prefer this option and have tried to use it as much as possible, there is a point at which its repetition begins to overwhelm the other aspects of any given sentence. Another option is to use the non-gender-specific terms *dancer* and *breaker*, which I have also done, mainly in cases where I can no longer stand to repeat the phrase "b-boys and b-girls." The negative aspect of this choice is that these terms, while used in the community, are not the norm, and their overuse—to me at least—starts to read as ostentatiously gender-neutral, to the point of being judgmental. Also, of course, the term *dancer* doesn't refer specifically to dancers in this style, so its use here is imprecise. The final option is to simply use the term *b-boy*, with the explanation that this is widely viewed in the community as a generic term that includes women. While this may appear to be begging the question, I would argue that the ambiguity of the term reflects an actual social ambiguity: to what degree, and in what senses, is a b-girl a kind of b-boy?

Another significant issue has been the relationship between b-boy culture and ethnicity. Clearly, ethnicity and its expression through culture are major themes of most scholarly writing about hip-hop. But b-boying presents some complex challenges in that area, for several reasons. First, a central theme of b-boy ideology is that the culture is a meritocracy. The assumption of unbiased competition is the basis of almost all b-boy philosophy; the idea that such a competitive practice should favor individuals of one ethnicity over another runs directly counter to the ideals of the dance. Of course, this is not absolute: aesthetic ideals such as "flavor" and "soul" implicitly have a cultural element to them. As I will discuss, the expectations of b-boying clearly derive from an Afro-diasporic world view, but one need not be of African descent to understand or follow them. Moreover, even if that issue is put aside for the moment, the relationship between the African diaspora as a general concept and the influence of specific ethnicities is far from clear.

The conventional narrative among dancers is that b-boying was invented by African Americans, but was only popular in that community for a few years. By the late '70s, it had been adopted by Latinos, who became its primary practitioners. And, while the '90s saw an influx of dancers from a variety of ethnicities, Latinos remain by far the most dominant ethnicity in b-boying to the present day (at least in New York City). If, just for the sake of argument, we say that b-boying was invented and performed primarily by African Americans for 5 years, then developed and maintained primarily by Latinos for 30 years, which group does the dance really "belong" to? This question is significant not so much for its answer (I have no idea), but for the issues it raises: what does it mean for a dance to belong to an ethnic group? Why is it important that b-boying should be credited to one and only one ethnic group? If Puerto Ricans and African Americans are both peoples of African descent living in the same neighborhoods and participating in the same culture of hip-hop, in exactly what sense do they constitute different ethnic groups?

Part of the power of b-boying is that it complicates these questions; it has drawn its foundational movements and concepts from African American culture, the cultures of the English and Spanish Caribbean, and Africa itself. B-boying is truly and deeply a dance of the African diaspora. Even the music that gave birth to the dance is notable for its fusion of cultural elements drawn from both African American and Latino musical traditions, including Latin percussion and song structure, African American melodic and vocal techniques, and an overall aesthetic that speaks to the struggles and aspirations of urban youth of the early 1970s. And the fact that the musical soundtrack to b-boying is still primarily drawn from recordings produced between 1969 and 1974 suggests that this fusion—and the tradition it gave birth to—is still highly valued almost four decades later.

# 2

## "The Original Essence of the Dance"
### History, Community, and
### Classic B-Boy Records

I was introduced, basically, to James Brown, Jimmy
Castor Bunch, and the rest of my life listened to that
music and enjoyed that music and did the dance that
went along with it. . . . I believe it's important to learn
to that, to break to that, because that's the original
essence of the dance. It was inspired by that music. So,
I think, in order to have the original style, you would
have to be able to rock to that. And make it look good.
All the intricacies of the horns and the snares and
the toms and all that. If you can't finesse those basic
sounds, then . . . you're not really b-boying. You need to
be able to do it. It's important to do it. It's keeping the
culture alive by doing it. You gotta keep doing it. . . .
 We were passed down those records, and now it's
our time to pass those records down.
—Phantom (Ready to Rock, Mighty Zulu Kings), a
b-boy in his mid-20s

Every hip-hop deejay knows the cuts that b-boys favor: a few energetic, bongo-laden tracks from the early '70s: "Apache" (1973), "Give It Up or Turnit a Loose" by James Brown (1969), "T Plays It Cool" by Marvin Gaye (1972), "It's Just Begun" by the Jimmy Castor Bunch (1972), "The Mexican" by Babe Ruth (1972), and a handful of others. These songs can be heard at any b-boy event, on the soundtrack to virtually any video that shows b-boying, and on a variety of b-boy-oriented mix tapes and compact discs.

They are not hip-hop songs. They are the rock and funk songs that b-boying's originators danced to in the half-decade between hip-hop's emergence as a sociocultural movement around 1974 and the development of an associated musical genre in 1979. For those who see hip-hop as a wild, anarchic expression of youthful abandon, brutal materialism, criminality, or even political change, this may seem odd. Could today's rebellious b-boys really be so mindful of history—so culturally conservative—that they insist on dancing to the *exact records* that brought the form to life 35 years ago, long before most of them were even born?

In both scholarly writing and the popular press, hip-hop culture is often presented as a response to the disruption of a tradition, a kind of cultural scab that formed over the wounds of African American and Latino youth in New York. An implicit corollary of this premise is that any social or cultural coherence that can be found in hip-hop is primarily a result of a common opposition among practitioners to some outside force. Whether these strange bedfellows are using their shared aesthetic of disjuncture to address concerns in the social (Erskine 2003; Rose 1994), musical (Krims 2000; Lipsitz 1994; Walser 1995), or ideological (Perry 2004; Potter 1995) spheres, the essential mechanism remains reactionary. In cases where active cultural continuity is emphasized, it is to be found in hip-hop's relationship to broader cultural patterns, such as gender (Gaunt 2006), Afro-diasporic identity (Keyes 1996, 2004), and Latinidad (Rivera 2003). But hip-hop culture is now over three decades old: does it not have its own internal continuities?

If it does not, then hip-hop constitutes not only a new musical genre, but truly a new *kind* of cultural practice. But if it does—and it does—we should not shy away from applying conventional methodologies and theoretical models to its study. Nor should we retreat from the commonalities that such methodologies may reveal between hip-hop and other expressive practices around the world. In other words, the question is not so much *whether* hip-hop has developed its own conventions, stylistic norms, and historical self-consciousness, but *how* it has done so. In this chapter, I will argue that the establishment of an honored repertoire of records that b-boys prefer to dance to—in effect, a canon—is one way in which hip-hop has developed its own set of cultural traditions.

B-boy songs hold several elements in common: they tend to date to the early '70s, feature Latin percussion (especially bongos), have relatively fast tempos (110 to 120 beats per minute), use horns and guitars in a percussive way, use stop-time at various points in the song, and feature a formal structure that builds to decisive musical peaks. But, most important, they have breaks.

B-boying began with the break, the part of a song where all instruments except the rhythm section fall silent and the groove is distilled to its most fundamental elements. In the 1970s, when kids began throwing rebel street parties in the Bronx, people from different neighborhoods came together for the first time since the gangs had taken over, and there was one thing they all agreed on: the break was an opportunity. It was a moment on a record that was so powerful that it could actually overpower day-to-day reality and become an environment unto itself. The power of the break was so evident that DJ Kool Herc even began to play two copies of the same record on separate turntables, repeating the break over and over again, giving the dancers more time to showcase their most devastating moves. Before long, Herc and other pioneering deejays like Afrika Bambaataa and Grandmaster Flash were playing nothing *but* breaks. And the dancers responded by creating a new dance form that was nothing *but* devastating moves: b-boying. Some even began dropping to the ground and spinning around. Hip-hop music and b-boying were born as twins, and their mother was the break.

By the mid-'70s, the musical break in the song had taken on a new life as a historical break between the end of soul culture and the beginning of hip-hop culture. It became a psychological break between the b-boy's pre- and postdance identities. And it became a break from everyday life, allowing the dancer to enter a heightened world where ideas about time and space and spirituality and style could be addressed through raw physicality. The break is the original essence of the dance and the seed of its tradition (it is also where the much-disputed term *breakdancing* comes from).

In discussing a somewhat different phenomenon, the syncopation of samba rhythms, Barbara Browning has articulated a fundamental aspect of the relationship between movement and "suppressed" elements of a composition. "This suspension leaves the body with a hunger that can only be satisfied by *filling the silence with motion*," she writes:

> Samba, the dance, cannot exist without the suppression of a strong beat. . . . In fact, the breaks in rhythmic structure, the ruptures in the pattern are the points at which the full complexity of the original pattern becomes evident. But the break precisely points out all that was inherent or potential in the texture before the tear. (Browning 1995:9–10; emphasis added)

Browning is addressing a rupture in rhythm created by suppressing particular beats, while the break is a rupture in form created by suppressing particular instruments (and, by extension, their melodic and rhythmic contributions to the groove). In both cases, the suppression serves to accentuate musical absences, creating a sense that a contribution is required from listeners to restore the music to its proper state. In both cases, that contribution takes the form of dance. B-boy records are songs that have breaks which—in a visceral way—impel b-boys to dance.

A version of this process that is closely related to hip-hop occurs in many musics of the African diaspora, especially mambo and salsa music. In his autobiography, for example, legendary rock promoter Bill Graham reflects on his experience dancing to Machito, Tito Puente, and Tito Rodriguez during their legendary tenure at New York's Palladium in the late 1950s: "In the middle of a song, the orchestra would suddenly stop playing except for the bass line," he remembers. "But nobody would stop dancing. We'd all clap our hands and keep the clave beat and everybody simply surrendered to the passion of the music—thousands of us.

We'd keep perfect time till the solo was over and the entire band would come back in and take it on home. *Thousands* of us. And everybody felt good. Everybody felt *so* good" (Graham 49).[1] The fact that Graham, who was not Latino, would single out this element of the performance for special mention suggests that the break, whether called by that name or not, was appreciated by New York dancers for at least several decades before hip-hop emerged.

Latin music was also influential on a more immediate level. In the '60s and '70s, notes pioneering Bronx b-boy Trac 2, "There was no 'dusk to dawn,' when the parks were closed. You would hear that conga—boom boom boom, boom ba-boom—and the people jamming. 'Cause that's what was called a 'jam' back then. It was an outdoor music session" (Trac 2, interview).

As Raquel Rivera explains, "The long-standing tradition of street drumming among New York Puerto Ricans and Cubans—in which African Americans also have participated—strongly influenced the music that was recorded as soul and funk, which was later played as *break-beats* at hip-hop jams" (Rivera 2003:35; emphasis in original). If one views this influence from the dancers' point of view, Rivera may even be understating the case. Since early hip-hop jams took place in the same spaces as street drumming—sidewalks, parks, public beaches, and schoolyards—the experience of dancing to an extended, Latin-style percussion break played by a deejay in a park would have been extremely similar to the experience of dancing to live drummers in that same park. It would have been surprising if youths who suddenly found themselves dancing to an extended recording of congas and bongos extracted from the center of a James Brown song *didn't* turn to the Latin drumming experience for guidance. Such moments—combining the street drumming environment with funk records—represented a cultural activity that fit equally well into both Latino and African American traditions.

Ned Sublette sees the increased prevalence of conga drums in the African American music of this era—one of the foundations of the break, and thus of hip-hop itself—as itself reflecting such a fusion sensibility:

> [In the 1970s], conga drums had become one of the signature sounds of African American musical nationalism, ultimately even acquiring a faux-African pronunciation unknown in Cuba: *kungaz*. Along with the one-chord groove tune that the conga helped define, the instrument was an important part of the sound of another of America's great cultural achievements: funk.
>
> When I asked Bobby Byrd (James Brown's music director in the glory days) about funk, I had expected that, being a pianist, he might say something about the harmony—the insistent use of sevenths, or something like that. Instead, he told me: "It was the syncopation of the instruments—everybody playing a different part. Okay now we winded up with a seven piece band, but everybody had a different part to play. That's where the funk part of it became. Everybody playing a different part and it's all fitting together like a glove."

That's exactly what Latin bands did, and exactly what American bands up until that time did not do. Funk polyrhythmicized the R&B combo the way the mambo had earlier polyrhythmicized the jazz band. But then, Bobby Byrd and James Brown, like Chuck [Berry] and Bo [Diddley], like Elvis [Presley], came of age in the mambo era. The example of Cuban music was everywhere in those days. (Sublette 2007:91)

The break, then, is an interruption of an integrated groove. In a very real sense, by inviting the dancers to "fill the silence with motion," the break is reaching out to the listener. And by interacting with the dancers in this way, the break provides a way for recorded music to serve many of the same functions as live music. There is a general sense among b-boys that, despite being prerecorded, a good b-boy song can be animated by the way its rhythms interact with dancers, to the point where it almost *does* become a live performance.

Pioneering hip-hop promoter Michael Holman describes James Brown's b-boy classic "Give It Up or Turnit a Loose"—one of the songs Bobby Byrd was referring to in the above quote—as if it is intentionally helping dancers every time it's played. "'Give It Up or Turnit a Loose' is designed to let you ride on it," he points out. "To let you dance. It's like it cuts your work in half, you know? It's like a galloping *anthem*. I like to associate it to [the] William Tell Overture because they're both anthem-like. And they're just, like, this galloping, charging, *martial* music, in a way" (Michael Holman, interview).

Holman's use of the word *martial* is no accident: part of a b-boy record's job is to make dancers want to go to war. The tempo, intensity, and aggressive feel of these songs elicit battling rather than socializing. As Alien Ness, a b-boy in his early 40s who is president of the Mighty Zulu Kings (the b-boy division of hip-hop's oldest and most respected cultural organization, the Universal Zulu Nation), states flatly, "I can't break to happy songs. My stuff has to be all down.... That's what I like. I like down. I like 'car chase' music, you know what I mean?" "Now one of my favorite songs in the whole wide world is [the Jackson Sisters'] 'I Believe in Miracles,'" he continues:

I will dance to that song all night. Let the deejay play it all night, I will dance to it all night. Will you see me breaking to it? *Hell* no. Why?...It's happy. That's how I feel when I hear that song. I feel happy. I feel good. I don't feel like breakin'.... That's not something I'm trying to rip somebody's head off in a cypher[2] on. (Alien Ness, interview)

One song that does feature the qualities Ness seeks is 1972's "It's Just Begun," by the Jimmy Castor Bunch. "'Just Begun' is the *epitome*," he stresses:

"Just Begun" *personifies* the b-boy mentality. From the opening words to the final words: "*Watch me now* / Feel the groove / Into something / Gonna make you move." That's *gangsta*. That's exactly how you feel when you breakin'. I don't

Alien Ness. Photo © Martha Cooper.

care what song you're breakin' to. But when you're breaking, subconsciously you're singing "Just Begun" in your head. Subconsciously, you understand what I'm saying. 'Cause it's the b-boy mentality. (Alien Ness, interview)

Jorge "Fabel" Pabon, a popper, locker, and uprocker in his early 40s who is vice president of the best-known b-boy organization, the Rock Steady Crew, emphasizes the sheer intensity of the song's musical setting, "'Just Begun' sounds like a bat outta hell! It's like a car chase, you know? Like a *crazy* car chase!...So imagine trying to dance to that intensity!" (Fabel, interview).

Eddie Luna, a Queens-based b-boy in his early 40s, agrees that these songs are distinguished by the emotions they spark in b-boys. He says that the songs are so powerful that they can make b-boys dance when they don't even want to:

> That is the adrenaline. If you know b-boying, that's like *anthems*, you know? This is where you stand up. This is where you gotta do what you gotta do. I mean, when I hear—to this day—the beginning of "Just Begun," "Apache," "The Mexican" during its breaks...and "Drummer's Beat," when it starts, when you hear those bongos going, it's just—oh, *man!* It's *war time*. It is. It's just this *rush*....Like, you don't care no more, you just go ahead and *do it*. Doesn't matter what it costs! You didn't even practice this move! You're at the point, I mean, whatever comes out is gonna come out, you know what I mean? You have a black eye or a scratched arm or whatever. Because the adrenaline rush that you get from the music...."Apache"? Forget it! I can't listen to "Apache." I just—I start sweating, you know! And I get angry! And it's like, I wanna hit the floor! (Eddie Luna, interview)

The vibrant relationship that b-boys and b-girls maintain with these songs belies easy stereotypes about the relative value of live versus recorded music. In fact, the "recordedness" of these songs—the way they seem to capture the time and place in which they were made—is an important part of their appeal. This sensibility is similar to that of hip-hop deejays and producers who value the sound of recordings over that of live instrumentation (see Schloss 2004:63–78).

Many b-boys feel that these emotions—and the environment that produced them—were literally encoded into the songs by the original social context in which they were recorded. As Richard "Breakeasy" Santiago, a Brooklyn-based b-boy in his early 40s who serves as a mentor to many younger dancers, explains:

> If you were to go back in time and...listen to that record being played while the conditions and the environment are around at that moment in time, you [would] understand why is it that we move[d] the way we did. A lot of people, when they just hear the music, they don't understand that that music is played by a group of people that were somehow affected by their environment to express that train of thought. The words, if there's words. In the rhythms and beats, because the energy of that music can be hardcore, like just letting it all go out, or it can be a guitar just wailing and stuff, just to self-express and experiment or go into a zone. There's so many different things involved in just that piece of music....if you

understand that, you're gonna ride that drummer going crazy 'cause he wants to vent it out. Then you're gonna move your feet to that rhythm. (Richard Santiago, interview)

When the song is blasted through huge speakers—and properly danced to—that time and place are virtually reconstituted. The songs paint a three-dimensional picture of an environment that b-boys can then enter through the dance. By engaging with the music, the dancer can experience the emotions of the original musicians—and the original b-boys.

"When I really like a song—especially all these ill breaks, the classic breaks from back in the days—I feel like the artist put their heart and soul into it to deliver me that ill fuckin' song," agrees Waaak:

> That ill, classic, timeless...piece of music. So when I go out there to dance to it, I gotta do it justice. So every time I go out and I dance to these songs that I like, I put emotion to it. Because, to me, I gotta match that level of that song....I mean, when you're hearing a ill piece of music, a masterpiece of music, and you're watching somebody dance that song correctly? It's what b-boying is. It's pure. It's beautiful. And I don't throw that word around like that, but that's what it is. (Waaak One, interview)

"I think that music is there just to remind people," says Ru, a Brooklyn-based b-boy in his 20s:

> That's just basically what that music is there for. It's just a picture book, you know,...to remind them of that world, but to have it in a way where they would *feel* it. You know what I'm saying: instead of actually seeing it on a picture. 'Cause [if] you see it in a picture, you're like, "Wow, man, that was back in the days," but you can't feel why...they were like that. Why they were dancing. What made them tick....Music's mad powerful. It is. (Ru, interview)

"It's not like a secret," says Tiny Love, a Brooklyn-based popper, uprocker, and b-boy in his 20s:

> But nobody talks about it. It's the real deal: basically, these songs have a message. The '70s songs, they talk about something that would change the world....Those are classics and those beats have life. You see, we play the same music on and on and we don't get bored of it. That means that, basically, it's not going to our minds; it goes to our soul, you know? It's gonna keep on moving, you know? We're always gonna listen to that. Those beats have life. (Tiny Love, interview)

And yet there were other songs recorded in the early '70s that had similar qualities, but which are not considered b-boy cuts (the song "A La Escuela" [1974] by Malo is a prime example—it even has a break). This is apparently a result of a series of lost decisions that were made by hip-hop practitioners at that time. In other words, we may not understand or remember why one song was included and another was not, but it's too late to go back and change it now. The fact that these choices are still adhered to more than 30 years later suggests a deep respect for the community that made those decisions, as well as the tradition that has preserved them over the ensuing decades. That, too, is encoded into the sound of the songs. As Philip Bohlman points out with regard to the European art music tradition, the reason that one would single out songs in the first place is precisely to define a vision of the past that has utility in the present. "Perceptible in a work of music," he writes, "should be some model of the past, expressed as formal similarity, aesthetic context, or mythological purity," all of which obtain in the case of b-boy songs (Bohlman 1992:204).

As Fabel reflects, b-boys do view the use of these particular songs as a cultural tradition, an outlook that he explicitly ties to that of a broader Afro-Caribbean world view:

> For the younger people, I think those who have had the privilege to watch older people get down to it, that's a definite inspiration. The minute you see it, you're gonna say, "wow, that makes sense." Just like when you see someone doing real dope mamboing to mambo music, or a salsa dancer who's right on. You know ... *it's the native music of the dance* ... the old-timers do it and still love it and keep it alive, because, honestly, I think that it's part of the ritual.
>
> [Like] when certain drummers drum the same patterns, whether it's *guaguancó* or whatever: for Afro-Caribbean communities and people who sort of keep folk-loric culture alive, there's no questioning about, "Hey, are we gonna break the pattern?" Maybe they'll build on top of the foundation, but the main base of it all is still the same....
>
> So I think the young people do it because they see the value in its tradition. (Fabel, interview)

The Dynamic Rockers' KaoticBlaze, a New York b-girl in her 20s who has appeared as a kind of coach on the b-girl episode of MTV's *Made*, confirms this interpretation. "It's important, in the aspect that it does have history behind it. And to think that you're getting down to the same beats that the pioneers of the dance got down to before. Like the *killa* beats from back in the day ... it's important to remember not to forget songs like that. It's history" (KaoticBlaze, interview).

B-Girl Emiko, a Philadelphia-based dancer in her 20s, expresses a similar outlook, despite (or possibly because of) the fact that she was not born when the songs were recorded and was raised in Japan, half a world away:

> That gives me the ... hypeness. Especially ... "Just Begun." It's just one of the songs. Being the b-girl or b-boy, no matter where you're from, once you listen to the song, you just get *crazy!* I don't know the reason why. I didn't live in the time when the music came, but I just feel it—feel that energy of the music. Just say "Aah!" Just start battle rock[ing] to each other. (B-Girl Emiko, interview)

DJ E-Rok also emphasizes the idea of tradition, comparing b-boy songs to folk songs:

**Joe Schloss (author/interviewer):** There's probably a lot of tunes that you *could* b-boy to, but there's like five songs that people *always* play, you know what I mean? Why do you think that is?

**E-Rok:** You're talking about, like, "Apache"? "It's Just Begun"? I think those are just handed down from generation to generation. Say, like, if you're a kid who's b-boying, you're looking up to the older generation, who you're getting your learning from. And you're watching how they dance. But then you're also listening to the type of music they're playing. You become accustomed to dancing to that particular song. So it's almost like old folk songs handed down from generation to generation. (DJ E-Rok, interview)

Rock Steady Crew DJ DV-One suggests a more abstract idea of "energy," which seems to conflate rhythm and social history into single concept. "I'm sure there's [other] upbeat songs that you can dance to or that you can break to, but it just doesn't feel the same," he notes:

If you're on the inside—like, if you're a hip-hop head—even a 15-year-old could feel the energy in "The Mexican" or in "Apache." You know, you can feel that. I'm sure you can find some, like, house record or even some R&B record...that has the same tempo or the same speed. It's just not the same as b-boying to the original joints. (DJ DV-One, interview)

Note that DV-One specifies that the listener must be "on the inside" to feel the "energy" of the b-boy songs. In other words, their value, while powerful, is not inherent; one must have some preexisting knowledge to be able to appreciate it. And part of what one is appreciating lies in the play between the practical value of the song as it's being danced to *right now* and the historical value it carries as a hip-hop classic.

Again, it seems to me that a productive way to address this interplay is by viewing these songs collectively as a canon. As Edgar and Sedgwick observe, the term has several distinct connotations:

Typically, the term is used to encompass what are generally recognised as the most important works in a particular artistic tradition (most usually of literature or music). It is derived from its original use, dating from the fourth century, to refer to the authoritative and definitive books of the Christian Bible. Defenders of the notion of a canon would argue from the position that there are universal aesthetic values (albeit that these values may unfold over time, with the development of the tradition). Individual works are therefore included in the canon on the grounds that they best express these universal values. The canonical works are therefore the finest expression of a particular language, and may indeed be taken as the expression of a culture's or a nation's identity. (Edgar and Sedgwick 1999:51–52)

There are a number of reasons that b-boy songs could be viewed as a canon. First, the group is a collection of specific songs, as opposed to a generic profile or type of song that is good to b-boy to. Second, the songs are described via a discourse of quality; they are presented as being "the finest expression" of the b-boy song genre. Third, the fact that b-boys would want to specify the finest expression of the genre in the first place requires agreement about both the values of the community and, more fundamentally, the actual existence of a community of b-boys. Fourth, the status of the songs is axiomatic. That is, elements of the canon cannot be questioned, because the criteria for what makes a good b-boy song are derived from these examples in the first place.

If we view these records as being analogous to "texts," Robert Alter's comments on the biblical canon are useful:

> A canon is above all a transhistorical textual community. Knowledge of the received texts and recourse to them constitute the community, but the texts do not have a single, authoritative meaning, however much the established spokesmen for the canon at any given moment may claim that is the case. After all, even within the community of traditional believers, the biblical canon has been imagined to endorse as a matter of divine revelation rationalism, mysticism, nationalism, universalism, asceticism, sensualism, determinism, free will, and a good deal else. (Alter 2000:5)

What gives these interpretations both their power and their audience is their derivation from the canonical texts in the first place. In other words, it is the canon itself that allows such a diversity of opinion to assemble itself under the single phrase "the community of traditional believers."

Literary theorists in particular have made valuable analyses of the ways in which canons—particularly the Western literary canon—reflect the social and ideological relationships between art and community (see Guillory 1993). In the case of the b-boy canon, negotiations are mainly embodied in, and mediated by, the relationship between b-boys and the disc jockeys who provide the music for them to dance to, many of whom are themselves current or former b-boys or b-girls.

Guillory's comments with regard to the Western literary canon are particularly relevant to the question of how contemporary b-boying practice is related to the idea of a "classic b-boy songs" canon. "The canon is itself a historical event; it belongs to the history of the school," he writes:

> If there is now a need to rethink and revise what we do with the curriculum of literature, this project will entail not only reading new works, or noncanonical works (both of which it should entail), but also reading in a better way, by which I mean reading works for what they say and do in their place and time, as well as reading the *difference* between those meanings and the meanings which have been imputed to them by virtue of their being canonical works. (Guillory 1990: 244)

The b-boy canon is ripe for such a reading because the *idea* of canonicity—of tradition—actually plays an integral role in the musical practice. That is partially due to the historical factors I discussed above and partially because b-boy songs operate as familiar "frameworks for invention" in a manner similar to the role that so-called standards play for jazz musicians:

> Lee Konitz has performed standard compositions "like 'All the Things You Are' for over forty years now" because of their unlimited substance as frameworks for invention, inspiring him to probe ever more deeply into their "possibilities." And Charlie Parker explained to Red Rodney that he routinely practiced formulating solos "on the blues, 'Rhythm' and 'Cherokee' in every key." Over artists' lives, mastery of form resulting from the repeated performance of favorite compositions obviously contributes to their extraordinary fluency as soloists. Konitz adds that improvising on familiar repertory also serves players "as a measuring device" for assessing their creative powers "at that moment" in relation to their recollection of their past improvisations on the composition.[3] (Berliner 1994:226–227)

B-boy songs are valued as frameworks for the act of b-boying because they combine practical factors that facilitate the particular dance style (including fast tempos, loud drums, rhythmic horns, and breaks) with sociohistorical associations that place any given performance in the context of b-boy history. A good deejay, then, is one who is able to properly deploy these factors to help the b-boys accomplish their goals for the dance. In other words, the interaction is not simply one of b-boys appreciating the deejays' choices on an abstract aesthetic level. Rather, it is the deejay giving the b-boys the tools to express themselves and the b-boys validating the deejays' choices by making use of those materials.

In addition to the pragmatic value of the rhythm fitting the steps of the dance, which I will discuss in a moment, a major part of a given song's value as raw material for performance is that it is canonical, that it is known to be a b-boy song. This is especially striking when one considers that none of these songs was originally written or recorded for this purpose. Their status as b-boy classics was something that developed organically as a result of the relationship between deejays and b-boys. It is no exaggeration to say that hip-hop *itself* was a result of this relationship.

The earliest b-boys danced to these songs in their entirety, saving their best (or most hostile) moves for the break; that was why the deejays began to focus on the breaks in the first place. This focus soon led to the innovation, credited to DJ Kool Herc, of using two copies of the same record on two turntables, a process which enabled the deejay to repeat a given break endlessly, by rewinding one copy while the other was playing. It was the deejays' recognition of, and service to, the b-boys' needs that prompted the birth of hip-hop as a discrete performance practice. As Nelson George has noted:

Records such as Jimmy Castor's "It's Just Begun," the Incredible Bongo Band's "Apache," and Herman Kelly's "Dance to the Drummer's Beat" didn't become hip hop classics in a vacuum. DJs played them, and often unearthed them, but it was the dancers who certified them. It was their taste, their affirmation of certain tracks as good for breaking, and their demand to hear them at parties that influenced the DJs and MCs who pioneered hip hop's early sound. (George 1998:16)

One example of this "certification" process is the case of the 1972 recording "The Mexican" (performed by the British rock band Babe Ruth), which b-boy and popper GeoMatrix explains is specifically "for" uprock, an aggressive precursor to b-boying in which an individual directly confronts an opponent who is dancing simultaneously. As he says, "'The Mexican'...[is] more for fighting. The Brooklyn uprock....Really, people don't really break to it, but they just uprock to it....That's the type of song, you just wanna uprock. Like when you doing 'Mexican,' man, you always wanna go out there and just *fight*. Like *battling*" (GeoMatrix, interview). Although the song's performers had certainly never heard of hip-hop or uprocking when they recorded it (since hip-hop didn't exist and uprocking was limited to teenagers in a few neighborhoods in Brooklyn and the Bronx), "The Mexican" has become so associated with uprock that whenever GeoMatrix hears it, he is immediately filled with an aggressive competitiveness that compels him to perform the dance.

Shortly after conducting that interview, I attended the Universal Zulu Nation's 30th anniversary celebration in Harlem.[4] At one point in the evening, the deejay played "The Mexican," and b-boys in the crowd began uprocking within five seconds. This suggests that the association of this particular song with this particular dance is literally embodied knowledge; when "The Mexican" is played, a b-boy or b-girl's body is simply inclined to uprock.

The idea of uprocking as a preconscious—though learned—*physical* response to hearing "The Mexican" is consistent with Bourdieu's notion of the habitus as a "system of dispositions" (Bourdieu 1977:82) or an "acquired system of generative schemes objectively adjusted to the particular conditions in which it is constituted" (Bourdieu 1977:95). Ken Swift, often described as "the epitome of a b-boy," sees the development of this kind of b-boy intuition as the central value of designating a canon in the first place: "I think it's important to know those songs. *I think it's important to know those songs.* 'Cause you never know when they're gonna come up.... You don't want to think about the song. You wanna react to the song without thinking about it" (Ken Swift, interview).

In Ken Swift's opinion, the existence of an agreed-upon repertoire of b-boy songs allows dancers to develop the ability to react instantaneously to each in a manner that reproduces the aesthetic principles of the b-boy community. From the moment this ability becomes a part of any given dancer's disposition, that individual carries a piece of hip-hop history in his or her physical being and recapitulates it every time he or she dances. When he introduces "The Mexican" on his underground mix CD *Throwback Breaks and Beats* (Grandmaster Caz 2004), DJ Grandmaster Caz mentions neither the name of the song nor the artist.[5] As the song begins, he simply declares, "If you don't know what this is, you don't need to know! You just wasn't there!"

In addition to the general emotional power of a song like "The Mexican," a good dancer also responds to the lyrics, interesting musical figures, and the pulse of the rhythm. "I dance according to what the music tells me," says B-Boy Phantom, a New Yorker in his 20s. "So, if there's a horn...that's going on a quarter note, you're gonna dance to that the way you hear it. That's how I express my dance to the beat" (B-Boy Phantom, interview). The establishment of a discrete set of b-boy songs aids this process by limiting the repertoire of songs that dancers need to master, so they can direct their energies toward learning the details of each.

On a more general level, encouraging b-boys to gear their dancing to a specific song necessarily promotes the idea that the relationship between music and dance is important. This is by no means a foregone conclusion in the b-boy world. The rise of air moves and power moves (demonstrating acrobatic ability and strength, respectively) has led to a significant portion of b-boying being arrhythmic. The underground b-boy DVD *Power Moves*, for example, contains instructional material on how to perform these impressive feats, footage from three b-boy contests (including one called Chico Got to Get His Share, named after a lyric from "The Mexican"), and interviews with well-known b-boys and b-girls. But the video begins with the following voiceover: "It's cool if you've got the most incredible power move in the world. That's cool. That looks hot. But the shit gotta have neatness to it and structure.... Remember, this is a dance.... This is not a gymnastics event; you not being judged on your flips and how many flares you do. So remember, this is dancing" (*Power Moves* 2004). Trac 2, who is credited with the introduction of gymnastics moves to b-boying in the mid-'70s, could not be clearer about this issue: "I incorporated gymnastics into the dance," he says. "I didn't put the dance into gymnastics" (Trac 2, interview).

"You can't really dance without listening to the music," agrees Phantom. "It's an acrobatic dance, yeah, but—exactly—it's an acrobatic *dance*. You have to dance first, *then* get acrobatic. People don't understand that and it's a shame. I tell this to people, 'look, get some rhythm first.' Make your toprocks look good before you decide to jump into a windmill" (B-Boy Phantom, interview). The promotion of the b-boy canon works as the promotion of b-boying as dancing rather than gymnastics.

In addition to this general sensibility, the b-boy canon also works to promote the use of specific rhythms. Many b-boy songs share the same implicit rhythmic pattern. Like the clave in Latin music, from which it may well be derived, this pattern is sometimes articulated in the music, and sometimes not. But it can always be felt by the dancer. And while there is no standard term for it, several b-boys have described it to me with a phrase from KRS-One's 1993 song "Boom Bap," which seems to serve as a mnemonic device: "Boom! Bap! Original Rap!" Essentially, it is a slightly modified cha-cha-cha, a fact which is not insignificant. As Ned Sublette has noted, the cha-cha-cha pattern pervades postwar American dance music (Sublette 2007). (Here, and throughout the book, I will try to represent rhythms as they are conceived by b-boys and b-girls.)

| | 1 | and | 2 | and | 3 | and | 4 | and |
|---|---|---|---|---|---|---|---|---|
| Rhythm mnemonic | Boom! | | Bap! | | O-rigi- | nal | rap! | |
| Cha-cha-cha | one | | two | | cha | cha | cha | |

The close association of this rhythm with the dance has two effects: it allows the dancer to lock in to songs that share the rhythm, and it makes it difficult to dance to songs that do not fit the pattern, especially songs that are too slow. The speed at which gravity acts on the human body alone exerts a decisive influence over which songs can be used. As b-boy GeoMatrix notes, this is actually one of the reasons that the canon is so essential. "This type of music represent[s] breakin'," he says:

> When you play this type of music, people already know. And you could play, like, "Apache," already the b-boys gonna say to themselves, "this is our music—we gonna go down."[6] 'Cause nowadays you can go to a party and you can't break to hip-hop. And [if] you don't give 'em this type of beat, the b-boys always gonna stay, like, just chillin'. But if you give 'em that beat, they're like, "nah, nah, I gotta go for it!" (GeoMatrix, interview)

Due to the nature of the movements, the music cannot be significantly sped up or slowed down without altering the form of the dance. In fact, when the tempo of hip-hop music began to slow down in order to better emphasize the words of its emcees, b-boys collectively decided that, rather than change the dance to fit the new tempos, they would actually *reject* hip-hop music. To this day, dancers rarely break to contemporary hip-hop, a choice which has had two related results. First, it has reinforced the dance's estrangement from rap music, and thus from the money and fame associated with it. Second, it serves to continuously reemphasize the stylistic relationship between the dance and the social world from which classic b-boy songs originally emerged: New York City in the '70s.

Of course, tempo is important to almost all dance forms, but it is all the more so with b-boying since many of its moves consist of jumps, hops, and shuffles that incorporate leaping or falling. For example, a sequence of movements is sometimes decisively concluded with a "blowup," a category of move in which the breaker leaps into a frozen position, usually one that requires a high degree of balance (the most common blowups involve variations on a one-handed handstand). For the blowup to be considered successful, it must be landed precisely on the beat, a feat which requires that gravity be taken into account in two ways: the initial leap must be timed so that the dancer touches down at the right moment, and then the dancer must be able to balance in the position for several beats, returning to her feet at a rhythmically appropriate moment as well. The most successful blowups coincide with decisive beats in the song. At one battle I attended in 2005, the entire contest was won with such a move. The dancer leaped into a one-handed handstand and aimed an imaginary gun at his opponent with his free hand. The song to which he was dancing—chosen spontaneously by the deejay—contained a gunshot sound at exactly the moment he assumed the pose.[7]

Another example of how this works can be found in toprocking, the upright, rhythmic cross-stepping that precedes "going down" to perform breaking's characteristic floor moves. The simplest toprocking step is known as the "Indian step," and it consists of the following movements, beginning from a stance in which both feet are parallel, about shoulder width apart:

1. The right foot crosses in front of the left and takes the body's full weight.
2. The weight is shifted back to the left foot.
3. The right foot swings back to a position parallel to the left and takes the weight again. The dancer has now returned to the original position. The process is then repeated to the right side.
4. The left foot crosses in front of the right and takes the body's full weight.
5. The weight is shifted back to the right foot.
6. The left foot swings back to a position parallel to the left and takes the weight again.

The step is performed in double-time so the entire process (to both sides) fills one four-beat musical measure:

| 1 | | 2 | | 3 | | 4 | |
|---|---|---|---|---|---|---|---|
| right | left | right | – | left | right | left | – |

| 1 | | 2 | | 3 | | 4 | |
|---|---|---|---|---|---|---|---|
| right | left | right | – | left | right | left | – |

This rhythm makes physical sense, because it takes twice as long for the leg to cross over in front as it does to step back (on the 1 and the 3), since the crossing leg's return trip is rhythmically divided by the other foot's step. When I initially learned this movement, I was instructed to associate the rhythm of my steps with a "boom boom bap" rhythm. (When describing hip-hop's rhythmic patterns, the onomatopoetic "boom" is conventionally used to represent the sound of a kick [bass] drum, and "bap" is used to represent the sound of a snare drum.)

If we lay this rhythm on top of a typical drum rhythm from a b-boy song and the general rhythm mnemonic I discussed earlier, it is easy to see how they fit together. Moreover, since the overall rhythm concept is held in the mind, the drum is heard in the ears, and the rhythm of the dance step is manifested in the body, the resulting groove—at its most potent—can actually integrate all three aspects of the dancer's being:

| | 1 | and | 2 | and | 3 | and | 4 | and |
|---|---|---|---|---|---|---|---|---|
| Foot rhythm (body) | boom | boom | bap | | boom | boom | bap | |
| Drum rhythm (ears/music) | boom | | bap | | boom | boom | bap | |
| Rhythm concept (mind) | X | | X | | X | X | X | |

This rhythm is well suited to the dance: it is sparse at the beginning, but then speeds up as it goes along, culminating in a decisive emphasis on the fourth beat of the measure, which is then followed by a short rest that allows both the dancer and the observer to absorb what has just happened before beginning the process again. This also creates a distinct call-and-response feel, with the first half of the phrase building tension and the second half resolving it. Furthermore, once this pattern is established, the dancer can then work against it to create new tensions and grooves, a process known as "rocking the beat."

As I will discuss extensively in chapter 7, the term *rocking* is an evocative one in the b-boy world. It has many senses, but perhaps the most potent is when it's used to suggest that someone has used her creativity to demonstrate control over some area of life: a microphone, an audience, clothing, a beat. It represents the nexus of creativity and power, an important intersection for hip-hop. So when dancers are said to be rocking the beat, the implication is that they are actually using their dance skills to wrestle with the song itself, to actually force the rhythm to conform to their desires.

Conceptually, this ties in to some of the deepest aspects of hip-hop philosophy. The idea that something as seemingly unalterable as a prerecorded piece of music could be changed by dancing to it requires an extremely abstract view of the situation. From the b-boy's standpoint, however, the song is not the recording; the song is the recording being played by a particular deejay through a particular sound system in a particular room to particular people at a particular moment in a particular musical context. The song and the social experience of hearing it become one and the same. And that experience—like any social circumstance—can be *rocked*. The idea that one's creativity can allow them to change situations that might appear to be unchangeable is an extremely powerful one. That b-boying should serve as a form of training in how to do this is an equally significant concept, and I will discuss this process more thoroughly in the chapters that follow. What is important here, however, is that b-boy songs are chosen for their conduciveness to being rocked in this way.

The canon, then, is the site of mutual influence: b-boys who wish to maintain these steps as part of their dance will show a strong preference for b-boy songs. At the same time, the continued prevalence of b-boy songs preserves such steps as an integral part of b-boying. Issues such as speed, openness to improvisation, and the original conditions under which the songs were recorded all influence this process.

In addition to the rhythm and tempo, another factor that comes into play in the canon is the formal structure of the songs. On one level, the formal structure is used in much the same way as the rhythm itself—as something to be rocked. Major moments in a b-boy's set, especially the moment when the dancer drops to the floor, will often be timed to coincide with significant structural moments in a song, such as the beginning of a new verse. But song structure can also be significant on a more general level. When Fabel discusses "Apache," for example, it is noteworthy that the first thing he mentions is his appreciation for its formal structure. "I love 'Apache' because it has a lot of buildups in the song," he says. "The hype of anticipation, a lot of times, is what did it...knowing, 'Oh shit—here it comes!' And wondering what's gonna jump off, a battle or whatever. Or if anyone in the crowd that you don't know is schemin' on you, you know?" (Fabel, interview).

In his comments, Fabel places the specific formal characteristics of "Apache" within a broader social context: the sense of "anticipation" that arises as musical peaks approach is based on listeners having heard the song before; otherwise, they wouldn't know they were coming. Moreover, the knowledge that these peaks are significant is based on the expectation that certain kinds of social interactions—"a battle or whatever"—will take place at that point in the song.

There is a general understanding that the high-energy point of the song "Apache" will be one of the most important moments of any given b-boy event. Anyone who has something significant to do—debut a spectacular new move, resolve a long-simmering dispute with another breaker—will often wait until that point in the evening to do so. This, in turn, means that when the deejay chooses to play this song, the energy in the room will rise noticeably as b-boys look around and wait to see what will happen. The power of being able to deploy this song at the appropriate time is not something deejays take lightly.

When I asked deejay Mr. Supreme if there were specific moments when he knew "Apache" was called for, his answer was immediate. "Oh, for sure!" he said. "Certainly. I mean, just the other night was a perfect example....I was playing some salsa stuff, really, and it had a lotta Latin rhythm and percussion in it and these cats started b-boying. So I knew: 'Yeah, OK, now's the time.' And it worked, you know?" (Mr. Supreme, interview).

From the deejays' point of view, it is the song's dance-floor effectiveness ("it worked, you know?") that sets it apart. In 2002, for example, hip-hop journalist Smokey D. Fontaine zeroed in on the power of "Apache" to inspire b-boys when he listed the song as one of the best singles of the 1970s: "This cornucopia of psychedelic keyboards, conga drums, and spaghetti western–like trumpet playing became one of the main building blocks of the break-dancing movement. Thirty years later, every riff in this manic workout will still incite spontaneous acts of backspinning at a park near you" (Poulson-Bryant and Fontaine 2002:7).

The ability of this song to move b-boys is apparent, as Mr. Supreme continues:

That particular song is *the* b-boy anthem. The *one*. . . .

I usually have that record with me, everywhere I go. Just because you never know. It's just one of those records that I always take with me. . . . It's a powerful song, there's lots of energy in it. The change-ups and the orchestrated [horn] hits and everything. . . .

It's the energy of the song and the way that you feel the song. I mean, I'm an original b-boy, you know what I'm saying? . . . And it's like, feeling that song within your body, when you hear it, the energy that just—it makes you wanna dance. More so than any other song.

Even, like, the other night, when I was spinning, these guys started b-boying. Everybody got all happy, they gathered around and there was lots of energy. But it seemed like—even though there was that much energy—when I dropped "Apache," there was even *more* energy. It was like the turbo boost. (Mr. Supreme, interview)

Mr. Supreme cites many valuable aspects that "Apache" offers: its rhythm, its horn arrangements, its energy, and the way it seems to animate the human body. For the deejay, though, all of these aspects are subsumed to its functional value: it can be depended upon to make a good social situation even better, which is why Mr. Supreme specifies that it is "one of those records that I always take with me."[8]

The ability to bring forth fun, energetic social gatherings is the deejays' stock in trade. Having canonical songs at their disposal is one tactic that is often utilized:

It all depends on the vibe of the moment, the spirit of the energy, and what's happening at the moment. It's kinda like a half-improvised and half set-up thing, the way that I do it. And I'll bring some cuts that are definitely the classic joints, but then I'll also bring a set of cuts [that] are kinda like warm-up cuts. Say, like, if I'm deejaying a b-boying [event], right? If I'm deejaying the whole thing, I'll definitely bring some warm-up cuts. Something not too hype, something just kinda like mid-tempo, but upbeat at the same time. Get everybody warmed up.

But, all of a sudden, when I feel and I see the b-boys getting really into it, and you see, like, two guys or two crews really getting into it and starting to battle, that's when I'll throw on the really hype cuts, the really serious cuts that the b-boys would really enjoy the break to. Whether it's like "Just Begun," "The Mexican," "Apache." It's whatever song at the moment, what the b-boys are feeling. From then, I'll just hit 'em with song after song after song, where it's basically, you know, I just want them to lose their mind[s] when they're breakdancing. (DJ E-Rok, interview)

It is useful at this point to compare the work of the contemporary hip-hop deejay to that of the "selector" in Jamaican dance-hall music, as described by Stolzoff (2000), from which the role of the hip-hop deejay is derived:[9]

Choosing what songs to play is no simple matter. Competent selectors think about tempo, key, texture, genre, mood, and theme, among other things, when deciding which record will follow the one they are playing. These "intelligent" selectors keep the crowd on its toes by the seemingly improvisational ordering of his selections, yet his selections have to "make sense" and are far from random. In actuality, the selector draws on both established sequences of songs as well as spontaneous gut feelings about what song should go next. (Stolzoff 2000:203)

As I mentioned earlier, the development of a framework of songs that is responsive to the needs of b-boys at any given moment is one of the major goals for deejays at b-boy events. Moreover, the ability to deejay b-boy events, once developed, can also be deployed strategically by deejays to bring the b-boy sensibility into other performance environments, such as nightclubs. DJ DV-One, for example, does this as a conscious strategy:

Part of being a deejay is being kind of in tune, or really responsive, to what your crowd is doing. So if you're deejaying and then you see someone in the corner b-boying, maybe you play like two or three more b-boy cuts in a row, to see how many other b-boys are there. See who else is gonna start b-boying. Or, you could have people b-boying and come up to you and be like "Yo, play some b-boy cuts." And then that would start off your b-boy set. (DJ DV-One, interview)

The deejay can use the symbolic power of b-boy songs to create an exciting environment in non-b-boy contexts. This is not insignificant. One of the hallmarks of good deejays is that the audience trusts their judgment with regard to which songs are appropriate to play at any given time; they know how to rock a crowd. Their understanding of how music serves various social needs is the primary reason that fans pay money to hear them. While other factors may come into play (e.g., institutional status, the size and diversity of their record collection, whether they have a radio show), they are all secondary to the deejay's ability to facilitate positive social situations in general, and a sense of group cohesion in particular. Again, while a deejay's actions occur in real time, his or her split-second decisions are informed by years of experience, as well as by conscious planning. This experience, it is worth noting, is the mirror image of the crowd's experience. What has historically worked for deejays is, by definition, what crowds have enjoyed. And crowds enjoy watching b-boys and b-girls.

As I mentioned earlier, the different varieties of hip-hop often overlap. For those who view hip-hop as a cultural practice, there is a general understanding—originally developed by Afrika Bambaataa, the Zulu Nation, and the Rock Steady Crew—that hip-hop comprises four elements: deejaying, emceeing/rapping, b-boying, and graffiti (Bambaataa subsequently added a fifth element: knowledge). Adherence to the elements mythology is one of the primary factors that hip-hop traditionalists use to distinguish themselves from those whom they see as having a more superficial interest in the popular music aspect of hip-hop. Taking into account that, by its nature, graffiti does not come into play in a musical performance, it is worth noting that the pop music aspect of hip-hop (i.e., rap music) is composed of emceeing and deejaying (or some deejaying substitute). Therefore, an environment that contains only emceeing and deejaying is a rap environment and thus ideologically ambiguous from the point of view of traditionalists. But an environment that contains emceeing, deejaying, *and* b-boying is a hip-hop environment, that is, one concerned with history, tradition, and community values. B-boying alone is enough to tip the balance. And canonical songs speak to and for the b-boys. A song like "Apache," then, can actually alter the environment for all participants, even those who are not themselves b-boys or b-girls.

Moreover, not only do these songs promote b-boying and the environment it creates, but they are also fun for others to dance to as well. "The key to the whole hip-hop culture is built on the deejays playing for the dancers," observes Michael Holman. "And not just the b-boys and b-girls, but...the club dancers. You can have a very good time dancing to 'Give It Up or Turnit a Loose' without having to breakdance. Believe me" (Michael Holman, interview).

These opportunities, while valued for their own sake, are also viewed functionally by deejays. If they can use the b-boy canon to create a sense of group cohesion in the moment, then they can count the evening as a professional success, a step toward greater respect and earning power. While most deejays believe their work can be art, they are well aware that an economic imperative may take precedence if conflicts arise:

> In your club, you pretty much have to be really really selfless. You know, 'cause you can't go to a club and play for a crowd of people and expect to play your personal favorites because, you know, a lotta people might not be feeling you. So you have to play pretty much what people wanna hear, and then you have to manipulate it in a way to where it's the way you like to hear it. So, if it's a song you

don't like, maybe you can juggle it. Or mix it with a different song or just speed it up, slow it down, however. But you pretty much have to be selfless and play to the crowd in a club-type setting. (DJ DV-One, interview).

But this does this not exclude the promotion of ideas about tradition; in the case of the b-boy canon, it virtually demands it. As DJ E-Rok puts it:

It's definitely something like a ritual that you do. And it kinda keeps the culture alive....These songs were very important songs of...hip-hop culture. And as a deejay you try to play those songs, and you try to educate that these were the songs that made a lotta noise during the golden age of hip-hop. And, basically, you wanna get a crowd response to that. (DJ E-Rok, interview)

The b-boy canon is a tool of tradition building as much as it is a result of it. The existence of a b-boy canon is one of the things that makes b-boying a single community. By dancing to "Apache" or "It's Just Begun," any contemporary b-boy or b-girl is arguing that communal values are shared by anyone who has b-boyed over the last four decades. The fact that such gestures are not unique to hip-hop is not a weakness on hip-hop's part, but a strength. If hip-hop uses its historical consciousness to achieve the same goals as any other musical culture, that only gives us the opportunity to dig more deeply into the specifics of how it does so and what those choices can tell us about hip-hop culture, its values, and its concerns.

The existence of a b-boy canon represents a particular perspective on tradition and a particular way of engaging with it. Specifically, it advocates two general premises: that there should be a close relationship between music and choreography; and that this relationship should serve as a conduit that allows b-boys and b-girls to transfer the historical associations of the music to their dance and, by extension, to their bodies.

In terms of the first premise—the advocacy of a close relationship between music and dance—several significant themes emerge. The first of these is the clear fusion of African American and Latino cultural outlooks. The recordings themselves are drawn primarily from African American musical genres, particularly soul and funk music. But within that tradition, the chosen songs tend to be the ones with the most obvious Latin connections. Not only do the recordings themselves contain many obvious Latin elements, such as the use of Latin percussion, but they also have a deeper conceptual foundation in Latin music, making use of such ideas as the cha-cha-cha feel and the clave concept. The use and significance of breaks also points to a world view influenced by the experience of dancing to Latin music. The fusion of Caribbean and African American approaches, in turn, suggests a broader, more Afro-diasporic approach to dance. The break's invitation to fill the silence with motion and the idea of integrating music, mind, and body through rhythm patterns both speak to a view of performance that sees music and dance as being two facets of a single greater activity.

In terms of the second premise—the idea that these songs allow b-boys and b-girls to carry history in their bodies—a number of issues also appear, the most obvious of which is the historical significance of the songs themselves. The fact that these specific songs are associated with the early history of b-boying is an explicit part of their appeal. But beyond that, there are other elements that come into play. The emotions that the songs evoke—particularly, aggressiveness—provide a deep connection to that history as well. The form of the songs also serves to maintain the social form of the event. These songs have special moments in them, which are manifested in real time every time the songs are played. On top of that, b-boys and b-girls are encouraged to develop the ability to rock the beat of a record, in essence to interact with the original musicians in a way that transcends historical time. Moreover, the fact that dancers actively train themselves for these goals reinforces the effect. Developing a feel for how to dance properly to a specific song is to have the culture in your body.

To dance well to the chosen songs is to live in hip-hop history. The existence of a recognized group of b-boy songs from another era represents a relationship between individual skills and collective history. The b-boy canon serves as an almost spiritual connection between modern proponents and the historical essence of the dance, giving strength, energy, and legitimacy to modern devotees. Or, as Alien Ness puts it, "I think, just for the sake of spirituality, you should get into those beats. Because those are the beats that moved the original b-boys, and it had to be for a reason. Without a doubt. So just for spiritual reasons, you should try to get into those beats and really see what it is about that beat that moved people and moves *you*" (Alien Ness, interview).

# 3

## "Getting Your Foundation"
### Pedagogy

> Battle, learn, but also teach. Don't just take.... It's
> like, if you're taking the harvest, and you constantly
> eat from the harvest but you don't replant. You don't
> have nothing to harvest any more. And that's the thing
> with hip-hop: a lot of people, they take, take, take, but
> they're not replanting what they're taking.... My thing
> is that I always tell them: *teach everybody*.... Because
> the main thing is that hip-hop, breaking, graffiti is
> about the people.
> —Anthony Colon, b-boy, graffiti writer, and martial artist

While knowledge about many elements of hip-hop—rap music, especially—is primarily developed through television, radio, the Internet, and recordings, b-boying is almost always learned through personal interaction. This may seem so obvious as to not be worth mentioning, but it is significant for several reasons. First, it is important to remember that there are still elements of hip-hop that are not primarily situated within the mass media, a fact that is rarely reflected in either the popular press or hip-hop scholarship (aside from some excellent work on graffiti; see especially Austin 2001; Castleman 1982; Miller 2002).

But even when noncommercial hip-hop is discussed, it is almost always within the context of a self-consciously "underground" approach where people are specifically rejecting commercialism. But, as I mentioned earlier, this mainstream-versus-underground distinction simply doesn't apply to many aspects of hip-hop. B-boying, for example, is for the most part noncommercial, but not *anti*-commercial. Since career opportunities for b-boys or b-girls are relatively rare, few individuals would become involved in b-boying primarily for that reason. As with anything else, individuals who enjoy b-boying do seek out opportunities to make a living at it. But for the most part, people become b-boys or b-girls primarily because they simply like to do it. Nobody takes up b-boying to get rich.[1]

Faced with a choice between placing b-boying in a category that doesn't really fit, or—more commonly—ignoring it altogether, it may be more valuable to rethink the distinction itself. A useful approach may be to view these issues in more practical terms, that is, to distinguish between hip-hop that is primarily devoted to the creation of a product and hip-hop that is primarily an activity performed for its own sake. Hip-hop of the latter variety—hip-hop culture—will tend toward the unmediated, noncommercial, and communal, but more as a practical matter than an ideological one.

Besides alerting us to such issues, personal interaction is also important because the way the dance is taught exerts a profound influence on the way it is experienced. It affects the way individuals understand the history of the form and their own place in it, the way they express their individual and group identities, and the way they pass this knowledge on to others. The previous chapter provided one example of this: b-boys and b-girls learn to feel history in their bodies through certain songs. By understanding these processes, we can develop a more nuanced vision of other unmediated aspects of hip-hop.

Finally, since almost all b-boys and b-girls learn about the dance through participant observation (though they wouldn't call it that), my use of that approach in the preparation of this work is consistent with b-boying's own learning style. This became clear to me in a conversation I had with Buz, an uprocker from Brooklyn in his early 40s, when I mentioned that I was almost finished with the first draft of this book. "Oh yeah," he replied, "I forgot you were doing that" (Buz, interview). Apparently, my constant inquiries about dance history and aesthetics were not significantly different from those that Buz had heard from others. The shape of the knowledge in this book reflects my personal experience to a great degree. But that experience—while distinctive in its scholarly orientation—is far from unique among b-boys.

Although I had witnessed b-boying many times since the early 1980s, my introduction to the rich philosophy behind it came in the spring of 2003, when I taught a course entitled Hip-Hop and Performance at New York University. Taking advantage of the opportunity afforded by teaching a hip-hop class in New York City, our small graduate seminar was graced with the presence of a variety of hip-hop figures, including producer Steve "Steinski" Stein, "media assassin" Harry Allen, journalists Jeff Chang and Elizabeth Mendez-Berry, scholar/musician Kyra Gaunt; and dancer, activist, and hip-hop historian Jorge "Fabel" Pabon.

The previous fall, I had seen Fabel speak at a Zulu Nation panel in Harlem, where he impressed all in attendance with his deep historical knowledge and nuanced analysis of issues facing the contemporary hip-hop community. At one point, he noted that Puerto Rican hip-hoppers needn't feel that the Spanish part of their ancestry was in conflict with the African and native Caribbean aspects, since Spain's culture was itself heavily influenced by that of Africa during the Moorish era (711–1492 CE). It was a far cry from the "yo, yo, yo, you know what I'm sayin'?" discourse imagined by so many of hip-hop's detractors. In addition to the many similar insights he provided to our class, he mentioned that he taught formal classes in popping and locking (West Coast hip-hop dance forms known collectively as "funk styles").

That summer, I began attending Fabel's classes. I had chosen popping and locking over b-boying for two reasons, the first being that Fabel was the only hip-hop dance teacher whom I knew and that is what he taught. The second reason was that, at age 35, I felt I was both too old and too fat to become a b-boy. In Fabel's class, I soon became friends with a fellow student, Francis "Mysterio" Rodriguez. As he quickly advanced beyond me, Francis decided to begin private lessons in popping with GeoMatrix, also of the Rock Steady Crew, and graciously invited me to join him. Geo rented teaching space from some kind of semi-legitimate Russian modeling agency on 35th Street in Manhattan, about which the less said the better.

At my request, GeoMatrix, who was a b-boy in addition to being a popper, began teaching me b-boy foundation at the end of each of our popping lessons. That fall, Francis and I went to support GeoMatrix at the New York finals of the B-Boy Master's Pro-Am in the South Bronx, where he was competing in the popping division. At that event, Francis introduced me to Ralph "King Uprock" Casanova, who ran a weekly afterschool b-boy practice at P.S. 93 in Ridgewood, Queens. The following spring, I began to attend these practices, where I started learning b-boy and uprock techniques in earnest. Within several months, I had lost 20 pounds without any dieting at all, and I haven't looked back since. Subsequently, I have studied with several teachers and participated in numerous b-boy jams, practices, and parties. I have internalized many b-boy values, and I am the better for it. I have learned that there is a b-boy way to be in the world.

The nature of my ethnographic engagement with the New York b-boy community went beyond simply participating; the experience actually made me rethink aspects of my own personal history, dating back to my childhood in the '70s. Since many of the elders of the b-boy scene began their careers as teenagers in the late '70s and early '80s, many are still only in their late 30s or early 40s, making them my contemporaries. As someone who grew up in Connecticut with two parents from New York, this meant that many of my childhood experiences—such as watching Saturday afternoon kung fu movies on channel 5, visiting relatives in New York, and forcing my parents to take me to what were in retrospect some pretty dicey martial arts supply stores in the city—had unknowingly occupied the same time and space as the foundational hip-hop moments described by my consultants. While I was not in any way involved in these moments—or even the cultures that gave birth to them—I had wandered

GeoMatrix. Photo by author.

obliviously through them three decades earlier. At one point in my research, I found myself walking around the Upper West Side of Manhattan with Amigo Rock, discussing the gangs that had controlled this area during the early years of hip-hop. Suddenly, I realized we had just walked past the building where my grandmother lived before she moved to Florida in the mid-'70s. Some of my earliest memories are of looking out that window at the street life below, and it was an extremely odd sensation to realize that Amigo could have been one of the kids I had seen playing so many years before.

I am suggesting that, since hip-hop was actually designed to incorporate concepts and experiences from diverse sources, these kinds of revisionist moments are not just artifacts of my own mind. They are actually typical of the way hip-hop enables its practitioners to reinterpret their lives through individual aesthetic creativity and skill. Several years ago, for example, I read an interview with graffiti pioneer FUZZ ONE, in which he noted that he had "kinged" his elementary school at the age of eight. In graffiti terms, the word *king* refers to someone who is recognized as the most prolific writer in a particular area (traditionally, a specific subway line). It is semantically interesting for two reasons. First, it presumes the status of king as an objective fact, rather than an opinion that reasonable people could disagree on (to this day, graffiti historians can tell you who was the king of a specific subway line at any point in history). Second, by transforming it into an active verb, rather than part of a passive construction—he didn't "become king" of his school, he kinged it—graffiti writers reinforce their ideology of self-reliance. When someone kings something, it is his own accomplishment, not something that is bestowed upon him by others. But it is unlikely that FUZZ ONE would have been initiated into the complex ideologies of graffiti writing when he was eight (around 1970), not only because he was eight—which is reason enough—but also because the ideologies themselves were not yet fully formed at that point in history. Rather, what his assertion suggests is that, when he later looked back at his experience of writing graffiti in elementary school, he realized that it was consistent with the concept of kinging an area, and he retroactively included that experience on his graffiti resume.

What I am suggesting is that hip-hop culture gives its participants the power to redefine themselves and their history, not by omission or selective emphasis, but by embracing *all* of their previous experience as material for self-expression in the present moment. "That's why the dance form is so phenomenal," says Trac 2. "Because it allows anybody to take this dance form the way it was founded and add what they are. And *who* they are" (Trac 2, interview). And if some of the most appealing aspects of b-boying are the lessons it teaches about how to turn your own life experiences into the raw material of artistic expression, it must also be noted that that itself is a kind of ethnography.

Some of the most powerful lessons I have learned concern the way one is to carry oneself in life, particularly with regard to the relationship between creativity and self-confidence. Self-assurance is the bottom line of b-boying: one must project an absolute certainty that, if one does something valuable, no matter how subtle, it *will* be appreciated. As Will Straw has noted, this attitude is the foundation of "hipness":

> Hipness and nerdishness both begin with the mastery of a symbolic field; what the latter lacks is a controlled economy of revelation, a sense of when and how things are to be spoken of. Hipness maintains boundaries to entry by requiring that the possession of knowledge be made to seem less significant than the tactical sense of how and when it is made public. Cultivation of a corpus (of works, of facts) assumes the air of instinctuality only when it is transformed into a set of gestures enacted across time. The stances of hip require that knowledge and judgment be incorporated into bodily self-presentation, where they settle into the postures of an elusive and enigmatic instinctuality and may therefore be suggested even when they are not made blatantly manifest. (Straw 1997:9)

When Alien Ness told me that his approach to dance was inspired by kung fu movies, for example, I half-jokingly asked if he had a "drunken" style, referring to a common theme of Hong Kong action movies. In the movies, many kung fu styles have alternative, "drunken" forms, in which the practitioner imitates intoxication to confuse his opponent, and it occurred to me that this concept could be equally effective in the context of competitive dance. "Of course," Ness replied and quickly found a videotape of a battle in which he had integrated the general approach and several signature moves from Jackie Chan's *Drunken Master* (1978) into his performance. It wasn't until later that I understood that, as a b-boy, he *had* to wait for me to ask the question before he could show me the video. And it wasn't until much later that I realized that, in doing so, he was teaching me a valuable lesson about the b-boy mentality: part of being prepared is not to let your opponent know exactly how prepared you are.

B-boying—and hip-hop in general—is like baiting a series of intellectual traps. If they told you where the traps were, that would defeat the whole purpose. Unfortunately, many academic observers of hip-hop assume that, just because hip-hop principles often go unstated, they therefore do not exist. One of the main reasons that Alien Ness created his drunken style was so that, if anyone ever asked him if he had a drunken style, he would be able to say yes. He—like many b-boys—has left literally hundreds of similar markers in the world, awaiting the day when one of them will become useful. And that is precisely the attitude he projects when he begins to dance. The b-boy attitude is not false bravado: it is the intellectual confidence of a master strategist who believes that he has every possibility covered. And, of course, this is a valuable life skill for anyone to learn. The pedagogy of b-boying is designed to teach precisely these kinds of lessons.

Virtually all b-boys and b-girls were introduced to the practice by friends. B-girl KaoticBlaze describes a typical experience:

My best friend saw me [dancing] and she was like, "Oh, you would be a dope b-girl." And I'm like, "What do you mean? A breakdancer?" You know, cause I wasn't. I was in hip-hop, but I wasn't in the scene like that. She's like, "Yeah! You have rhythm! You have motion!"...

I was like, "OK, I'll try it." And I was never an acrobatic person. I played basketball. Like, that was my thing, playing basketball. So I started trying it. You know, I liked it. I started practicing with Zulu Nation in Tampa, in Florida—that's where I'm from. And met a lot of people and just kept on breaking for about seven months. I ended up moving to New York and stopped completely, 'cause I wasn't involved in the scene. I didn't know anybody. Everybody that I did know was back in Florida, so I stopped breaking....

One of my best friends...knew that I would throw down every now and then, a little bit. And once you start, at least once you fall in love with breaking, it doesn't leave you. Even though you could be 80 years old, you probably throw a little uprock. But he was like, "Yo, there's this practice spot over here in Queens, I want you to come." It was King Uprock's spot. So I went there.

The first time I went there, they had a dollar jam battle. And he was like, "Enter, enter." I was like, "I haven't breaked in freakin' two years! How am I gonna break?" This was January of last year. And so he convinced me, and I entered and there was only one other girl that entered. It was like the weirdest situation....

So I was like, "Fuck it! I'ma do it! Whatever!" Cause I have, like, a[n] attitude sometimes. Like, it's *b-girling*, you know! So I entered...and even 'til this day, people will come up to me: "Yo, you're from that King Uprock battle? You did *nothing* good on the floor, but you were coming at her like you wanted to murder her! You lived up to your name!" (KaoticBlaze, interview)

This story contains many of the major elements of the typical experience: the role of friends in bringing a new dancer into the fold, the fact that when she moved away from her breaking friends she stopped doing the dance, the significance of the battle, the centrality of style. But perhaps the most important aspect of her story is that, despite her lack of practical ability at the time, people were impressed with her attitude and encouraged her to continue on that basis.

B-boy and popper Tiny Love had a similar experience of being introduced to the dance through an ill-prepared battle. He characterizes it as the way he actually became a b-boy:

I became a b-boy by [going] to this place...[the] Tunnel, in the '90s, and they had like a b-boy event. A b-boy battle. So I didn't know what's b-boying. To me, popping is b-boying. To me, waving is b-boying, you know? Back then, you know? So I entered the battle and I battled a b-boy. And in the first round, I burned him. He did some, like, freezes with a little footwork and some toprock. And, you know, I did my popping.

Tiny Love. Photo by author.

Basically, I did, like—I used to have a blowback, you know like I would turn on my back and come up, it was like a power move. And I basically did that to him and everyone went "oh" and I burned him. And I was the only popper in the event to pass to the second round. (Tiny Love, interview)

Battling was also a significant part of Alien Ness's education. In his case, the process was the result of strategic thinking about how to manage defeat. "[When I started,] I used to be scared," he remembers:

> Like, I would battle, but I would never battle one-on-one. I would battle crews. I would call out whole crews, 'cause then even if you look stupid, you're still a winner. You understand what I mean? Or me and my partner, Chino in those days, we used to go and challenge whole crews, and we'd bite from the people we battled. We'd get smoked, but we'd always get little bits of props, here and there, because we was battling whole crews. (Alien Ness, interview)

Knowing that, as a beginner, he was bound to lose anyway, Ness maximized the benefits of the situation by challenging groups rather than individuals. As a result, despite losing the battles, he was able to get credit for his bravery and also learn the moves of those he challenged. Such strategic thinking about social situations is itself a major part of the attitude that b-boy culture tries to produce in its adherents.

The idea that it is possible—much less common—to begin a b-boy career through competition says a lot about the form itself. In the DVD bonus section of the groundbreaking film *Style Wars*, graffiti writer, painter, and Rock Steady Crew b-boy DOZE is strident about the value of feeling and soul over technical ability: "Style versus technique, style will always win," he says. "*Always*. And that's what a b-boy is: style, not technique." B-boys feel that an individual with style can learn technique, but the opposite is rarely the case. It is for that reason that such trial-by-fire moments tend to figure prominently in the stories of most b-boys and b-girls; it is those moments that most clearly demonstrate whether an individual is cut out for b-boying. B-Girl Emiko describes another typical experience:

> In 2000, I went to B-Boy Summit in L.A.... That was my first event ever. Then I saw so many b-boys and -girls. And I saw this b-girl Little Bear from Canada. She was really, really nice to me. She was good and I was just a beginner, but she was like, "Oh, just come into the cypher," you know, "don't worry about whatever you do." So I was like, "OK," so I got comfortable in the cypher, but I couldn't go to other cypher because I was scared. But me and my friends with the crew were like, "we have to go into the cypher." We all, like, from, you know, countryside. Like, we have to do it, and they were so scared. All the b-boys were so scared. I was like, "Ah, forget all you guys, I'm just gonna go in." I was the weakest one, but I just went inside. And they're like, "Oh my God, Emiko went, then we have to go in too!" So everyone just started going into the cypher, and it was just so fun. We decide to practice every day after that. (B-Girl Emiko, interview)

This idea—that attitude comes first—goes back to the earliest days of b-boying, as in the case of BOM5, an early b-boy and graffiti writer, who learned from the original Zulu Kings in the early '70s:

As a little kid, I would go to the handball courts and I would see these guys dancing. I didn't know what they were doing, but they were rocking from the top, like we would rock in a gang, to the bottom, doing helicopters and swipes and all that. And one-shot head spins and stuff like that. And I was like, "Hey, what's going on here?"...I tried to speak to Beaver and them. Those are the guys that put me on. The funny thing about them, I used to go out to the handball court, but they thought I was too small to get with them....They wouldn't bother me, but they would just say, "Kid, can you move over and step to the side?" Either on the basketball court or the handball court. They would practice on the cement. On the concrete.

And I would ask them a couple of times, "Yo, can you teach me?"

"Kid, come on man. You wanna watch? You watch. But just please get to the side...."

One time they had a...party in Bronx River...a park jam.[2] And I went there in the park jam and they had a circle....So I was nervous, and I was on the edge of the circle and all of a sudden my cousin pushed me. So I was in there, and I was like a jackrabbit: I just went wild! I was rocking, sliding on the floor....I didn't know what the hell I did, I just went crazy!...I was trying to copy everything I saw. The helicopters...I even tried to do a headstand, but I couldn't even spin on my head. And then the other guys pushed me out, right?

So after a while just standing there, that guy Beaver came up to me, saying, "Hey, don't I know you? Where you got that stuff? You biting moves?" You know, "You copying moves?" He said, "Yo, who's teaching you?"

And I said, "*You guys* teach me!"

And that's when they were like, "*What?*"

And I said, "Yeah: you, you, that one, you know, the big guy..."

And they were like, "Wait, wait, wait..."

And I said, "Yeah, don't you [recognize] me? I'm that little kid."

"You're that little fuckin' Puerto Rican kid that comes every day?!" And he's like, "Yo, you really interested in this?"

I said, "Yeah, man, I want to do this!"

And he said, "All right. Come back, man....We're usually here at this time, after school."

So I started going there and just hanging out with them more. And I got to be really close and cool with Cisco Kid, El Dorado Mike, Simmons. And Robbie Rob....They're all, like, motivating me and teaching me....They took me as, like, a little brother, and they started teaching me more. And I felt happy and motivated. (BOM5, interview)

When Character, a b-boy in his 20s, speaks of his introduction to b-boying, it quickly becomes clear that entering a social circle was almost as important as learning the actual moves:

I met up with a guy named Mikey Love who was from a crew called Total Control Breakers. He kind of helped me out in the beginning. Teaching me like some of the basic stuff. Then, after that, I moved on to another crew called Full FX, which I

BOM5 and Ralph "King Uprock" Casanova. Photo by author.

just recently got out of two or three years ago. They're still around, but I was hang-ing out a lot with Kid Glyde, which is one of the guys from Dynamic [Dynamic Rockers, an old-school b-boy crew], right now he's the leader of Dynamic. And basically helped him begin second-generation Dynamic. And was very influenced by the culture and everything that they were telling me; [it] was really inspiring. I ended up meeting his father, Glyde. That was a big inspiration. And ended up meeting this guy Kid Freeze, Spinner, and a lot of people. And he showed me a book by Martha Cooper, which kind of helped me fill in the gaps of the missing links of time. (B-Boy Character, interview)

Character's depiction of his b-boy education consists not only of learning basic moves, but also meeting members of the influential early b-boy crew the Dynamic Rockers and learning the history of the dance, including from books. Most b-boys and b-girls refer to these subjects collectively with the term *foundation*. "Foundation is the combination of the mental approach, philosophies, the attitude, the rhythm, style and character combined with the move," explains legendary b-boy Ken Swift in a recent interview on a Korean b-boy Web site (Swift 2007).

"Foundation: the first thing is energy," adds Anthony Colon:

Spirit. Attitude. Without that? Nothing. You could have a hundred head spins. Doesn't mean anything. If you don't have energy in your dance? The spirit of the dance? It's like a singer that can sing a high note, but the song has no feeling, and then you have a singer that doesn't sing high notes, but you feel the music. Feel the energy. And they ride the music. And you're like, *damn*. You feel that music.... And they don't have that operatic voice, but you feel that there's something there. You're like, "wow." It touches you. And breaking's the same way. (Anthony Colon, interview)

"Not trying to sound like a philosopher or anything like that... but to me, foundation means the beginning of life," says Waaak:

No matter what that life is. Foundation is the first thing that happens for anything. You have to have the foundation.... Whether you believe we came from God, or we came from monkeys or we came from dust and a comet that exploded, it started from somewhere. It started from something. Whether it be an idea, whether it be minerals, sperm, semen, whatever it is. We started from something. And that's what foundation is. If you don't have foundation, you can't exist. That's the way I see it.... You can't build a building without foundation, right? For everything that you do that's technical, you have to have some foundation. You want to be an engineer? You want to be a scientist? Math and science, those are things that you need: that's your foundation of what you do. So I don't understand how people argue [about] foundation.... You shouldn't be able to argue that. It goes without saying. (Waaak One, interview)

There is an almost mystical connotation to the term, particularly in the context of teaching, where it provides a clear lineage for each student. From the teacher's point of view, this relationship represents a legacy, much like that of other apprenticeship systems. "Why is it that certain people can do other people's movements?" asks b-girl Seoulsonyk. "Because it was passed down specifically from one b-boy to another, saying, like, 'Yo, I'm teaching you my shit right now, and you're basically gonna carry my torch'" (Seoulsonyk, interview). Most b-boys can tell another dancer's lineage from her style alone.[3]

In literal terms, a strong foundation gives a building balance, stability, and durability over time. It is what allows it to rise without being toppled by its own weight. Similarly, the idea that b-boying is founded not only upon a series of physical movements, but also on attitude, rhythm, style, character, strategy, tradition, and philosophy makes a profound statement about the way b-boys and b-girls wish the art to move forward. It saturates movement with history and sets clear aesthetic boundaries for future innovation. For someone with a proper sense of b-boy foundation, a move that lacks the correct rhythm or character is unacceptable. But dancers who do have a strong understanding of foundation can be boldly innovative, knowing that they are well grounded in the tradition. In fact, when b-boys and b-girls are criticized for being overly abstract or experimental, their first line of defense is usually to demonstrate—either verbally or physically—their knowledge of foundation. It is notable that this defense, if properly executed, is almost always accepted.

B-boy Ru sees foundation on a more practical level, as a system that has been designed to balance the energy and expressive potential of b-boying with physical safety:

> A baby, he has to learn how to walk. But before he can walk, he has to crawl. So basically, the foundation is steps towards not hurting yourself.... These guys are not getting hurt because they started slowly developing a foundation, which is basically a structure to increase their passion, but do it in a way that they stay safe and elevate to a different level. (Ru, interview)

Since the concept of foundation combines physical discipline with philosophy in a sophisticated way, it should be no surprise that many compare their b-boy educations to martial arts training. Many b-boys include Bruce Lee in their list of dance influences, and it is probably not a coincidence that the birth of b-boying dates almost precisely to the year in which Bruce Lee achieved popularity in the United States (1973). "I try to be like myself, like Bruce Lee did," says King Uprock. "He took all the styles and he made one. I took all the styles, I made one."

> **Joe:** Was Bruce Lee a big inspiration to you? I notice you mention him a lot.
>
> **Uprock:** Oh, of course. He's always been, since I was a kid. I saw him once: that was it! He became like my idol. (King Uprock, interview)

"If you read [Bruce Lee's] *Tao of Jeet Kune Do*, it applies to b-boying," says Alien Ness. "He talks about rhythms, broken rhythms, the importance of footwork, the importance of foundation, you know? In competition—or in combat—the need, or *not the need*, of all this flashy stuff that all the other martial arts are made of" (Alien Ness, interview). It is not surprising that Bruce Lee would be an influence on b-boying. He was arguably the best-known nonwhite action hero of the '70s, he developed fighting strategies that are directly applicable to b-boying, and he represents an attitude toward apprenticeship that is respectful without being subservient. On a more direct level, Hong Kong action movies that depicted martial arts training were a mainstay of youth culture in New York in the '70s and '80s. Many theaters in Times Square showed kung fu movies at that time, and one of New York's independent television stations, WNEW (now Fox affiliate WNYW), had a long-standing policy of playing these films as a regular feature on its Saturday afternoon *Drive-In Movie* programming, which ran from 1981 through 1988.[4]

Like kung fu, the b-boy educational system not only offers a traceable educational lineage, but often a strong, accomplished mentor. "Trac 2 just started schooling me, mentally," Alien Ness remembers. "All the important lessons in b-boying, I have learned from Trac 2. And he has shown me those lessons without ever having to touch the floor once. You can quote me on that.... He has never had to touch the floor once. Ever. In teaching me. And that's why I still say Trac 2 is one of the greatest b-boys that ever lived" (Alien Ness, interview). B-boy Ru expresses a similar perspective about his own teachers. "I've had, actually, great teachers," he says:

> And basically all these teachers had their own cypher.[5] They never knew each other, but they all had their own cypher in the mind. And basically what it was, was that *you must learn your foundation*. And it's not just moves, it's also mental. 'Cause once you get the mental part of it down, it's like no matter if you stop training, you're always training. (Ru, interview)

Tiny Love takes a similar tone when speaking of his teacher, Kwon. "Kwon...started teaching us about b-boying," he remembers:

> Basically, drilling us like crazy. I used to leave from there, I used to have marks— like heavy-duty marks—on my back. Scrape. That floor was so dirty, I used to eat the floor. I used to sweat, like the whole floor was full of water. It was nasty. For one year, I learned from him. One year, drill[ing] me on b-boying. And all that he would play...was James Brown. James Brown, hardcore. Just James Brown. James Brown. So that gave me, like, a real b-boy foundation. Like, people might think of me that "Oh, he's just a popper." But behind it, I have a real b-boy foundation from Kwon....He's like the Bruce Lee of b-boying. (Tiny Love, interview)

In addition to disciplined training, Alien Ness sees "actual combat" (i.e., competition) as an important component of his own teaching strategy, giving him the opportunity to demonstrate the effectiveness of different approaches to his students. "The day that I can't battle any more, I'm gonna be a miserable person," he predicts:

> Because then there'll be no way of me proving what I'm trying to teach....The only way I could teach people is in actual combat. I lead by example. You know, I don't sit there and tell people, "You're doing this wrong. Foundation is better. You gotta learn foundation." No, I'm gonna show you. I'm gonna enter your battle and I'ma show how I can go all the way to the finals doing nothing but foundation. (Alien Ness, interview)

Interestingly, hip-hop is now old enough that foundation can actually be passed down literally from parent to child, as in the case that Character alluded to above. The Dynamic Rockers' Kid Glyde, one of New York's most prominent b-boys, was taught by his father, Glyde. And B-Boy Phantom actually learned the dance from his mother, who was an early b-girl. "My mother was into b-boying," he notes:

> She was actually a b-girl. She knew the basics. Basic Indian step. Basically, just dancing. Basic rules, basic chair freeze, and basic footwork. And then from there, I kind of expanded and did my own thing....She was the one that basically introduced me to the dance and introduced me to how it's supposed to be done, pretty much.[6] (B-Boy Phantom, interview)

As with martial arts, the learning process in b-boying is not only one of teacher-to-student transmission. Most teachers have multiple students who encourage and critique each other. Often, these cohorts of students assemble themselves into crews. Even in the absence of a teacher, crew members can inspire and motivate each other. As b-girl Seoulsonyk, a student of Richard "Breakeasy" Santiago, notes, "Our crew will literally be coming up with routines, and we'll ask, 'What would Breakeasy do?'" (Seoulsonyk, interview).

"We try to drill ourselves," explains B-Boy Character. "So we'll come out with drills. Like, we'll first do just straight-up toprock to footwork. No freezes, no nothing. And then from there, we'll just do footwork to freezes. And then from there, we'll go into our power moves and air moves and stuff from that" (B-Boy Character, interview). As a practical matter, this kind of disciplined, systematic practice would be difficult for an individual to maintain alone. Part of the value of a crew is that it allows breakers to combine socialization with practice, making the necessary repetition more interesting.

As Amigo Rock, a b-boy and uprocker in his late 30s, reflects, socialization was a major factor in early b-boying. "We used to pull out a radio," he remembers:

> You know, have a little boombox. Hook it up right there. Sit right there on the benches. And at night, too, after 10, 11 on, like, a Friday night. You know, we'd get together, we'd hang out. And as we're hanging out, you know, drinking beers, smoking, we'd do our little thing. It wasn't like an official thing. . . . you know, we practiced while we hanged out, basically. . . . it was more fun that way. (Amigo Rock, interview)

This reflects the way that preexisting social relationships—and different kinds of social relationships—were naturally integrated into the culture of the dance. As BOM5 notes, early b-boying was only one of many activities that a group of neighborhood youths might engage in; a b-boy crew of the late '70s could easily have the identical membership to a graffiti crew or stickball team. "B-boy crews were [also] graf crews," he says:

> Because a lot of the people that [were] involved are writers too. So almost every-body did everything at one time. When you were dancing, you . . . danced and then you did something else. Like you did deejaying. Or you'd try to emcee. Or you'd try to do graffiti. It was always something else. And martial arts. Getting involved with martial arts was a big thing at that time, too. (BOM5, interview)

"The thing is that people may not see the connection with breaking, but it's a huge connection," agrees Anthony Colon. "Because everything that started coming out at that time, you did it together. . . . Whether you did the graffiti, the bombing, you did it together. You went together. . . . You played manhunt, you'd climb the roofs, went roof to roof, you did it how? *Together.* It was always a pack of kids, like a pack of wolves" (Anthony Colon, interview). Ultimately, as Richard Santiago points out, "It's a [collaborative] thing; it's not just one or two. 'I' is hip-hop? No. *'We'* is hip-hop" (Santiago, interview).

Buz and Amigo Rock. Photo by author.

While the immediate effect of this philosophy is obvious—you're more likely to practice if it's fun—it also seasons the dance itself with subtle social implications. The relationships between the members, as well as the contexts in which those relationships are forged, the other things they do together when they are not b-boying, all become encoded in the way the dance is performed. To this day, the kind of solidarity that such relationships can produce is a valuable aspect of breaking. It is particularly valued in the context of battling, when the group is expected to move seamlessly between improvised individual runs and prearranged group routines. These transitions are not merely a matter of smooth choreography, but also bring into play such things as what the collective vision will be for the routines, how the individual expressions will relate to that collective vision, and how confidently the two can be brought together.

This relationship—between spontaneous dancing and choreographed routines—is a common one in many expressive forms, and it has a particular resonance with jazz improvisation. Part of the movement through time involves negotiating opportunities to shift from organized group expression to improvised individual statements, with each framing the other. In jazz, this can be seen in so-called head arrangements, in which the band plays one or two choruses of composed material that is then followed by a series of solos, before concluding with a recapitulation of the composed theme. Within a single tune, musicians move from being part of an ensemble, to being part of a supporting group (when others are soloing), to being the soloist themselves (when their turn comes), back to being part of the ensemble. Part of the b-boy education is learning how to make similar shifts within the context of the b-boy crew. As with other aspects of b-boying (many of which I will discuss in the next chapter), the expertise and confidence that b-boys and b-girls develop through such practices are directly applicable to other areas of life. They develop a subtle feel for group dynamics and particularly how to maximize their individual accomplishments in a way that works to the benefit of the group.

"The crew member knows what the people in the cypher gonna do because they always see [them] in the practice, and they know... their style very well," explains B-Girl Emiko:

> So if they know that he's gonna hit the freeze, they would do something to support the freeze, you know?... Like, let's say, do some footwork and going to chair freeze or something. But usually people will do the same way to get to the freeze, because that's a way to get it comfortably. So once the crew members see that little step, they're like, "oh, that's coming next." (B-Girl Emiko, interview)

When that connection is not there, she notes, the loss is felt:

> Crews should be just the people who [you] always hung out with. It's not the people who just battle and then say "bye," you know? You go there, battle together, and maybe after the battle you go eat together. When you're off, maybe go to see [a] movie [or] something like that. That's the way it should be. That way, when battle comes, it will be tighter. (B-Girl Emiko, interview)

In many cases, even nondancers also have an important role to play. According to Amigo Rock, nondancing friends provided a sort of focus group that allowed his crew to test out ideas before exposing them to the public at large:

> So then, these guys, whenever we used to have circles, they were there. And you know how loud they are. They would see it and they would just fucking go bananas, you know? And they were fair—they weren't always on my side. I mean, if a guy did a move on me, they would have had no problem being like "aaaaah." So it was not like, just because they were my boys, they were on my side. They gave credit where credit was due, unfortunately!... Which was good, it made you not depend on that.... These guys, they kept you honest, 'cause a lot of guys depend on their crew to pull them through. (Amigo Rock, interview)

These kinds of interactions also help to define the relationship between b-boys and others in their neighborhood. Again, b-boys would—through their dance—attempt to create an image for themselves. This image could then be either accepted or rejected by onlookers. In cases where it was accepted, it set in place an implicit agreement: the b-boys and b-girls, by virtue of their physical skills, had earned the right to define their own places in the neighborhood's social world.

Although modern-day b-boying is not nearly so geographically specific, the same principles still apply. Crews now routinely draw their members from different neighborhoods and even, in some cases, different cities. But vestiges of the neighborhood-based philosophy still remain. Crews are still almost always identified by their location of origin, even if that is now a city or a country rather than a city block. And the kinds of social relationships and roles that once developed in the environment of New York's city streets, having been encoded into b-boying's DNA, are still an important part of the dance.

The dance form was created under specific social and cultural circumstances, and its characteristics— by either design or natural selection—reflected those circumstances. As a cohesive aesthetic developed, those characteristics became valued for their own sake. As a result, those characteristics were maintained, even as the circumstances changed. The social values of the original practitioners thus remain encoded in the dance. I will address this process in a variety of specific areas, but what underlies all of them is the general emphasis on defining one's own identity through a superior dance style and membership in a crew.

As we walked around the Upper West Side of New York, Amigo Rock took me to a somewhat hidden playground in Central Park, where his crew, the Sureshot Boys, used to practice in the '70s:

> See that little part? That's where we used to go practice. Sureshot Boys used to go practice there. Away from everybody. There was a lot of biters. A lot of spies back in those days. I mean, it sounds ridiculous, like, "shit, who would go out of their way to...?" But you don't know, bro.
>
> Shit was so competitive, man. Other crews used to send people out there to see what the hell you were doing. Like the freaking spy wars, nation against nation, Stratego, and shit. You know, "Find out what they're doing! We got a battle next week—let's see what they're up to!" I mean, people wouldn't believe how involved it really was.
>
> Even though it's petty—to a lot of people, it's petty. But, yo, to us, it was like *life and death*. You know, it was amazing, man. I guess importance is what you give it. (Amigo Rock, interview)

Years later, Amigo Rock—now a successful currency trader—has developed an interesting sense of perspective about the seriousness with which b-boys took their enterprise. While he marvels at the lengths to which he used to go, he still remembers why it was so important. As he notes, "importance is what you give it." When winning or losing a dance battle can profoundly change the way you are perceived and treated by your peers for the foreseeable future, it must be approached with the utmost seriousness. It is no different than any other activity that would have similar results for an individual, whether that is a local dance contest or an international business deal.

One of the first things that beginning b-boys or b-girls learn from their peers is not to refer to the practice as "breakdancing." The issue brings together a number of questions concerning authenticity and historical consciousness, since most feel that the term was part of a larger attempt by the mass media to recast their raw street dance as a nonthreatening form of musical acrobatics. Although this occurred in the mid-'80s, the repercussions are still being felt in terms of public perception, and b-boys respond accordingly. Those who are unfamiliar with the culture may be surprised at the vehemence of b-boys' feelings about the term: "I don't use the word 'breakdance.' It's an ignorant word," says Waaak:

> It's like a stereotype. I look at it as like a racial slur, you know?...[When] I work with people, I make sure that anything they write about me, to pass out to parents or whatever, don't use that word "breakdancing." Not even in quotations. Write "b-boying." They got any questions, you tell 'em they can talk to me....I don't break- dance and I don't want to be affiliated with breakdancers. (Waaak One, interview)

B-boy Ru, who is African American, casts this distinction in even harsher terms: "Basically, when they started calling it 'breakdancing,' it was kind of like saying the word 'nigger,'" he says:

> And then, after, when people started getting used to saying the word "breakdancing," it was kind of like saying the word "nigga" now. Like, before, you said the word "nigger," it was like, "Awww, that was a bad word." But then it's like, now, you say, "Oh, what up, my nigga?" It's the same thing, like breakdancing. If you say "break- dancing," a lot of people will still be like, "ehhh," but there's not really much you can do about it. It's kind of just bringing the bad with the good. (Ru, interview)

In its earliest incarnations, the dance had a number of different names, includ- ing burning, downrocking, going off, scrambling, the boyoing, and probably quite a few others. Many of these names, in retrospect, only referred to spe- cific aspects of the dance. "Burning," for example, referred to dance moves that insulted or topped other dancers. "Downrocking" referred to any aspect of dance done on the floor. "Going off" applied to especially crazy moves. "Scrambling" referred to crazy moves done on the floor. "The boyoing" referred to the process of getting down to the floor and back up again. The fact that there seems to have been no single word to describe the whole dance suggests that it was not viewed as a complete, self-contained dance style at that time.

As it coalesced into a standardized form in the early '70s, however, the dance took on the name "b-boying." By most accounts, the verb was derived from the noun DJ Kool Herc used to describe this particular kind of dancer: "b-boy," short for "break-boy." There is even disagreement, however, as to what the term *break-boy* actually means, specifically whether it refers to someone who dances to the percussion break of a funk song, or someone who, in keeping with the slang of the time, temporarily loses his mind, or "breaks," and then expresses that in the dance.

B-boy pioneer Trac 2, however, strongly disagrees with the "break-boy" derivation:

"There's only three terminologies that I would accept. 'Bronx-boy,' because that's where we come from. 'Battle-boy,' because that's what we were. Or a 'beat-boy,' because that's what moved us."

**Joe:** So not "break-boy."

**Trac 2:** No. No no no no no no no. Those three terms actually fit that environment back then. You know, like I told you, a b-boy lives and thrives for the battles. So we were battle-boys. You know, we lived where? In the South Bronx. The Bronx. We were Bronx-boys. All right? We were rockers and the things that moved us was specific beats. Beat-boy.

"Breaking"? No. It doesn't really make sense. Because you can't mis-interpret "break-boy." OK, now if you say "break-boy" 20 times real fast, it's [still] gonna sound [like] "break-boy." If you say "beat-boys" 20 times really fast, you can see that it's starting to sound like "b-boys." So what they say is the terminology really doesn't make sense. . . . Because you can't misinterpret "break-boy," but you *can* misinterpret "beat-boy." (Trac 2, interview)

In a reminiscence of his life in the Bronx, essayist C. J. Sullivan gives a supporting explanation for this view: "While all the swells at Studio 54 in Manhattan were 'getting down' to Chic, a crew of ghetto kids were charting the course music would be take [*sic*] up to the present day," he writes:

Thus developed a new B-Boy culture. The origin of the name can be debated, but when I first heard it used by some Zulu Nations [*sic*] dudes back in the 1970s it meant Bronx Boys because the blacks of the Bronx always felt slighted by the blacks of Harlem. They felt Harlem got all the props for black culture in New York, and they wanted Harlem to know that the Bronx was here and it was happening. (Sullivan 2007:83)

Ru takes a more ecumenical approach to the issue, suggesting that the term was actually *designed* to be open to multiple interpretations:

B-boying is, of course, its true name. It stands for "bad-boy," "break-boy," you know, "best-boy." You know, it stands for many things. That's the reason why it's just *b* and "boy." Because the *b* is actually a universal. You know what I'm saying? A universal letter for b-boying. And also b-girling as well. That's why they always have that *b* at the front. (Ru, interview)

When the dance became a fad in the '80s, the story goes, it was assigned the term *breakdancing* by cultural outsiders who wanted to give it a broader appeal. Exactly who it was that initiated this change—and exactly why they thought the term *breakdancing* would be more appealing than *b-boying*—has been lost to history. Regardless, to this day, use of the term b-boying is seen as an indicator of authenticity, while the term breakdancing connotes exploitation and disregard for the dance's roots in hip-hop culture (interestingly, the term *breaking* does not have this connotation and is considered acceptable by most b-boys and b-girls).

It addition to its general association with commercialism, the term breakdancing is also problematic on a more practical level. Unlike b-boying, which refers to a specific dance form that developed in New York City in the '70s, breakdancing is often used as an umbrella term that includes not only b-boying but also popping, locking, boogalooing, and other so-called funk-style dances that originated in California. The instructional book *Breakdancing*, published at the height of the b-boying fad of 1984, explains, "Breakdancing...has three main parts: *Breaking, Electric Boogie* and *Uprock*" (Elfman 1984:13; emphases in original). While the terms *breaking* and *uprock* are defined relatively accurately in the book and have maintained their definitions to the present day, the term *electric boogie* is more problematic. It is used in Elfman's book as a synonym for popping, a West Coast dance form that uses sharp, rhythmic muscle contractions to punctuate large, sweeping, circular motions and was primarily performed to the sound of synthesizer-based funk music. But to its practitioners at the time, electric boogie was a specifically East Coast variation of popping, which was often performed to the same raw breaks that b-boys favored.[7] But no matter how they are defined, neither uprocking nor electric boogie is b-boying, a fact that the book acknowledges by placing them alongside the term breaking. In other words, Elfman presents b-boying as only one of several varieties of "breakdancing." The fact that the term breakdancing conflates a variety of different dances that developed in different communities, in different parts of the country, at different times, under different circumstances, suggests that those who use the term are not concerned with the specifics of the dances' history nor—by extension—with the cultural traditions they represent. Since the way one becomes a b-boy or b-girl in the first place is to engage with the culture on a practical level, it would be unlikely for a b-boy to adopt a term—such as breakdancing—that minimizes the importance of that culture.

"It's a marketing tool," explains Trac 2:

It's a corporate way of promoting something that's urban.... All street dance, they labeled it "breakdancing." So they put it out to the mass media, who really don't know what it is, because they are not from that area or they never followed the evolution of each specific dance. Then it was easy to just lump everything together as a form of urban-style dance, and label it and market it as such. But each dance has its own pioneers, has its own origin, has its lingo, has a reason why, the type of music they dance to, and all that. It's much different. But again, when you are in a position to make money, then the label is brought out to the masses. And then the guys who are dancing at that time, just to be noticed, just to be accepted as *something*, they accept the label. So it was easy to exploit it. (Trac 2, interview)

In speaking with contemporary dancers, it quickly becomes clear that sensitivities about exploitation are the real reason that this terminological distinction has maintained its power, as the following explanation from b-girl Seoulsonyk indicates:

OK, the difference between a b-boy and a breakdancer. The rhetoric, like the party line from any underground b-boy, is that a breakdancer is someone who doesn't live a b-boy lifestyle. Someone who just learns the moves so that they can go to an audition and get a job based on the fact that they can do windmills, right? But they don't understand. Like, they literally learned it in a studio from somebody else, who taught them step-by-step. They didn't have to go to a club. They didn't have to go to practice. They didn't have to go to fuckin' sticky-Bushwick-floor practice every day and hurt themselves. They just picked it up and they used it.

So it's like two people can do the *exact same movement*, right? You have Breakdancer A doing windmills, and then you have, like, Junior Jiggz doing windmills. And there is a *huge* difference. Physically, it's exactly the same. But...one is loaded with all these symbols and history. And [the other] one is just movement. (Seoulsonyk, interview)

At the beginning of this short statement, Seoulsonyk presents a somewhat critical assessment of the distinction, referring to it as "rhetoric" and "the party line." Yet within a few sentences, she finds herself emphatically endorsing it, arguing that b-boying is "loaded with...symbols and history," while breakdancing is "just movement."

Waaak takes a similar position:

I could use the word "breakdancer" to describe some people. Some people, I look at them and go, "you're a fuckin' breakdancer," you know? You're not a b-boy. Some people just don't live the lifestyle. Just because you do the dance don't mean you're a b-boy. It's more that goes into that. It's knowledge of self, you know? It's knowledge of the culture. It's *contributing to* the culture. It's living that lifestyle. It's a lot more than just wearing the outfit and saying, "this is the dance that I do, so this is what I am." (Waaak One, interview)

From this perspective, b-boying and breakdancing do not represent different attitudes on the part of the *observer*, but on the part of the *dancer*. A breakdancer is someone who has learned the dance for mercenary reasons, while a b-boy has learned it through a commitment to the culture. But if breakdancers are professional dancers in another style who have learned a few b-boy moves to make themselves more commercially appealing, they would be unlikely to see breakdancing as a significant enough part of their lives to identify themselves by such a term in the first place. And if they did, then—by definition—they would be b-boys or b-girls. The "breakdancer," in this view, is essentially a straw man, designed to allow b-boys and b-girls to emphasize their dedication to the culture.

Michael Holman, however, has a different take on the issue. Holman was the manager of the New York City Breakers, a crew that was instrumental in the dance's brief mainstream popularity in the '80s. Previous to that, he helped to define the general perception of hip-hop culture itself, with his nightclub, Negril, and the short-lived but much-loved television show *Graffiti Rock*:

> I had this club, [the] first hip-hop club downtown: Negril....It could arguably be *the* first hip-hop club. Why? Because there were other clubs of course...but they didn't *know* they were hip-hop clubs, they were just uptown clubs. And if Busy Bee Starski rapped there, that's where he rapped. I mean, that was where it was happening. If somebody played a Treacherous Three record there, that's where they played it. But nobody was saying, "OK, now we're gonna have graffiti, and then we're gonna have b-boys, and we're gonna have..." You know, that was something that needed to come from someone like me, an outsider, who could see this culture, the forest from the trees. And so could see ways to package it. And I stand guilty if that's what anyone wants to accuse me of. (Michael Holman, interview)

Holman attributes the popularity of the term b-boying specifically to Crazy Legs, the president of the Rock Steady Crew, b-boying's preeminent group, and characterizes it as a later—retrospective—change in terminology. In his telling, the dance *was* originally called breakdancing, and it is only a recent need to distance themselves from the commercial world that has led b-boys to embrace the term b-boying. He speculates:

> Maybe what Legs is doing is saying, "I want to reeducate the marketplace and make them see that everything that came before was 'breakdancing' and what's going on now is 'b-boying.' And it's all under *my* control and auspices and whim and whatever." And so it's a cleansing; it's like an etymological purging....But it's smart, because it's a paradigm shift in which he now is not just a player but is a kingmaker. A kingpin. So, you know, props to him for that.[8] (Michael Holman, interview)

In Holman's view, the use of the term b-boying represents a strategic purism—almost a branding exercise—on the part of those who have promoted it. And not incidentally, it is one that is intended to work to their own benefit just as much as the term breakdancing worked to Holman's benefit in the '80s. On one level, it's not difficult to see why he would feel that way; his analysis casts the two terms as representative of different constituencies (his own and Crazy

Legs') that both have equal legitimacy. Both Holman and Crazy Legs are trying to sell ideas about b-boying; it's just that the ideas themselves are different. Moreover, all parties pretty much do agree on the basic distinction: Holman is promoting "breakdancing" as a flamboyant style of dance; Crazy Legs is promoting "b-boying" as a culture, essentially the distinction that Seoulsonyk expresses above. While, in my experience, older b-boys and b-girls do seem to have less hesitancy about using the terms b-boying and breakdancing interchangeably, the larger analysis appears to be unique to Holman. As seen above, the community in general overwhelmingly feels that b-boying is the original term.

To make the issue even more complex, the term b-boy took on another meaning in the early 1990s, when it began to be used to describe the rebellious attitude not only of dancers, but of hip-hop fans in general. A typical example can be found in Nelson George's 1993 collection of critical essays on hip-hop, *Buppies, B-Boys, Baps, and Bohos: Notes on Post-Soul Black Culture*. George defines the b-boy as an "African American character type," who has been

molded by hip-hop aesthetics and the tragedies of underclass life.... The B-boy has rightfully been the most celebrated and condemned of these figures, since he combines the explosive elements of poverty, street knowledge, and unfocused political anger. B-boy style has flowed far from its ghetto base and affected language, clothes, music, and damn near everything else. (George 1992:2)

In response to the shifting meaning of the word, b-boy elders Ken Swift, PopMaster Fabel, Crazy Legs, and Mr. Wiggles published a sort of manifesto in the *Source* magazine in 1993 requesting that the word be restored to its original meaning. "As B-boy and Boogie-boy pioneers of this culture," they wrote, "we feel obligated to preserve and maintain true historic understanding of terms and facts connected with hip-hop. From reading articles and hearing certain rap records, it has become clear to us that the word B-boy has come to be a catch-all term for a hip-hop fan, and this is incorrect." After a brief history of the term and its implications, they concluded with their demand: "Kool DJ Herc was referring to a dance movement and not a hardrock image or a fashion statement when he conceived the term B-boy. Those who consider themselves true members of the hip-hop culture need to respect and understand not only our history, but the proper use of our terminology as well. PEACE" (Gabbert and Pabon 1993: 6). As of this writing, in the early twenty-first century, all four of these individuals remain major educators in b-boy culture, and all still feel strongly about the use of the term b-boy. In a section of his Web site devoted to common misconceptions about hip-hop, Mr. Wiggles still rates the issue as number three. "Rappers are B-boys," he writes:

No! No! No! No! Noooooooo!!!!! Unless you can do top rock footwork and freezes you are not a B-boy!!! You have a title, sh#t you have two titles (rapper, mc). Leave ours alone, B-boy means Break boy, Beat boy, or Bronx boy. Why do rappers insist on using our name just to legitimize their careers? I don't know. (Clemente 2007)

In addition to placing the focus on general attitude rather than dance, it is noteworthy that the b-boy archetype George describes is also specifically African American. This shift, part of a larger embrace of black nationalism in the hip-hop culture of the late '80s, did not go unnoticed by Latino b-boys. In fact, many people whom I spoke with took this change very personally. At that time, notes Anthony Colon:

> [Hip-hop] was more geared to the black community. *Only* the black community. Not really the Latino.... Which was kind of messed up, because when you look at how everything evolved, Latinos were there in the trenches ... growing up in the ghetto, growing up in poverty, growing up Section 8.[9] Cheese line days. The cheese and the powdered milk. You know, the starvation. You know, the tough days. We all went through the same [experience]. But then we got omitted. We got pushed out. (Anthony Colon, interview)

The authors of the *Source* article are all of Latino heritage; the extent to which that has affected their position on the changing meaning of the word b-boy is not clear, but it would be surprising if it did not have some influence. (I will discuss this issue in more detail in chapter 7.)

My intention here is not to take a position on what the dance should be called. What is of significance here is that—for those who *do* wish to consider themselves b-boys or b-girls—learning the "proper" use of the term and its many implications are a significant part of their education. When one takes on the label b-boy, one is taking on all of its resonances, even the ones that are contradictory or in dispute. A b-boy or b-girl is representing a relationship between dance and musical form (a "boy" or "girl" who dances on the "break," or to the "beat" of a record), a reaction to the psychological stress of poverty (one who "breaks," emotionally), a commitment to the culture and symbolism of the dance over commercialism (b-boy versus breakdancer), a commitment to dance over other aspects of hip-hop (as in the *Source* manifesto), and a sense of geographical and class pride ("Bronx-boy" versus, presumably, "Manhattan-boy").

It is also important to note that the term b-boying is gender-specific in a way that breakdancing is not. Many, though not all, b-girls refer to what they do as "b-girling," but this implies that the *activity itself* is different from b-boying simply by virtue of the gender of the person doing it. In other words, is it possible for a b-boy to also practice b-girling in his spare time? If not, why not? The way the term is used seems to imply a sort of gender essentialism—that the dance is, in some fundamental way, an expression of one's gender identity.

"Is b-girling a different dance form than guys'?" asks b-girl Seoulsonyk:

> We haven't really talked about it as women.... But at this point, the women that have been dancing and been active and visible on the local, national, international

scale are the women who are *physically* accomplishing what men are accomplishing. But they're not setting the standards for everyone, [regardless of] gender. The guys are still the one[s] that are setting the standards. So, I don't have a problem, personally. I don't think it's like we're being less of a person, we're not being proactive women by calling ourselves b-girls all the time. If people are like, "Oh, that's b-boying," I have no problems with it. (Seoulsonyk, interview)

Complicating the picture even more, as Seoulsonyk notes, is that b-girls often refer to what they do as "b-boying," but b-boys *never* call their dance "b-girling." This suggests not only that the term b-boying is normative, but that so is the projection of masculinity itself. This can sometimes put b-girls in situations where their dedication to the (often masculine) ideals of b-boying comes into conflict with their identity as women. When I was talking to B-Girl Emiko, she noted that the atmosphere at the We B*Girls battle, sponsored by Martha Cooper, was much more sociable than other breaking events she had attended. "As a b-girl, I felt when I went to the We B*Girls battle, it was an event for specifically b-girls," she says:

And I've been to many just "breaking" jam, and it was so different. Because when I go to regular jams, there's just the cypher going, people moving around. No talking. But when I got there...I start stretching and practicing. Dancing. A couple girls came, [and]...they start talking to me, asking me a lot of questions. Females talk a lot.

B-Girl Emiko at We B*Girls battle. Photo © Martha Cooper.

At this point, I expected Emiko to comment on how much more supportive the atmosphere was than conventional b-boy jams, but that was not the point she wanted to make: "So they start like, 'Oh no, I don't get my footwork faster.' 'My freeze is weak.' And blah, blah, blah. I said, like, 'That's your concern. But now is not the time to talk.' That's how I felt. Like, *it's not the time to talk.* We just dance" (B-Girl Emiko, interview).

In Emiko's eyes, the other b-girls were violating battle protocol by attempting to be sociable before the competition. And by making these overtures on the basis of gender, they were not only forcing Emiko to choose between two aspects of her identity (woman versus b-girl), but also doing it in a way that was specifically detrimental to her ability to compete in the battle that was about to happen. If she tried to support her fellow b-girls, she would not only be losing part of the character she was trying to project in the battle, but would also have to carry around the knowledge that she had done so because she is female.

The idea that a b-boy or b-girl should be judged on their skills rather than their gender (or any other factor, for that matter) is central to the ideology of the dance. At the same time, it sets a clear standard that can be carried over into other aspects of life: if you expect to be taken seriously, you should be prepared to compete on an equal footing with anyone. "When I started teaching the b-girls," says Richard Santiago:

> I was [teaching] them the same way I would do b-boys. "You want to be a b-girl? That's it: you gonna do the same training."...I don't care [if] you're a girl....This is the game. When you're in that cypher, it's no "b-girl cypher" or "b-boy cypher." No. It's a cypher! There's no gender breakdown, this is what you got. You want to do it, you do it! (Santiago, interview)

B-boying's essence—its foundation—is passed on from teacher to student in a highly personal context. And, as with any form of cultural expression, the teaching context can profoundly shape a student's understanding of the material. The idea of the student as a disciple of the teacher—and thus of his or her style and lineage—is similar to that of various martial arts traditions. This system teaches its students important lessons about the dance, about life, and about the relationship between the two. By encouraging the dancers to see themselves as b-boys and b-girls rather than as breakdancers, the teacher instills a sense of pride in the culture and community from which the dance emerged. Similarly, the idea of foundation presents cultural values as a concrete part of the dance. In this conception, the qualities that foundation comprises—style, boldness, attitude, rhythmic fluency, musical sophistication, historical awareness, even gender identity—are all facets of a single, larger, concept. This, in turn, creates an intimate and mutually influential relationship between the elements of the dance. Improved rhythmic fluency is presumed to improve your style, attitude improves your flow, and knowledge of b-boy history makes you physically safer.

But perhaps the most important thing that foundation teaches is how to develop your own individual identity in the context of the group, which necessarily entails understanding your own strengths, weaknesses, and personal history. Foundation allows you to bring your own past experiences into your present identity in a way that is specifically designed to work to your advantage. While this is primarily done to avoid liabilities in a battle situation—you should not have skeletons in your closet that an opponent could exploit—developing the ability to fold any previous experience into current needs gives you the confidence to move forward without being caught off guard by your weaknesses. And this is clearly a valuable life skill outside of the cypher as well.

This is also a good example of how b-boying can alert us to aspects of hip-hop culture that have been underexamined in other elements. Many other hip-hop practices besides b-boying are based on similar mentoring relationships, and understanding the values implicit in these relationships can provide important insights into the cultural values of hip-hop in general. Graffiti writers, for example, often use specific letter styles as tributes to their teachers, while stylistic lineages are also valued—and can be heard—in hip-hop production.

The focus of media and scholars alike on rap music is the main reason that the effect of this mentorship has rarely been studied. And even this is the result of several specific misconceptions. One is that emceeing is something that people "just do." While that is true in some cases, other emcees take great pride in the craft of their work and will easily give credit to those who taught them about song structure, rhythmic and tonal variations, and literary devices, particularly different varieties of metaphor. Another, broader misconception is that, since rapping is a form of popular music, it can be understood at a distance, without looking into the practical realities of how it is made. This naturally tends to deemphasize the craft aspect, as well as how it was learned by the artist. In reality, mentoring is significant to all forms of hip-hop.

To understand a particular mentoring tradition, of course, it is important to understand what people are being mentored about. How does the teaching style reflect the values of the art? How can personal relationships provide subtle guidance to artistic nuance? What kinds of expression, ultimately, are the mentoring relationships designed to produce?

# 4

## "We Have to Be Exaggerated"
### Aesthetics

Hip-hop is a colorful culture. It's vibrant. It's a culture
that just has to be larger than life. When you look at
the graffiti characters and you see the way they're
exaggerated, you know, *we* have to be exaggerated
as b-boys.... We have to be blasting out off the page.
Off the circle. Off the crowd. Off the blacktop. Off the
wall. That's what it's about.
—Ken Swift (Breaklife, Seven Gems), legendary
b-boy

B-boying, like most other aspects of hip-hop, is often portrayed as being
devoid of abstract aesthetic principles (see Schloss 2004:65–66 for discussion
of this issue with regard to sampling). In the case of b-boying specifically,
this is partially due to its being seen as a pop culture fad of the '80s, partially
the result of social prejudice toward the communities from which the dance
emerged, and partially due to the way hip-hop tends to keep its aesthetic principles to itself.

The reality, however, is that while not all b-boys and b-girls feel that it is
necessary to articulate a cohesive aesthetic of the dance, many clearly do:

I have my five elements, which I got from the *I Ching*, but I use it in b-boying. And
I apply b-boy philosophies.... You got Fire, Earth, Air, Water, and Ether. Ether's
what holds everything together in existence. If there's no ether, our molecules
would be breaking apart. But Fire's your intensity. Your heat. How you come into
the dance. Then you got Earth, which is all your ground moves. Back rocks, body
rolls, footwork. All that stuff, that's Earth. Air is all your air moves, including
swipes. Swipes, flips, airflares, windmills, those are all your air moves. That's Air.
Water is your flow. Trying to keep everything in one consistent motion. 'Cause too
many people are stuck with "step one, step two, step three, step four," and there's
no flow in it. And of course Ether's what holds everything together, and that's the
rhythm. (Alien Ness, interview)

Perhaps the most telling phrase in this quote is "And I apply b-boy philosophies," which takes as a given that a body of abstract thought about b-boying already exists. In other words, Alien Ness is presenting his five-elements concept not as a totally new way to think about the dance, but more as a system that attempts to synthesize preexisting aesthetic principles.

Looking at these principles and their function within the b-boy community, it is apparent that practical considerations reflective of b-girls' and b-boys' lives in general have become encoded into the aesthetics of b-boying and have remained as artistic preferences even after their practical significance has been lost. Through this process, which is to some degree intentional, modern b-boying is able to serve as a symbolic arena in which those issues can be addressed.

Writing about another frequently overlooked practice of the African diaspora, Kyra Gaunt has characterized African American girls' clapping games as "oral-kinetic lessons in black musical style, behavior, and social identity formation," going on to call for

> a somatic historiography of black music and dance.... The stories that the body can tell are not the same conversations that we speak or sing. They are visual and kinesthetic. We feel them polyphonically and polyrhythmically. We resist letting these "stories" be analyzed, for fear of dissecting the whole so much that the spirit of the music and people are lost.... These game-songs are embodied scripts of music, inscribed into space, experience, and memory. (Gaunt 2006:186)

In the case of b-boying, these aesthetic lessons allow the dancers to define various aspects of their identity, develop strategies for integrating that identity into a larger social world, and then actually practice doing so. This is done in a variety of specific areas, including the choice of a name that expresses one's b-boy or b-girl character, the clothing one wears, the way one carries oneself physically, how that attitude is reflected in the way one interacts with a given piece of music, improvisation, and the structure of the dance performance.

B-boying, like all art forms, reflects the circumstances in which it arose. At the risk of stating the obvious, people develop art forms that are consistent with the material conditions of their particular environment. This just makes sense, because why would people create an art form that they can't do? For reasons that are something of a mystery, this issue seems to be almost always over- or underplayed; artists of all varieties are often portrayed as being either completely free from material restrictions or completely constrained by them. In reality, of course, most people express themselves as creatively as possible within the boundaries that life has given them, and those boundaries then become integrated into their overall aesthetic. So, for instance, due to a variety of cultural and economic factors, New York youth of the '70s chose to use turntables rather than more traditional musical instruments as the medium for their expression. While this decision is often portrayed as a symptom of poverty, one rarely hears this decision portrayed that way by deejays from that era. They are more inclined to view it as a conscious artistic choice based on a creative use of available materials, not substantially different from the choices made by any other artist in any other circumstances. Eventually, the philosophies that artists develop to contextualize their expression become abstracted into aesthetic principles, which are then maintained even after the material conditions change. In the case of the above example, the use of live instruments actually came to be viewed by purists in the '90s as a violation of hip-hop's "two turntables and a microphone" aesthetic (see Schloss 2004:63–78). In other words, once the rules of the form had been established, other options were then accepted or rejected based on their perceived compliance with the aesthetic expectations of the form. As a result, the aesthetic principles of an art form not only can tell us about the conditions that led to particular artistic decisions being made but also can provide insight into the community's abstract understanding of—and approach to—those conditions. This is certainly true of b-boying, and one area in which these connections are very apparent is in the choice of a b-boy's or b-girl's name.

It is unusual for b-boys and b-girls to dance under their given names. More commonly, they will choose a name that suggests the qualities they wish to project in their dance, and they may go through several names before they find the one that really fits them. Many include the honorific title "b-boy" or "b-girl" as an actual part of their name much in the same way that emcees (MC) and deejays (DJ) do in other elements of hip-hop. Some do not. In many cases, the name is given to them by a mentor or other dancer who they respect.

"It's a character—it's definitely a character," explains Richard Santiago of his b-boy alter ego, Breakeasy:

> My first birthright as a b-boy was just probably "Easy" because of the way I flow. "Breakeasy" came out a little bit later...because they associate it with the dance. You know: "Break." "Easy." And not only that, but "break" would mean to just lose it or to go off. So when I was younger, yeah, I used to lose my temper a lot. But I was a hotheaded kid and stuff. I mean, anybody that knew me back in the days knew that I would hit first, talk later. That's it. (Richard Santiago, interview)

B-Boy Character outlines a similar process. "Every time I used to dance," he says, "I used to always, like, do freezes in the air and stick out my tongue, and make funny faces. And I was very emotional when I danced. So people started calling me a character. 'Oh, you such a character'" (B-Boy Character, interview).

B-boy Ru's name is a good example of the process I discussed in the last chapter, in which dancers take preexisting aspects of their personality and reinterpret them through the culture of b-boying. Although "Ru" was a childhood nickname, he added deeper layers of symbolism to it when he became a b-boy. "Ru stands for 'Radical Unit,'" he explains:

I've always had Ru for a long time, but Radical Unit, I got that, actually, in high school. That was when we were at the point of doing radicals...in math....But then I always used to watch this show...this kid's name was Radical—it was a cartoon—and he would always kind of bend the rules a little bit; he would always go out and do something extreme. So that's what I used to do, I used to do that a

B-boy Ru. Photo by author.

lot. I used to flip off rocks in Central Park, those big ones. I would jump turnstiles and stuff like that. (Ru, interview)

Similarly, b-boy Waaak's name began as a graffiti tag. "I came up with a whole bunch of different tags, WAK being one of them that stood with me," he remembers. "And my older brother, he gave me the acronym Weird-Ass Kiddo because, you know, I was a weird-ass kid. Being that he gave me that, that's the one that stuck with everybody.... All his friends would call me Weird-Ass Kiddo."

The, problem, he soon realized, is that WAK sounds like "wack," a hip-hop synonym for "bad." But rather than develop a new name, he chose to embrace it as a challenge:

Everybody would always try to change my name. And that kind of pushed me as a kid—as a toy[1]—to get better.... And when it came to the b-boying thing, it was like, "Oh, *Wak*?" I remember I would sign up for competitions, and people would *not* want to call my name.... They're like, "Uhh, Wake?" "Uhh, Woke?" I'm like, "No, it's Waaak."... Same thing with the graf thing: I mentioned I got better with the graf thing so people couldn't say I was "wack." B-boy thing was the same thing. (Waaak One, interview)

The name, then, not only represents his graffiti work, it also symbolizes his dedication to overcoming obstacles and his relationship to his brother.

For b-girl KaoticBlaze, the process was somewhat more intentional:

It was, like, maybe a month into me first learning how to break. And [my friend] was like, "you know you gotta come up with a b-girl name, right?" Cause everybody has these dope names. I was like, "you know what? I wanna have a *dope* name. I wanna have a name that when they hear it, it's like, 'oh shit! she's gonna throw some shit down.'"...

So I was in English class, and I was just sitting there, like, zoning out and just thinking of how I dance and just everything in general. And... I always carry a thesaurus usually with me when I'm writing. I don't like repeating words. So I was just thinking about something crazy, wild, and I'm looking at the thesaurus: "Crazy." It says, "chaotic." "Oh, that's dope." Chaotic. *Kaotic*. I could spell it with a *K*. Yeah. And I was like, "No, that's too short—I need something else." I was thinking, I'm a Leo, like, that's my sign. It's a fire sign. And, you know, like, "Oh, she's hot—she dances hot." First I was thinking of "Wildfire." I was like no... fire... fire... Blaze. I was like, "oh, that's dope: KaoticBlaze."...

It's crazy. My full name is Margie Stephanie Flecha. Like, ewww. And I hear "Blaze," I'm like "what's up?" My name is me. My name is powerful. (KaoticBlaze, interview)

Even in cases like Blaze's, where dancers choose their own names, it must be approved by their peer group. As a result, the name reflects not only the dancer's self-image, but the fact that the self-image has been verified by the community. This is a mantle that is not taken lightly, as Santiago explains:

> The name [Breakeasy]…is not something that I picked by choice. It was something that my own community gave me. And that's what stuck, you know? And that's something that I kind of like: that my community is the one that gave me that name. Built me that name. And now I'm stuck with it, and I have to live up to that character. But, you know, I'm thankful for that, because it made me live up to that character now. And now I see that I have a responsibility. To myself, first. To my community, second. And then to the kids within my community. (Richard Santiago, interview)

BOM5's name ties him not only to his community, but to a whole history of social interactions and artistic choices. He describes how he moved through a succession of gang, graffiti, and b-boy names until he finally found one that struck the perfect balance: "They used to call me 174 SPIDER. That was the name Blackie [Mercado, president of the Savage Skulls] and my cousin SEE2 gave me in the Skulls. Because I was small and I was fast. And I lived on the block of 174th Street."

> **Joe:** So you mentioned that in Jeff's book [Chang 2005], right? You put the 174 first.
>
> **BOM5:** Right, because my block comes first. And when you protect your neighborhood, your neighborhood comes first. Not you. The unity counts more than the individual.[2]
>
> The guy that really taught me my wildstyle was this guy named BILLY 167 (R.I.P.).[3] He was an Irish kid. [What] a lot of people don't know about BOM5 is that I used to hang out with everybody: from the blackest of the black, to my own people, all kinds of Hispanics, and all kinds of whites, were my friends. So this kid BILLY was a nasty style master of graffiti, and I was lucky to meet him in '76. And he taught me my wildstyle, after CHINOMAL0174 [and] SMILY149 (R.I.P.) taught me the beginning of graffiti. History. And my cousin SEE2.
>
> So after that, I wanted to have a name instead of SPIDER.…People [were] doing [cartoon] characters for their letters. So most of the guys who would do characters usually had names with an O.…So I was trying to get with that too. You can't do it with SPIDER.…
>
> They had an original writer named BOMB1.…So BOMB was already quitting by that time, so BILLY introduced me to him. The guy said, "I give you my blessing. You can have the name."
>
> But when I left with BILLY, I said I didn't feel well.…'Cause I said, "You know, this guy—he's already famous. Everybody knows BOMB1.…What, I'm gonna have a BOMB? BOMB2?" And I said, "Graffiti's all about being original."
>
> So he said, "At least when you get it passed down to you from the original guy, it's OK." But when I went home, I still didn't feel good about it.…

But, then, for some reason, I liked that name, BOMB...so I went to the dictionary and I found out that *bomb* is really spelled BOM, because the other *B* is [a] silent *B*. So I said, "Hey, I'm gonna become BOM." And I took that name, and since I got the name in 1976...I started writing BOM76. And it became good and I was loving it....

I was more known for my fighting, since I'm a little kid....When I went to some boys of mine, they said, "Yeah, you be dropping people like bombs." I said, "Yeah, that's two things: I got BOM because I got respect, and it's also a good name to do a piece, and not only that, they know I knock out guys and they call it 'dropping bombs.'"...And I thought deeply, and I found out that it's my fist that protects me in my neighborhood. So it's five fingers that makes a fist [and so now my name's BOM5]. (BOM5, interview)

BOM5's names represent a powerful series of statements about his identity and his relationship to the larger communities around him. They represent aspects of his personality that include neighborhood pride, the value he places on the group over the individual, his physical appearance, his speed, his fighting ability, the diversity of his circle of friends, his respect for older graffiti writers, artistic considerations about letter shapes, and the value of originality and creativity. B-boys and b-girls take their names extremely seriously. They represent deep truths about their characters and personalities and their relationships to their peers. And that's before they even start dancing: once the name is established, it also represents the reputation that a dancer has developed in the b-boy community. In fact, this is taken so seriously that, if two b-boys take the same name, it is still standard practice to battle over it, with the winner receiving sole rights to use the name from that point on.

This relationship between the individual and his or her community is seen in other areas as well, such as the way one carries oneself. In comparing b-boys to graffiti characters at the outset of this chapter, Ken Swift was not only pointing to the dramatic personalities that they are expected to display, but also to a specific set of aesthetic expectations for how that personality should come across to spectators: "colorful," "exaggerated," "vibrant," "larger than life." In other words, they should stand out as individuals, in the same way that an effective graffiti piece stands out from the wall or train it is painted on. This opinion is widely held. Tiny Love clearly considers the graffiti comparison to be one of the highest compliments that can be given to a b-boy. In describing his own teacher, Kwon, he proudly states, "You know, he got his character, b-boy character, all the time....You just have to see him, *he looks just like a graffiti character*" (Tiny Love, interview). Part of what Tiny is complimenting is that this is something that Kwon has achieved through his own effort. By practicing b-boying, he has actually *become* visual art.

The idea that this can occur not only in a broad abstract sense, but actually according to the specific principles of graffiti—the visual art of hip-hop—implies an aesthetic coherence that is far beyond the comprehension of hip-hop's critics. Many b-boys are also graffiti writers, and the principles of both forms overlap to a great degree. In the case of names, this has two components: choosing (or being given) a name that symbolizes significant aspects of one's personality and then publicizing the name through bold and creative action. As Ivor Miller notes, the motivations of graffiti writers are very similar to those of b-boys:

> The themes of praise naming and self-praise are fundamental to the culture of New York City writers, where newly created names are intended to contribute to their positive identities. Many New York City writers are masters of self-praise, their traditions involve getting the name up around the city to inspire awe, as well as the praise of their communities. In a social context where excellence is not expected of them, writers took pride in praising themselves. (Miller 2002:52)

"That ghetto celebrity status: that is the biggest key to what a b-boy wants to accomplish," agrees Trac 2:

> That's the ultimate gold for every b-boy: that ghetto celebrity status. The guy that's most feared. The guy that has that reputation. That's what you want to obtain. Amongst your community, you know, your own environment. But if your name travels on the other side of the Bronx, and these people have never seen you, you obtain that. Where your name supersedes your appearance. (Trac 2, interview)

Anthony Colon, who has been a graffiti writer, b-boy, and martial artist, notes that his first graffiti name was designed to encapsulate his approach to all three pursuits. "I used to write MAEZ in the Bronx," he says:

> It's a martial arts thing, from Bruce Lee. It means "Master at Eternal Zenith," which means the high point. I was 13, 14 years old. Back in the days, you always had a meaning for your name. Like, some kids write a graffiti name, but it has no meaning. For us, we had deep meanings for our names. There was a reason we wrote it. Because of Bruce Lee [and] martial arts, "Master at Eternal Zenith" meant: all the time, you have to be tip-top. (Anthony Colon, interview)

In the case of graffiti, projecting a name is done through "getting up," writing one's name consistently in public places. In b-boying, it is done through public competition. In both cases, the twin components of performing well and performing often are eqally valued. Someone who is creative, but rarely shows it, will not be respected. As Cooper and Chalfant write with regard to graffiti:

> "Getting fame" is the repeatedly stated goal of graffiti writers. Because there are so many thousands of writers in the city, to get fame an individual must stand out from the others. The competition is very intense. One can be "King" in several ways, such as King of the Line, or King of the Insides, or King of Style. A writer is judged by his mastery of painting and by the number of times he "gets up." All

Kevski and Anthony Colon. Photo by author.

new pieces on the line are subjected to close scrutiny by self-appointed critics. Uppermost in the minds of the kids watching trains is always, "Who burned?" That is, which piece is the best? Winners are declared and the choice is hotly disputed. (Cooper and Chalfant 1984:31)

The power of naming is well understood within b-boy circles, and it doesn't only apply to people; in an oral culture like b-boying, the power to name a dance movement represents a claim of authorship. When b-boys and b-girls refer to a plank freeze, a pose in which the entire body is extended and balanced horizontally between one bent arm and the top of the head, they are intrinsically paying respect to Ken Swift, who created and named the move. And to Swift, that is far from incidental. I was surprised to hear him cite it as one of the most important aspects of the dance: "For me, personally, that was something that you couldn't compare to *anything*," he says. "It was like, 'I can name this shit my own name?

Yeah? *Wow.'* ... That's the beauty of it ... you get street credibility.... And then you're like an instant celebrity if that move is off the hook and everybody starts doing it" (Ken Swift, interview). To call a movement by name is to honor the individual who created it.

As Miller noted above, for individuals whose economic or social circumstances predispose them to a life of anonymity, the idea that future generations around the world may openly acknowledge their creativity as artists—and thus as human beings—is an attractive one. This is also the reason that b-boys are scrupulous about knowing and preserving the names of specific moves: to change the name of a move is to break the chain of history that connects contemporary b-boys and b-girls to the original innovators who created their dance. Although the geographical diversity of modern b-boying has led to cases where the same move may have multiple names, individual b-boys are fiercely dedicated to certain names and are prepared to defend their choice with elaborate, often meticulously legalistic arguments. Alien Ness, for example, feels strongly that the move commonly known as cc's, essentially a rocking motion performed in a squatting position with one leg extended, should properly be called "Russian taps," since—he argues—it was derived from "the Russian," a move that imitates the iconic Russian dance step in which the dancer squats and alternately extends each leg (Alien Ness, interview). It is not the new name itself that prompts his emotional response, so much as the sense that the evolutionary connection between these two moves—a part of b-boying's history—has been lost as a result of the name change.

Similarly, when Anthony Colon refers to "helicopters"—a move in which the dancer starts in a squatting position and swings one of his legs in a broad circle, jumping over it with his or her other leg every time it comes around—he makes a point of emphasizing the name:

**Colon:** Helicopters. Now they got a different name for it.

**Joe:** Oh, it's "coffee grinders" now.

**Colon:** It's helicopters. *It's not coffee grinders.* Let me tell you something: in 1983, I was doing like 20 helicopters in the snow and I remember leaving, like, that snow mark.... That was 1983. *Helicopters* in the snow. That [move] ain't called coffee grinders. Somebody told me that, yeah. "Coffee grinders." It's not coffee grinders. *Helicopters.*

Notice that Colon's argument is based on a combination of historical chronology and personal experience. He cites the name of the move and the year it was called that and supports both of these statements with his personal experience. The implication is twofold. First, to challenge this assertion, someone would not only have to cite an instance in which the move was called a "coffee grinder" before 1983, but would have to be able to verify that instance with an eyewitness. And second, it ties the significance of the term to the significance of his personal experience. In other words, to call the move a "helicopter" as opposed to a "coffee grinder" is, in a way, to recognize and even honor his own experience as a b-boy, even though he did not invent the move and may not even know who did.

Another way that b-boys articulate and project their self-image is through their choice of clothing. B-boy style combines athletic functionality with artistic creativity. A b-boy's or b-girl's clothing must allow for an extreme range of motion without binding the body or actually ripping. The art of finding (and/or altering) clothing so that it is serviceable for b-boying and also looks flashy and unique is a subtle one. On a deeper level, b-boys' ability to mediate between these two concerns represents a more general ability to mediate between functionality and creativity in other aspects of life as well.

One of the specific arenas in which this plays out is the way clothing can provide a venue for demonstrating control over one's appearance and image. "You want to look right and you want to be comfortable. And you don't want to look like a bum either," says Eddie Luna. "It's almost like no respect for yourself. You gotta present yourself and have a little pride in yourself and what you're doing. For you to shine. . . . That was the whole purpose of it: being comfortable, looking sharp, and being ready. Because you're gonna wow a crowd" (Eddie Luna, interview).

As Richard Santiago notes, there were many reasons that this should be the case:

> Gotta be all clean and shiny. And if you break, let's break, but let's not get all dirty. It was about being able to be presentable and fashionable. Because you wanted to go out there as a teenager and look good. When you would go to a party, you wanted to go off on the break—'cause it was a dance—but you also wanted to make sure that you were clean enough that you can pick up the girls' numbers and date later on. That's what the idea was. That was the motivation for us to do that. (Richard Santiago, interview)

"I'd say clothing is important," agrees B-Boy Phantom:

> You can't really . . . expect to get respect if you don't look right. It goes with everything in life. You can't go to a job interview with holes in your shirt, you didn't shave, your hair's super long, and you're smelling bad, you have bad hygiene. The same thing with dancing. If you go . . . dancing and you got a crispy white outfit on and you didn't get it dirty and you just did 20 rounds, what does that say about you? The brother's obviously nasty. (B-Boy Phantom, interview)

This attitude—that you should make extensive efforts to preserve your appearance, while at the same time acting unconcerned—is a variation of the "cool" style that pervades the African diaspora (Thompson 1979). It manifests itself in other ways, too, most notably color coordination. It goes without saying, for example, that b-boys' and b-girls' sneakers should match their shirts.

This, in conjunction with the idea that sneakers should be spotless, requires that the dancer develop a substantial arsenal of shoes to choose from before leaving the house and put substantial effort into maintaining them.[4] "I will go to a jam wearing one pair of sneakers, but have my breaking sneakers in my bag," says b-girl Seoulsonyk. "I do want to look tight. I don't want to look like everyone else....If I do have a fresh pair of kicks, I don't want it to clash with the shirt that I'm wearing, for sure. Like, I do want my name on some shit...you know, 'let's put letters on this thing'" (Seoulsonyk, interview).

Part of the performance of fashion lies in manifesting the effort that went into one's appearance while simultaneously appearing not to care whether anyone notices or not, a similar function to that of Alien Ness's drunken style, noted earlier. At the We B*Girls battle, for example, one of the things that distinguished the Rock Steady Crew's Jeskillz was that not only did she change her shirt in between rounds, but she actually changed her shoelaces to match the new shirt. It is likely that very few onlookers actually noticed this subtlety, but for those who did, it represented a true triumph of b-girl style. Overall, b-boying may be the last element of hip-hop fashion in which creativity is valued more than cost. Again, on a deeper level, this is about learning to confidently express one's identity in a variety of circumstances. It represents a certain confidence about one's life and reputation that is easily transferrable to other life circumstances. Nowhere is this clearer than in the actual display of one's name.

As Seoulsonyk notes above, a b-boy or b-girl's name and the name of his or her crew are often displayed somewhere on their clothing. First and foremost, this is a way for b-boys to honor themselves, much in the same way as the name in a graffiti piece honors the writer. In the case of b-boys, the suggestion is that they are identifying themselves for the onlookers' benefit. The unspoken message is, "I assume you want to know who I am."

That such a public declaration of individual identity would be coupled with the name of their crew—a proclamation of group membership—is directly derived from the "colors," or gang vests, worn by street gangs of the '70s, a culture that was deeply influential on hip-hop. This is not to say that b-boys are in gangs or even that they are intentionally paying tribute to gang culture as such (if they were, they would certainly represent contemporary gang culture rather than that of three decades ago). But it is important to think about what it *does* pay tribute to.

First, it acknowledges the fact that many early b-boys were gang members (or affiliated) and modeled their social organizations on gangs. Second, it suggests that they did this for the purpose of emphasizing what they viewed as the positive side of the gangs: mutual aid, loyalty, respect, and responsibility for the welfare of their fellow crew members. Finally, it is a way for younger b-boys to honor their b-boy elders.

"The whole dance form and the whole battling scene was paying homage to what we grew up with, with the gangs and the rumbles," says Trac 2:

Even the look of a b-boy is paying homage to guys in our neighborhoods that we considered heroes. Pimps. And the drug dealers. And then we had the outlaws and the gang members. OK, a b-boy has an aggressive look like a outlaw. With the Lees [jeans]. You know, with the sweatshirt with the names [on] the back. And his crew name, representing colors like the gang. But then we also dressed clean. (Trac 2, interview)

Stylistically, crew names often were—and are—printed on the shirt in such a way as to simulate "rockers," the banner-like patches that proclaim the names of street gangs and motorcycle clubs. Traditionally, this means that the shirt will often include an upper rocker with the actual crew name and a lower rocker specifying the area the dancers represent. Moreover, as with gang colors, the crew name will usually appear on the back of the shirt rather than the front (the individual's name goes on the front) and will often be written in an Old English font or other outlaw-evocative typefaces.

"A lot of rocking crews were from M.C. cliques [motorcycle clubs, i.e., biker gangs]," explains Richard Santiago, referring to the transitional "rocking" dance style of the late '60s and early '70s (see chapter 7):

A lot of rocking crews came from that. Later on, in the '70s, you had rocking crews that were segregated from the M.C. cliques. These were your Touch of Rocks. Now they used . . . the iron-on letters to create their own look. But if you look at the fashion design in clothing, they had the mimic of the vests. The Old English letters and stuff. (Richard Santiago, interview)

Buz, the founder of the Touch of Rock crew that Santiago refers to, confirms that concern about being mistaken for a gang was the major factor in their choice to use iron-on letters, rather than patches, on their vests and T-shirts. Nevertheless, he notes, confusion still existed:

**Buz:** Well, what's with those guys wearing those letters . . . ?

**Joe:** 'Cause, like, people would see your crew shirts or whatever and think it was a gang.

**Buz:** That's why we never used the back [of the T-shirt]. The Dynasty [a Bushwick-based dance crew] style, using the back and things? Dynasty was probably the first to put rockers on. They were the first one to put that thing on.

**Joe:** And you guys didn't use rockers on your shirts?

**Buz:** We never did *anything* on the back. We had 'em, but they were like our undershirts. We use to use them, like, if we in the house, just in the neighborhood, whatever. But we never went out of town with Dynasty or any of those guys who were wearing it. And us, we would have vests [with our names on the front]. We would keep it, like, you know, "we're just a brother club." That was basically what I was trying to [tell the gangs]: we were just a brother club. (Buz, interview)

The seriousness with which this was taken may be startling to read today, but it speaks volumes about the environment in which hip-hop dance emerged. Buz specifies that his crew had T-shirts with their name on the back, but that they would only wear them in their own neighborhood. If they wore them outside, they risked being mistaken for a gang. It is worth noting that this concern was so severe that not only would they not do it themselves, they would not even travel with others—such as the Dynasty Rockers—who did.[5] Virtually every dancer I spoke with who was active in the '70s had at least one story about being chased out of a neighborhood by gang members who mistook their b-boy crew for a gang.

To this day, when speaking about wearing shirts with their crew's name on it, older b-boys almost always refer to it as "flying" the name. This term comes directly from the gang practice of flying one's colors (gang vest) or flying "cut sleeves" (indicating general outlaw status). Presumably, that term reflects the fact that gang colors were treated like a flag; they were the literal embodiment of the group's identity and, as such, were treated with supreme respect. Moreover, it was common practice in the '70s and '80s for b-boys to battle for shirts, much in the same way that gangs fought over colors. To have your colors taken was an almost unimaginable humiliation for a gang member (the exact equivalent of having a foreign army capture your flag), and the same mentality seems to have applied to crew shirts.

In the early days, crew identity was also similar to gang identity in that it was associated with a specific territory, something that does not apply today:

**Joe:** So it could get to even beyond taking your shirts or whatever, that they could actually take over the territory?

**Richard Santiago:** Yeah. They can take the territory. Yeah. That means that your colors would be rested [retired], and you'll fly under *them*. And [if a] battle comes down, you support that group and that squad. Or you become part of the battle squad and battle for them. To rep 'em. Or if they had a big meeting and stuff, you would all come down. (Richard Santiago, interview)

Notice that Santiago actually refers to the dance crew's T-shirts as "colors." Although they were designed for different purposes, the social organization of dance crews closely resembled that of the gangs, and in many cases individuals participated in both activities.

Interestingly, one way that this relationship was often managed was by splitting b-boy crews into two divisions, one that was the regular dancing crew and one that was more open to questionable behavior. As Buz reports, this format served several purposes: the "bad boys" could provide security for the dancers in various situations, give the crew credibility in their interactions with gangs, and advise younger members on street life so that they didn't have to turn to outside sources for information. It also provided a pathway for individuals to transition smoothly from gangs to dance crews:

**Buz:** We had two crews: we had Touch of Rock and Another Touch of Rock. It was all together, but Another Touch of Rock were the bad boys.

**Joe:** OK.... That's something that I'm starting to see, too. A lot of crews had that, like with Zulu and Zulu Gestapo.[6]

**Buz:** There you go. Yeah. And we were the only [dance crew] that did that. Another Touch of Rock and Touch of Rock. Another Touch of Rock were the bad boys.... I had a real communiqué with them, and I would turn around and say, "Hey, do me a favor, guys, man, don't do any of the stuff around my juniors." 'Cause we had juniors.[7] So they would meet up with [the] juniors and...that's where the juniors used to get the street life, from them. "Well, let me tell you something, I did this, this, this, man, but I'm gonna tell you, man—and I did this—but it's wrong...." And they were the eye opener among my younger guys.

**Joe:** And that would keep them from being drawn to people out in the street.

**Buz:** Exactly. So if you want answers, then go over there and talk to guys who keep it in the group or whatever. I know that I can trust these cats....

**Joe:** And then, also...the other Touch of Rock would kind of have your back in battle situations, too, if things got out of hand.

**Buz:** They were the ones that we used to—when we did a dance, they were like the bouncers. You know, they'll sit there, whatever.

**Joe:** 'Cause that was still in the gang era, too, right? So you had to be concerned about that: people coming in.

**Buz:** And these guys, again, the guys from Another Touch of Rock were guys kind of getting out of the gang and coming in. So you would go through Another Touch of Rock, and then slowly, "are you good enough to come into Touch of Rock?"...So it was almost like a "prospect" deal.

This practice was part of a larger phenomenon of social organization that is both fascinating and massively understudied: New York teens in the '70s and '80s lived within an elaborate patchwork of affiliations and loyalties that were self-selecting for different personality types. Dance crews were merely one arm of a linked series of social groups that included gangs, musical ensembles, sports teams, graffiti crews, and a whole variety of other groups. Richard Santiago, for example, outlines the extraordinarily complex web of "family" ties that he was affiliated with, starting with his dance group, Breaking in Style, which—like the earlier Touch of Rock—was divided into two factions:

Within our Breaking in Style family, that was just considered first, the dancing crew. The other side of our family was called S.M.D. This was the wild side of the family. S.M.D. meant "Suck My Dick." The president was called SHIT-3. The crew in the graffiti side that was down there was T.P.A.: The Public Animals.... There was another group called B.R.U.: Blunts R Us. Cause these guys used to be smoking joints, but then they went into what these guys call blunts—you know, like the cigars and roll it up. So there was a camp that did that. Each one structured internally differently than the other, yet the participants freely moved among them all.

So, yes, we were the b-boying side of it. But networked with us was T.S.P., The Street Partners, which is networked with The Public Animals, which is networked with Blunts R Us, which is networked with S.M.D.... So in reality, it was all the same family, but just different directions of who they want to associate with. (Richard Santiago, interview)

In other words, what we see is a series of affinity groups for every possible interest, legal or otherwise. On some deep level, they were all connected, so that individuals could move between them as their interests or attitudes changed without ever having to actually leave their "family" or have their loyalty called into question. It also provided any given faction with a huge support network that could be called upon if any conflicts arose with other families. The interaction between different forms of expression also naturally led to a kind of artistic cross-pollination that made each form stronger. "They'd feed off each other," recalls Anthony Colon. "You had segments. You had the writers. The writers may not have done the breaking, but they were associated with the crew" (Anthony Colon, interview).

It is this deep sense of community—and the principles, rules, and expectations that allowed it to function—that b-boys are honoring by the way they dress.[8] Waaak, for example, explains that his personal fashion sense represents not only his general attitude but also specific connections to both graffiti writing and a legendary Brooklyn crew of the '80s called the Lo-Lifes, known for shoplifting specifically Polo merchandise from department stores (members included underground emcees Thirstin Howl the 3rd and Rack-Lo). Waaak explains that he wears Polo merchandise not because of the image created for the brand by Ralph Lauren, but because, via the Lo-Lifes, it represents the wildness of Brooklyn in the '80s and early '90s. Similarly, he wears North Face to represent his graffiti days. "I wear Polo 'cause, you know, 'two *L*'s up,' I'm Lo-Life," he says:

I keep tradition, you know. And I believe in just being fly when I do it. I [also] wear a lot of North Face shit.... The jackets were good for boosting... 'cause they were big, they had a whole bunch of pockets. And they were perfect for being out late at night in the snow. Painting [graffiti]. In the cold. Walking the streets, you know? So that's the attire right there. B-boy attire for me is Polo, Nike, and North Face. (Waaak One, interview)

As Richard Santiago describes it, b-boys wore

short-sleeved sweatshirts, the individual [iron-on] letters, with the stars now as a symbol for the rocker, lightning bolt for the b-boy, Playboy [bunny] for the hip-hop contributor. It was a whole thing....Lightning for the b-boys, 'cause it was flash, energetic, boom, break-on-the-break. The stars were rock, like, "you're the one." And then the Playboy was, "you're just a regular b-boy head, a hip-hop par ticipant."...There's a lot of different things that people aren't aware of. (Richard Santiago, interview)

"There's so many different intricacies of how you had to sport your shit," he continues:

The idea of the cap. It's just a cap. You put it on your head, boom, that's it. But why aren't they wearing it correctly, with the brim forward? Because if you would get into a fight, all they have to do is drop the brim, and that's it. You couldn't see and then you get a beatdown. So that's why you move the brim to the side and off. To say you were ready to scrap. (Richard Santiago, interview)

The sideways or backward baseball cap, then, began as a practical necessity— not only to be prepared to fight, but to show it—but was ultimately encoded into the fashion expectations of hip-hop, where it remains to this day.

Beyond what the clothing looks and feels like in general, there is the issue of its role in demonstrating b-boys' control of the body. Specifically, a foundational value of b-boying is that good b-boys and b-girls should be able to dance with the utmost intensity and still have enough control to avoid damaging, scuffing, or wrinkling their clothing: "If I can get down the whole night, and I have white sneakers and didn't get one scuff on them," says B-Boy Phantom, "then I con- sider myself the victor. You see what I'm saying? Because it's like, 'I got this sucker here trying to battle me. I'm gonna burn him, and I didn't even get my kicks dirty'" (B-Boy Phantom, interview).

The ideal that this reflects—that one should be intense yet totally in con- trol—is at the heart of the b-boy attitude and is perhaps the single most signifi- cant aspect of the overall b-boy persona. B-boys should exude preparedness, competence, and confidence. They should not only be prepared to battle at any time, but they should look it. Several of my consultants have attempted to judge my familiarity with b-boying in general by asking whether I was yet able to distinguish b-boys from the general public simply by the way they carry themselves.

The attitude, like the dance itself, requires a controlled aggressiveness. Clearly, this expectation derives from the circumstances in which it arose: the New York streets of the '70s often required a posture of barely restrained violence, as reflected in the slang phrases "ice-grill" and "mean-mugging," and what BOM5 describes as the "deadpan look" (BOM5, interview). Like the backward ball cap, this basic survival mechanism has become abstracted as part of the b-boy dance. It also reflects on a deeper level the social circumstances under which the dance developed.

B-boys literally work for years to build their reputations. And to battle them is, inescapably, to strike at that reputation. Under those circumstances, a battle can become very personal. "A lot of it is like, if you go through struggles and you go through hardship, it's like somebody's challenging what you have," says Anthony Colon. "It's like, 'OK, this is mine. *This is mine.* And you're trying to take it away from me? *F— you.* You're trying to burn me? You're gonna take what *I* got? *You better kill me.*' And that's the mentality" (Anthony Colon, interview).[9]

"It's the essence of what a b-boy, b-girl, is: you know, rebellious," confirms Trac 2:

[They] have a lot of frustration, whether in the environment in which they live in, or the home in which they're being raised in. Peer pressure. And the dance form was basically an outlet for us to express ourselves....It's more of an ego, aggressive-type environment; you have to show that you can hold your own. And it represented the type of struggles that we were coming out of.

"So the look that we had was an aggressive look," he continues:

B-boys have a cocky attitude, a confident attitude. And when a b-boy comes in, he has a certain swagger, that you know he's a b-boy. Just the way he is, his appearance. He had that mean look, like, he can't be approached. He's waiting for that music to drop, he's waiting for that first guy to step into a circle. It was almost like a fight at the OK Corral! (Trac 2, interview)

In addition to a general sense of menace, another part of what b-boys and b-girls are trying to get across, of course, is their actual ability to dance. One way to do that is to allow your body to express the music's rhythms as if it were a musical instrument. Specifically, the ideal is to have the rhythms so present in your body that onlookers could feel the rhythm visually even if they could not hear the music. Beyond that, b-boys and b-girls should actually be able to create a groove between the rhythm of the song and the rhythm of their bodies, a technique known as rocking the beat. This oneness with the music can also be manifested with regard to the song form:

If you listen to a break record, there's a time to go down....There's a time to get up. There's a time to stop. There's a time to do it. And when you do it correctly, everything is rhythmically correct. You can't do no wrong. You're always gonna look tight. And it's all in counts. And once you start learning music—not learning it, *understanding* it—you don't even gotta know the record....I understand rhythms. I understand that everything in funk—'cause that's where the breakbeats come from—is all on four or eight counts. Every four counts, the music changes. So should we. Real simple. Every time the music changes, so should we.

It could be a song you ain't never heard in your life. I guarantee you…if it's got a dope breakbeat, it's a dope drummer, or it's got some funk in it, it's gonna change in four counts. I don't care. Bring me something that I ain't never heard in my life. And we'll sit there and count. One, two. On the fourth one, it's gonna change. It's gonna either climb, or break down. But everything is like that. You know, that's *it*. That's basically it. Just know that. And once you know that, you can never do no wrong. You can never do no wrong. (Alien Ness, interview)

In this quote, Alien Ness makes a subtle, yet important connection. He suggests that, to embody the relationship between the structure of the music and the structure of the dance is to open up the possibility of transcending them both: "you can never do no wrong." When the dancer's body becomes that connection, her natural—or even supernatural—instincts will *always* be correct.

The structure of the dance is deeply entwined with the structure of the music. The b-boying format, as mentioned earlier, operates within the cypher, a circle of b-boys and b-girls. Each takes a turn in the center (known as a "run" or "set") that lasts approximately 20 to 30 seconds, and proceeds through five types of moves. These are, in order:

1. toprock, upright rhythmic dancing that announces one's presence;
2. the go-down or drop, a creative way to move from toprock to the floor;
3. floor work, dancing low to the ground, which consists of footwork, intricate rhythmic movements on the ground; air moves, which demonstrate acrobatic ability; and power moves, which demonstrate physical strength;
4. the freeze, a concluding pose that punctuates the dancer's statement; and
5. returning to one's feet and leaving the circle (interestingly, there is no name for this, which suggests that it is not considered an actual part of the dance).

Beginning breakers can learn simple versions of each type of move and be able to perform relatively soon after they take up the dance. Improving one's breaking ability consists of developing this repertoire in three ways. The first is learning many varieties of each type of move so they can be strung together in different combinations as the moment requires. The second is learning (or creating) more difficult or distinctive varieties of each type of move. The third is learning to perform each move—simple or difficult—with greater precision and finesse.

B-boys and b-girls who have achieved all of the above have the ability to marshal these movements in the service of larger expressive goals. As Ken Swift explains, it is about creating narrative threads, which he actually refers to as "text":

> I like to really make statements when I dance that are designed specifically for certain [themes]. You know, like, for aggression or for humor or for skills. So the "text" would be taking the fundamental moves, the simple fundamentals, and doing the mathematics with them. Which means…I take 15 fundamental moves to deal with—anything from particular spins or a move or any element of original fundamental—and I paste them together. And I take 15 moves and I just rearrange them. The mathematics behind taking 15 moves and doing different combinations is very—you can do *a lot* of shit. So that's basically what text is. It's like putting everything together in between your topstyle and your ending.
>
> Similar to when you write a letter. You got your fuckin' opening. You got your body of your shit. You got your closing. And the text is like your statement…the bulk of what you're gonna say in the body. The ending, it's a flash statement.
>
> Text is more than one statement. It's like 10 different statements in a body. That's how I look at it. (Ken Swift, interview)

From Swift's perspective, a b-boy set has a clear narrative form: the toprock is the equivalent of the salutation of a letter. The dancer is addressing the crowd directly, defining his relationship to them, and giving them a sense of what he is about to do. The floor work is the body of the letter, in which the dancer explores a variety of themes. For Ken Swift, this process includes the idea of "mathematics," or systematically testing the relationships between different types of movement, in order to understand the emotional content that results from each combination: aggression, humor, technical skill, and so on. When a dancer tries several such experiments in a particular order, a kind of story emerges based on the success of each experiment and the order in which the emotions are released. The story is concluded with the freeze, which Swift characterizes as a "flash statement." In other words, the freeze serves as a kind of a punch line to the story.

"This is a vocabulary," agrees Alien Ness. "With commas and periods and capitalization and exclamation points and question marks and all type of stuff.…Every time I'm on the dance floor, I'm saying something. I'm saying *something*" (Alien Ness, interview). Keeping in mind that this entire process is improvised in response to whatever song the deejay happens to be playing at that moment, we can begin to see a sophisticated narrative form emerging.[10]

The toprock is a way of taking command of the space, setting a tone, and building tension for your turn. "That was like a way of getting the crowd antici-pating what you're gonna do," says Amigo Rock:

> People would go there, get in the circle, do their little dance steps, you know? Then the breakers come down, then they would hit the floor. But you know, meanwhile, a lot of people don't realize that when you get in the circle like that, before you

hit the floor, all eyes are on you. People are anticipating, "what the hell is this guy gonna do?" (Amigo Rock, interview)

The ideal is to toprock until the crowd just cannot wait for you to hit the floor. This is why Alien Ness specified above that knowing when to finish your toprock is a key b-boy skill. If you can time it so that you drop to the floor at a moment that is both the height of crowd anticipation *and also* a decisive point in the song, the resulting release of tension can create a momentum that carries you well into your floor work.

Floor work, in turn, is the heart of the dance. The foundational floor move is called the six-step, and it consists of the dancer moving in a continuous circle around her center of gravity in a six-count pattern. The pattern serves several purposes: it works as a launching point for other moves (most are designed so that they flow seamlessly into and out of a six-step); it serves as a placeholder that a dancer can return to while considering what her next move will be; and it establishes a circular momentum, both physically and artistically. The dancer can then choose to reinforce this momentum or redirect it, but either way it serves as a kind of theme to which specific moves can provide variation.

At the same time, the six-step—and its relationship to b-boy songs, all of which are in a 4/4 meter—raises an intriguing question: how do you perform a six-count movement to a four-count rhythm? B-boys and b-girls will generally answer this question in one of three ways. The first and most common approach is to perform the six-step out of time. This option emphasizes the sweeping circularity of the entire movement over the individual steps. The discrepancy between the movement and the music creates a tension that is resolved when the dancer moves from the six-step to a different movement that *can* be done in rhythm. This shift—from an arrhythmic dance to a rhythmic dance—also serves to emphasize the new move, as it locks into the groove.

Another option is to perform the six-step on beat, which reinforces the rhythm of the song but also creates a strange poly-meter. Since each complete six-step is three beats long (when performed at double-speed to fit the tempo of most b-boy songs), a dancer would complete four full rounds of six-steps for every three measures of music. Since this approach puts dancers at a different point in the six-step (and thus a different physical position) at the beginning of each measure of music, it presents them with two different sets of options for shifting from the six-step to other moves, depending on whether they shift at a specific point in the music or a specific point in the six-step.

If they make the shift at the end of a complete six-step cycle, they can choose which beat of the measure that will occur on, depending on how many times they perform the complete move. If they start the six-step on the first beat of the first measure of music, for example, it will end on the third beat of the first measure the first time around, on the second beat of the second measure the second time, on the first beat of the third measure the third time, and on the fourth beat of the third measure the fourth time. Alternatively, and more commonly, they can shift into a new move at a specific point in the music, by leaving the six-step before the full cycle is finished. While such calculations are rarely—if ever—performed consciously, their implications are internalized through practice. A good dancer simply learns what needs to be done in order for his body to end up where it needs to be at the right time. As above, the longer the six-step is performed, the greater the tension between the music and the dance; moving into other types of footwork resolves the tension, in a similar manner to the first approach. By the same token, however, the longer a six-step is performed, the more onlookers will begin to assume that the dancer can't think of what to do next. Accomplished dancers will rarely perform more than one complete cycle of a six-step at a time, before transitioning into another move. It is a subtle balance that all dancers must negotiate for themselves.

Finally, and perhaps most intriguingly, the six-step may be performed poly-rhythmically, with three steps allotted to each beat of the music (allowing the dancer to complete a full cycle every two beats, or two full cycles per measure). Since virtually all b-boy songs are in common time, this creates an ongoing three-against-two tension between the dance and the music that is clearly related to similar techniques in West African dance. In other words, while the song by itself may be in 4/4 time, the addition of the dance creates a 12/8 feel.

Although floor work can sometimes be choreographed (most commonly in the case of group routines), most breakers improvise this portion of the dance. "I don't work out sets," says B-Girl Emiko:

'cause I always forget. Unless it's a show, choreographed show—then I will remember. But as far as battle or dancing in the cypher, I might do [some of the] same stuff, but it's not a "set" to me. It's just really comfortable for my body. My body remembers the movement. So, without thinking, I just moving like that. But usually, I just think about how I getting into the floor. So I have a different way to get into the floor. From that, my mind move different way, or my body moves different way. So the movement would change. So mostly my dance is freestyle. Improvised. (B-Girl Emiko, interview)

One part of the value of improvisation is that one can discover new movements in the heat of battle that would never arise in a more controlled practice environment. From the point of view of choreography, this could be viewed as simply making mistakes. But part of the b-boy attitude concerns learning how to successfully turn a mistake to one's advantage. "A lot of people tell me this," observes B-Boy Character, "that a lot of times when I fuck up, I actually come up with better shit than I was planning to do.... If I freestyle, it's like, way more different, because I have the stamina and I have the capability of flexing my body to go from footwork to power to freezes and combine it and just really, like, flow. Flow with all my moves" (B-Boy Character, interview). But the main value of improvisation is that it allows b-boys and b-girls to respond to the music in the moment. That flow, the connection between the individual human body and the shared rhythms of the music, is the essence of the dance.

"Music really defines it," confirms Ken Swift:

I mean, lot of times if you see, like, certain songs come on, you're gonna see me come out of a shell. Certain songs come on, you're gonna see me wanting to act like I'm a Don Juan. Certain songs come on, you're gonna see me acting like I don't give a fuck, you know what I mean? And clowning, and not even being serious, just really finessing. And the music has always defined everything I do. Even finding moves is based on the music, 'cause some music just puts you overboard. And sometimes going overboard opens up new doors. (Ken Swift, interview)

"I remember I learned a lot about myself and about the dance the first time I got my heart broken," says Waaak:

All of a sudden—you know, you hear it all the time—"oh my God, every song I hear, it finally makes sense." A lot of the songs that…we listen to are disco and funk…and they speak about love and about women and relationships. So during that time, a lot of songs made sense to me. I finally understood the music. So I finally started understanding more of myself. Therefore, I evolved as a dancer. I got better. You know? So I credit that for me actually getting good. (Waaak, interview)

"Sometimes people can give you the idea, but they can't teach you how [to] do something, just because you're not ready to learn," he continues. "So once I finally understood the music, I understood more about the dance. It wasn't about moves, it wasn't about trying to fly and do power and all that shit; it was about the music. So I had growth within myself, had knowledge of self, so therefore I got better as a dancer."

While the connection between music and movement may be abstract in certain cases, it can also be specific in others. "Let's say even if you're dancing to a funk track and it has like a little blues guitar on it," explains B-Boy Phantom, "and it has, like, a little [string] bend in it. You could do something with your legs to represent that bend in that blues guitar.… That's [the] essence of b-boying." "The people you see do that," he continues:

you're gonna know: he's a b-boy.… That's what gets my respect, really: knowing the intricacies. Not the elaborate head spin or the elaborate windmill.… You can teach somebody, physically, to do a windmill, but you can't teach somebody to hear that quarter note and dance to the sixteenths. You can't teach somebody that. That's something that they'll hear and they'll think of. (B-Boy Phantom, interview)

Another technique that dancers use is to juxtapose different moves for their historical implications. Ken Swift, for example, feels that the combination of original b-boy moves with more contemporary additions to the repertoire is itself making a powerful statement. "I always try to add some sort of fundamental move in any combination," he reports:

> This way, I keep the traditions of the original style. You know, that's what I tell people to do. I say, "Look, you could do a shuffle, and it may mean nothing to you in a battle. But if you combine it with a lot of ill shit, you're maintaining the traditions of the dance...." The finesse behind fundamentals is *serious*. (Ken Swift, interview)

Finally, the freeze concludes the statement. As a static pose, the freeze calls attention to itself by decisively breaking the momentum that was set in motion by the floorwork. In doing so, it is expected to bring the narrative to a satisfying resolution. Alien Ness describes an incident in which Lil Lep of the New York City Breakers criticized him because his freeze failed to tie up the loose ends of his set:

> One time, I came up with a run where I pull out my gun, cock it, spin around, and blast you and end up in dead man's freeze. Everybody in the room was like, "Whoa! That's dope!"
>
> And Lil Lep was like, "That shit is wack!"
>
> And I'm like, "What?!"
>
> He's like, "What happened to the gun?"
>
> He said, "I saw you pull it out. I saw you blast me. But when you went into the freeze, you didn't put your gun away." That's how technical Lil Lep is. If you pull a weapon, put it away. Or throw it away. He's like, "I wanna see you throw it away, or put it back away, do something. But that, it looks wack, it's not believable."
>
> And that's what the problem with most b-boys are. They're not believable. They doing things that don't make no sense whatsoever. Some of them look like they're imitating somebody washing a floor.... And I'm like, "*What is he saying?*" (Alien Ness, interview)

The details of any given b-boy set, then, build on deep aesthetic principles in order to make complex narrative statements. The general aesthetic provides a context or frame, and the actual movement provides the statement of the individual within that frame. Together, these two elements allow dancers to make concise, clear statements about who they are and their relationship to the world around them at that moment. The fact that these statements are improvised in response to the songs of the b-boy canon (which was compiled specifically for this purpose) creates a system that provides an extraordinary array of options for self-expression. This self-expression, in turn, is further supported by a dancer's clothing, general attitude, and crew affiliation. B-boys and b-girls who project a distinctive swagger, wear clean sneakers and immaculate clothing (featuring their name and the name of their crew), and move through the different stages of their text with finesse, power, and creativity in response to a song that is associated with the South Bronx of the '70s can turn a 20-second performance into the equivalent of a thousand-page autobiography.

"My style of breaking is what fits who I am, as far as also how I dress and my attitude," says b-boy Ru:

> That should go for just about almost every b-boy, you know what I mean?...How I get down is I get down rough. I like to just do things to the point, and basically put a little comedy in there, and...just do my thing. Just get rugged. And that's how my style is....And that's what makes b-boying so interesting, is who you are. Your own style....It doesn't matter who you are: you dress however you want to dress, and you get down however you want to get down. (Ru, interview)

It is not hard to see similar imperatives in other aspects of hip-hop. All aspects of hip-hop, for example, push their practitioners to choose a performing name that expresses significant aspects of their identity. Striving to live up to that name represents a commitment to live up to the claims that they make about themselves, as well as the expectations of their peers. On a more specific level, the music of the deejay and hip-hop producer indicates not only their technical skill and musical taste, but their entire history as musical listeners, their skill at finding records, and their personal sense of which samples "belong" together. The emcees, in their use of words, are the most explicit in their self-presentation. But in addition to the actual contents of their lyrics, they also present an extraordinary amount of information about themselves through their style. This includes elements of literary style, such as slang and metaphors; musical style in terms of the flow, rhythm, and tone of their performance; and personal style in their clothing, jewelry, hairstyle, and so forth. And graffiti writers are perhaps the most conscientious of all in this regard, as they must make extravagant, highly personal statements about themselves that are specifically designed to be appreciated in their absence (and to disguise their true identities from law enforcement). These statements naturally tend to focus on their names, their styles, and the relationship of both to physical space.

The depth of b-boys' and b-girls' commitment to expressing their individual and group identities is impressive, but not surprising. The art that they have created gives each individual an opportunity to define and express a persona, while the standardization of the form allows each individual's story to be connected with all the others. This gives rise to a rich, almost three-dimensional social mosaic where each individual's expression also contributes to the beauty of the collective. This relationship and the sense of community it creates thus become self-reinforcing. But perhaps the most significant aspect of the b-boy aesthetic is the way that it trains b-boys and b-girls to take control of these factors. If a dancer learns how to project a positive self-image and build productive relationships with others in the cypher, it is that much easier to do the same thing in other contexts. As Waaak notes:

> Just the practice of it, of the art form, gives you discipline and gives you techniques that you can apply in the real world. Like decision-making techniques. Basic decision-making techniques that you can take into the real world. Like I tell people all the time: you don't gotta be a b-boy when you grow up... but there's no reason why you can't b-boy and be a doctor. B-boy and be an architect. B-boy and be a politician. And that's what we need. (Waaak One, interview)

# 5

## "In the Cypher"
### B-Boy Spaces

Dance is an art form that uses both time and space as its media. As a result, the dance may be in the best position to comment on the way concepts of space are addressed in hip-hop generally. But as Forman has astutely noted with specific regard to the musical aspects of hip-hop culture:

> [T]he links between ghetto or inner-city spaces and rap are frequently drawn without significant interrogation of the discursively produced value systems that always influence our social perceptions of these spaces. In many earlier instances, the ostensibly "raw" reality of hip-hop's formative spaces is valorized and roman-ticized, creating misperceptions that position its cultural expressions as the appar-ently organic product of a particular sociospatial milieu. (Forman 2002:xx)

The phenomenon that Forman criticizes—the presentation of hip-hop arts as the mechanical result of a particular set of social or material circumstances and the resulting characterization of hip-hop's pioneers as, at best, creative reaction-aries—is sadly typical of academic hip-hop scholarship. I have discussed this issue in regards to music elsewhere (Schloss 2004:25–30). What I would like to do here is exactly what Forman suggests: to interrogate the "discursively pro-duced value systems" of b-boying by investigating the theoretical approaches that b-boys and b-girls themselves have articulated to address their relationships to the spaces within which they operate. In other words, what should interest us is not so much *that* b-boys and b-girls engage with their environment through dance, but *how* they do so.

In the b-boying discourse, concerns about space usually manifest themselves most immediately in three areas: the dance surface, the shape of the dance space, and the size of the dance space. In each of these areas, b-boys and b-girls not only have articulated specific aesthetic concerns but have also explicitly connected them to broader symbolic issues. As with the aesthetic principles I discussed in the previous chapter, the way a dancer interacts with the space can be a way of metaphorically engaging with larger issues of history, community, and identity.

The dance surface comes into play in several ways. First, being able to dance on different surfaces is, in and of itself, considered to be a valuable skill. Unlike other dance styles, the ability to contend with unsuitable conditions is viewed as a core aspect of the form; complaining about a poor dance surface would be considered a shortcoming on the part of the dancer, not on the part of the environment. For example, I once saw Ken Swift dancing at a party in a style that was very different from his normal approach. When I asked him about it, he explained that someone had spilled a drink on the floor, so he could only use moves that were appropriate to a slippery surface. There are two notable aspects to this statement. The first is that he could have simply chosen not to dance at all, yet he rejected that option. The second is that he did not volunteer his rationale until I asked; he took it for granted that he was expected to dance on the wet floor.

When I asked him to expand on this issue several months later, it was clear that he saw this skill as a fundamental aspect of the dance:

> I look into my repertoire to choose...what I know would work with the surface. So, for example, you're on a floor that's sticky as fuck. You're not gonna try sliding knee spins. You're gonna pivot on your footwork and you're really gonna try to be, you know, pivoting. [If] you're on a slippery floor, you're not gonna try and do fuckin' back tucks. You're gonna slip...and crack your head.

Ken Swift. Photo © Martha Cooper.

So it's about thinking and knowing your stock [of moves]. So I know what to do. There's people that just did what they always do and fuck up half of everything because they didn't sacrifice. That's the beauty of having a lot of moves and a lot of different styles. You should have moves for concrete, you should have moves for a wooden floor. You should have moves for linoleum. And you should know what works on each. And that knowing, that requires practice. Knowing and adjusting to the medium. (Ken Swift, interview)

Knowing which moves work on which surfaces shows a b-boy or b-girl's skill in several ways. First, and most obviously, it allows dancers to choose moves that will work well on the surface they find themselves on. At the same time, by excluding moves that are not appropriate, they are minimizing their chance of having problems. A b-boy who *does* lose control, then, has actually committed two errors: the loss of control itself and the lack of strategic thinking that led him to attempt the move in the first place. As Ken Swift points out, this reveals an even deeper problem: the fact that he attempted the move suggests that the b-boy had a limited number of moves in his repertoire and thus could not afford to sacrifice any one of them to environmental factors. Skilled b-boys and b-girls, by contrast, can show off by *not* doing certain moves in certain situations, thus demonstrating that they can do without them and still triumph. This is as true in life as it is in b-boying: the more options you have in any given situation, the more freedom you have to choose the most appropriate one. It also means that you are not tied to any particular strategy and have the luxury of changing your approach as the situation changes. B-boying, then, teaches its practitioners exactly how to negotiate change. When this strategy is practiced and internalized through b-boying, it can become second nature in other contexts.

In addition to the general value of being able to dance under different conditions, certain surfaces have additional ideological value based on their being viewed as either especially challenging, more traditional, or—in the case of concrete—both. "If you break on the cement, you're, like, a raw motherfucker," says b-boy Tiny Love (Tiny Love, interview). "Especially if you do footwork," adds B-Boy Character. "And you have a nice pair of kicks. Definitely concrete is like fresh, yo. . . . [But] you don't wanna do like no elbow freezes or stuff like that 'cause you don't really wanna hurt yourself, so your footwork becomes more open" (B-Boy Character, interview). Again, in referring to "footwork," Character is talking about intricate, rhythmic moves performed on the ground. The term is used to differentiate those movements from air moves (which are acrobatic movements) and power moves (which are movements designed to display physical strength). B-boys whose style emphasizes one aspect or the other more decisively will naturally tend to prefer surfaces that support that aspect, particularly when they are competing.

Concrete surfaces specifically work to the advantage of more traditional b-boys and b-girls in three ways. First, as Character noted, concrete happens to be more conducive to footwork, which is emphasized in traditional styles of b-boying. Second, concrete is more unforgiving, leaving b-boys who unsuccessfully attempt air moves to nurse scrapes, sprains, and broken bones. The stakes are somewhat lower for footwork. Finally, the *idea* of concrete—and its association with urban environments (literally, "the streets")—has a certain rawness that reads as historical authenticity.

As I have noted, the relationship between raw, street culture and the socioeconomic conditions that gave birth to hip-hop culture is a common theme of academic hip-hop scholarship. But most academics who have addressed this issue have tended to view it from a rather general perspective: that hip-hop has been a way for people to struggle against neglect and poor living conditions. It is rarely acknowledged that these bad conditions didn't only provide a kind of general emotional inspiration for hip-hop; they also provided specific opportunities that creative youths exploited to create their art and their lives.

Trac 2, for example, notes that teenagers in the South Bronx often rehabilitated abandoned buildings into underground nightclubs, where they could create hip-hop culture away from the prying eyes of parents and teachers (Trac 2, interview). Another example can be found in the anthology *Total Chaos*, where Danny Hoch writes:

> If we're talking about aesthetics, let us not forget cardboard and linoleum. The 1970s saw an acceleration in manufacturing and a proliferation of cardboard packaging that had never been seen before. It was also a time when New York City apartment dwellers were replacing their linoleum floors of the '50s and '60s with carpet. The sanitation department was notorious for underserving poor neighborhoods and leaving heaps of trash in the street, along with copious amounts of cardboard and linoleum. The backspin, windmill, glide, and headspin would not have been invented were it not for young people reappropriating these two mundane items. They certainly didn't conceive them in a dance studio at Lincoln Center. They defied the ground by spinning on it, on their backs, on their heads, on garbage. (Hoch 2006: 353)

On a similar note, Anthony Colon explains that the lobbies of exclusive New York apartment buildings were a favorite b-boying environment for two reasons: they were larger than other indoor spaces that teens had access to, and they often featured smooth marble floors, an ideal b-boying surface: "You'd go to the apartment, put...the [boombox] on the floor of the buildings. 'Cause it was slippery—the marble floors. That's where we did our breaking...in the lobbies" (Anthony Colon, interview). BOM5 actually attributes specific developments in b-boying to this practice: "You know how the spins got a little better in the late '70s? Because we used to sneak into buildings, nice buildings....On the marble floors...in the building lobbies...you were able to spin better" (BOM5, interview).

In our discussions, both BOM5 and Colon specified that they snuck into these buildings, suggesting that their own residences didn't have such lobbies. Both further described a methodology known to any city kid: they would ring all of the buzzers and hope that at least one resident was expecting a delivery or a guest and would buzz them into the lobby without verifying their identity. I mention this because of what it indicates about the environment in which the dance arose: it was one in which poverty existed in close proximity to (relative) wealth, and it was one in which youths developed strategies to gain access to at least some of the benefits of that wealth when they needed it.

The conditions faced by working-class inner-city youth of the '70s and '80s were not only hardships to be overcome, but also opportunities to be nourished. In preserving the styles, moves, and attitudes that were developed under these conditions, modern b-boys are both memorializing these conditions and celebrating the creativity that their forebears developed to overcome them. B-boy theory on surfaces emphasizes that a b-boy or b-girl should always be prepared to deal strategically with different environments and situations and teaches specific strategies for doing so. As Trac 2 emphasizes, this attitude is at the heart of hip-hop culture:

> In an oppressive society, we had something that we needed to say, through this form of aggression. And . . . we wouldn't conform to what was the norm. We just adapted, overcame, and just excelled. The whole essence of what people portray as hip-hop is basically the youth recognizing who they are through self-expression. . . . It was innocent, it was pure, and *imagine that!* I mean, how innocent and pure we were in that environment . . . with all those abandoned buildings. . . .
>
> [But] this social environment basically let us identify who we were, as individuals. And it was empowering. You know, for a kid that's 10, 11, 12, going into his early teens, it became very empowering. It allowed us to be who we are and express it the way we wanted to express it. And, basically, the whole cultural movement was founded on that. (Trac 2, interview)

The second aspect of the b-boy space is shape. The quintessential b-boy environment is the cypher, an informal circle of onlookers, in the center of which b-boys and b-girls take turns dancing. The term comes from the Nation of Gods and Earths (known colloquially as the Five Percenters), a sect that separated from the Nation of Islam in the late '60s, whose terminology has been extremely influential in New York hip-hop (Allah 1993; Miyakawa 2005). Gods and Earths use the term *cypher* to represent anything associated with circles or cycles, including the numeral zero (0), the letter *O*, and especially the circles of people in which their lessons are propagated. It is this usage in particular that has made its way into hip-hop, most commonly referring to any hip-hop activity that is performed in a circle, particularly rapping and b-boying. A cypher can be "built" virtually anywhere at any time: all that is required is a group of dancers. It does not require a stage, an audience, a roof, a dance floor, or even a designated block of time. The cypher's very informality and transience are part of its power; it appears when and where it is needed, then melts away. Rhetorically, it is often referred to as "the" cypher, rather than "a" cypher, which suggests that all cyphers are, in some abstract way, connected. B-boys and b-girls view the cypher with an almost mystical reverence, befitting its status as the most authentic, challenging, and raw environment for b-boying.

Like the term b-boying itself, cypher has also become a verb—"to cypher"—and it is here that the social and spiritual nuances really begin to emerge. When b-boys and b-girls refer to cyphering, they are presuming that the space, the dance, and the relationship between the two are all part of one larger experience. It is distinguished from other dance settings, such as battles and stage performances, specifically by its informality. Essentially, cyphering is to b-boys what jamming is to musicians: a collective enterprise that mixes improvisation, competition, and mutual support, where everyone is presumed to be an insider simply by virtue of being there.

Writing about jazz musicians of the 1920s, the clarinetist Mezz Mezzrow could just as easily be describing contemporary b-boys:

> Through all these friendly but lively competitions you could see the Negro's appreciation of real talent and merit, his demand for fair play, and his ardor for the best man wins and don't you come around here with no jive. Boasting doesn't cut any ice; if you think you've got something, don't waste time talking yourself up, go to work and prove it. If you have the stuff the other cats will recognize it frankly, with solid admiration. (Mezzrow and Wolfe 1946/1990:231)

Almost 100 years after the events Mezzrow describes, event promoters B-Boy NYC would express a distilled version of this sentiment on their T-shirts: "Stop Talking, Start Rocking."

Similarly, in reminiscing about the early years of b-boying in the South Bronx, Trac 2 makes it clear that the demands of the cypher created social expectations that could—and should—be totally different from those of the outside world:

> We had fun.... We would play handball all day long. All day long. Or swimming in the swimming pool. The girls are communicating. I mean, when we were young, we would steal our parents' cigarettes. Find a dollar. We had guys on the corner selling loose joints for a dollar. We tried to get one of the older teenagers to go buy us a quart of beer or whatever. And go to the handball courts on the sneak side and kind of drink or smoke or whatever. And then have fun all day.
>
> But then a jam would come. And [you'd] go home and you would change, put on your crew shirt. And the same guy that you hung out [with] all day, he hits the floor? Man, *fuck you*. You know? I mean, it dictated who we were gonna be.

But after the jam was over, and we're walking the same way: "Yo, I'll see you tomorrow on the handball court."

"I got the ball. Make sure you got the court!" (Trac 2, interview)

Returning to Mezzrow, it is clear that this way of thinking about the role of competition in dance has existed in New York for decades, if not centuries: "These contests taught the musicians never to rest on their laurels, to keep on woodshedding and improving themselves," he writes:

> Dancers had the same kind of competitions, and so did most other kinds of entertainers. Many's the time some hoofer would be strutting his stuff in the alley outside the Lafayette Theater, with a crowd around him, and Bubbles would wander up and jump in the circle and lay some hot iron that lowrated the guy, then walk off saying "Go on home and wrastle with that one, Jim." There wasn't any room for complacency. Bubbles wasn't just showing off. He was making that cat work harder. (Mezzrow and Wolfe 1946/1990:231)

Such decisive statements of aesthetic superiority, known today as "burning the cypher," would be familiar to any modern-day b-boy or b-girl. "You know what's beautiful?" asks Alien Ness. "When you got a heated cypher and you break in that cypher. And you get up and you got that moment of dead silence and nobody goes out? That's when you know your job is done. That's when you pick up your bag and leave" (Alien Ness, interview).

The circle of onlookers as competitive dance space has a well-documented history, having been used throughout the African diaspora for dance (Daniel 1995), religious rituals (Epstein 1977), and martial arts (Obi 2008). As Gottschild has noted:

> Where the circle rules, there is an abundance of energy, vitality, flexibility, and potential. For one, there is always the possibility that the person who is an onlooker may be drawn into the action and become a performer. In addition, since there is no proscenium stage separating audience from performers, spectators may choose where to focus their attention, and performers may choose where to locate themselves while performing. Frequently there is more than one "performance" going on simultaneously. No one person is capable of knowing/seeing all that is going on at any particular moment in time. But this is not to be mistaken for chaos (a cultural bias emanating from those who see linear structure as superior to other possible alternatives). Instead, this is a democracy of structure that is characteristic of Africanist-based performance modes. (Gottschild 2002:9)

In terms of social space, to step into the center of a circle is to demand (or attempt to demand) the attention of everyone present. In other words, engaging with the cypher space requires b-boys and b-girls to develop strategies and sensibilities for projecting and maintaining a confident self-image. As Ken Swift relates, the aesthetic of the dance not only encourages confidence; in many circumstances, it actually demands it. "It was a unspoken-of thing that you had to have: the ability to clean up your shit if you fucked up, so that no one noticed it," he remembers. "I got up *many times* and nobody said *shit* and I'm like, 'Damn, I fucked that up.' But because I was agile and able to catch myself, and not show an expression, just stay confident? That's what's b-boying is about" (Ken Swift, interview). Dancing in the cypher forces b-boys to instantly incorporate mistakes into a larger framework that recharacterizes them as being correct, a skill that is arguably as important as performing the move correctly in the first place.

In Monson's *Saying Something*, jazz drummer Ralph Peterson, Jr., makes a similar point, albeit in the context of musical improvisation rather than dance improvisation:

> It's more musical to be wrong and go with everybody else's wrong and make it right from that point...than it is to stay *right* when everybody else is wrong... just to prove that you know where you are.... That's actually a very arrogant attitude...because in trying to show your knowledge you're really exhibiting your ignorance. (Monson 1996: 169)

In both cases, the message is that, to be responsive to a changing situation is more important than maintaining allegiance to a prearranged plan that is no longer relevant. In both music and b-boying, the practice trains the artist to make the shift so smoothly and confidently that an observer is unlikely to notice that a change has even occurred.

The cypher as a social space teaches many valuable lessons to b-boys and b-girls: a connection to Five Percenter spirituality and politics, a connection to other circle-based elements of hip-hop, the ability to overcome shyness or reserve, developing one's general ability to perform under pressure, the ability to project confidence, and the ability to seamlessly correct mistakes.

The third aspect of b-boy space is the size of the dance area. When I asked Alien Ness about the ways in which space is conceptualized within b-boying, this was the first issue he brought up. Specifically, he cited the example of the Octagon, a b-boy competition he founded. The competition is a traditional one-on-one battle, with one added constraint: each contestant's entire performance must take place within the boundaries of a seven-foot-diameter octagon, constructed from traffic cones and police tape. If any of the cones are disturbed, the contestant is immediately disqualified:

> The Octagon came across originally when one night I was hanging out with Lil Lep [of the New York City Breakers]. And I was like, "When you gonna train me?"
>
> And he's like, "I'll start training you right now!" And he pointed at the box in the sidewalk. He's like, "Get in that box and do a set from beginning to end." He was like, "Give me about 30 seconds' worth of footwork."...

And I did it, and I would hear him go, "Uh-uh. You messed up!"

And I be like, "What you mean?"

"You stepped out the box."...

Then he went on and telling me stories on how back in *his* days, you had venues that might've had a capacity of a hundred people? They'd fit in *two* hundred people. So when the break came in, you was fighting for space, and *God forbid* you stepped on somebody's shoes, or kicked somebody. So you needed control.

And that was one thing that I used to always look at when I used to...judge battles.... You know, these people are going crazy for this one person, and I'm like, "he lost." And everybody look at me like [I'm] crazy. I'm like, "he can't even control his own moves." *Part of mastering is controlling.* If you can't control your own moves at any given point, you're worthless. You're just doing moves. (Alien Ness, interview)

Alien Ness presents his abstract aesthetic principle—"part of mastering is controlling"—as a tribute, in a sense, to the socioeconomic environment in which b-boying developed (overcrowded dance clubs). In b-boy theory, as Alien Ness suggests, the size of the dance space is intimately connected to ideas of self-control. Control of one's moves is highly valued, and the most fundamental way to demonstrate this control is by not bumping into things when you're dancing. "I've seen really amazing b-boys who've just been dancing forever, like Richie [Santiago], literally be able to dance in, like, a four-foot-by-four-foot space," reports b-girl Seoulsonyk. "You know, that's one of his lessons. He's like, 'You've gotta be able to get down in any small amount of space. You have to be able to control your movements so much and adapt to the situation'" (Seoulsonyk, interview). (I have personally seen Santiago dance in a space of about three feet between a table and a wall in a small Korean restaurant in the East Village.) In any case, both of these statements point to significant elements of b-boy philosophy: it is important to be able to adapt to different situations, and self-control is a powerful tool for accomplishing this. Again, it is not hard to see how someone who learns this lesson through b-boying would be well prepared to apply it to other areas of life.

As Eddie Luna notes, b-boying was invented and practiced in tiny apartments (a clear result of the economic constraints of breakers' lives) but was often performed in larger venues. This, too, had both practical and symbolic advantages:

The tighter the spot to practice, the tighter you made your move. So that this way, when you go to make a move in a bigger space, that freedom—you still stay with that tightness—but that freedom just brings it out somehow.... And you don't have no fear no more about "I'm gonna hit this, I'm gonna hit that." So that's how it came to play, like, the sizes of the rooms and how it changes it between doing it in a spot like this [his apartment] and then going to a dance floor. You know, you're being careful *here*—of course, naturally—but in a dance floor, you let it all out. And making it so tight that when you're out there, it just stays tight. Except you got more room to move and breathe. (Eddie Luna, interview)

The development of discipline and self-control gives an individual more options in a small space. Taken on a more abstract level, it is not hard to see how this could help someone deal with an urban environment. The more self-control one has, the more freely and confidently one can move in a constrained environment. Size, in b-boy theory, represents both self-control and, in that, the preservation of the socioeconomic history of the community.

"That's something that people forget," says Trac 2:

That a b-boy created his or her own environment. . . . There's times I had to battle in a small and narrow hallway where I basically had to kick off the walls. You know? Because it didn't allow me to extend my footwork. . . . So I use what's around me as an element of my dance routine. . . . Any time any individual can take control of how they want to express themselves? That in itself is empowering. (Trac 2, interview)

As much as the cypher is situated in a physical space, it is also situated in an acoustical space. When asked about their early hip-hop memories, older b-boys almost always single out the echo of distant breakbeats as an important component of the overall experience. When jams took place in parks and schoolyards, they explain, the music could be heard for blocks. As a result, the booming echoes became linked in the minds of participants with the anticipation they felt as they approached the event.

"What we did is, we would go walk around and find out [where the jam was]," recalls Trac 2. "You know, we would basically *listen* to where the jam is at. Or somebody would call you up and [say], 'they jammin' over here.' And then you go, you take a walk, and you hoping there *is* a jam, and it gets quiet. And then you turn a certain corner, then you hear the music: 'Oh, yeah!'"

"When we heard the music that the deejay was playing, we heard it three blocks away!" he continues. "We heard it, and the closer you got, the more it moves you. You know? And that's when you're like, 'getting closer to the jam, yeah, getting closer to the jam!' . . . You know, it moved us" (Trac 2, interview).

To some degree, this phenomenon still exists, even in indoor venues, simply due to the nature of b-boy events. Since music is required for b-boying, a deejay will usually begin playing records when the first dancers arrive and continue uninterrupted until the end of the jam. As a result, music is already playing by the time the vast majority of participants appear. This, in turn, creates a consistent experience of being slowly drawn into the cypher by degrees. The dancers arrive alone or in small groups, approaching the venue. Soon, they hear the muffled sound of familiar breakbeats and follow the sound to its source. When they enter the venue, either by turning a corner or passing through an entrance, the music becomes substantially louder. At this point, before entering the main hall where the event is taking place (usually a school gymnasium), many will duck into a convenient bathroom to change from their street clothes into their b-boy clothes, as the muffled music continues through the walls. As they move from the street to the cypher, they are also moving from a social environment where they are likely to be called by their given names to a world where they are known by their b-boy or b-girl names. They transform both their names and their physical appearances at the sonic and spatial midpoint between outside and inside.

This accomplished, they then continue into the actual room where the event is being held, where they are suddenly confronted with much louder music, competitors, friends, and in the midst of it all, the cypher. At this point, there is a general expectation that they will make their way around the venue and greet each person whom they know. Then they will begin warming up around the edges of the space. Finally, when they feel ready, they enter the cypher, which is almost always situated either at the exact center of the room or in front of the deejay. The gradually increasing sound of the music runs parallel to the journey from street to cypher, from individual to group, from not-dancing to dancing, and actually guides and facilitates the journey.

This phenomenon is not unique to b-boying. As Ellingson has written, the idea of a space defined by sound emanating from a central point is found in many ritual traditions. "More concretely, the central spatiotemporal foci of ritual actions in the physical world may be highlighted by musical intensification, while movement toward or away from the center is marked by gradually changing intensity rather than a sharp boundary," he writes:

> For example, the religious and musical focus of a Sinhala Kohomba Kankariya ritual is in the drumming, singing, and dancing of the priests themselves; their sound is heard with decreasing intensity as one moves outward through the concentric row[s] of the audience in the open-walled ritual enclosure, through the fields of the surrounding district, which may be the ultimate space consecrated by their performance. (Ellingson 1987:170)

This idea—that the sound in a sense "consecrates" the space in which the dance happens—is a powerful one. It represents not only an interaction between b-boying and the greater environment, but a sense that music and dance can actually effect a spiritual transformation of that environment, if only temporarily.

To present the cypher as the center of spiritual transcendence may seem like a strange way to look at this phenomenon, but there are at least two arguments for doing so. The first concerns the elements involved: individuals coming together to dance in a circle in a tradition of the African diaspora; individuals changing their appearance and taking on new names as they move from "outside" to "inside"; and people using dance to present a narrative—a b-boy text—that physically manifests their sense of self at that moment. From that point of view, spirituality does seem like a plausible organizing principle through which to interpret the experience. Second, and perhaps more important, b-boys and b-girls themselves often invoke ideas of spirituality when they speak of these aspects of the dance. Alien Ness, for example, places b-boying firmly in the spiritual tradition of Africans in the New World:

> This is the only luxury that the slaves had, was the dance and the music. And, you know, they did it—if you look at the music that the slaves had, they had words and phrases that they used in exchange of saying "the master" or "the white man," or whatever like that. They used to clown their masters through song and dance. And other people in Brazil, they used to disguise their martial arts in the dance and came up with capoeira. That's all we had was the song and dance. 'Cause they stripped us of the religion. And a big part of that religion was song and dance. So the only thing that they were able to really participate in without getting whupped or killed was the dance. Because anything else would look too much like worshipping the wrong god. (Alien Ness, interview)

While it would certainly be going too far to present b-boying as a specifically religious practice, it clearly is informed by African spiritual traditions. Speaking of the Haitian *rara* tradition at a recent conference, Daniel Dawson raised the idea that such a pursuit could be thought of as a "secular activity in a ritual form" (Daniel Dawson 2008). A similar approach does seem to apply here.

Scholars often view local practices as specific manifestations of broader social, economic, or political forces. But it is equally important to understand local practices in the terms set by their participants in accordance with the details of their particular environments. This is especially the case for b-boying, as b-boys and b-girls attach substantial significance to the nature and use of space. The relationship between space and performance aesthetics is not just a by-product of economic forces, but an intentional and even cherished aspect of the form itself.

In the case of b-boying, the aesthetic conventions of the form promote a very specific attitude that is broadly applicable to life outside of the cypher. B-boys' and b-girls' understanding of their relationship to the dance space carries with it the history of the community from which it emerged, from tiny apartments to concrete streets to overcrowded nightclubs. At the same time, it models a relationship among music, place, and spirituality that is designed to open up a variety of options for personal transformation. And it trains them to project confidence, discipline, and preparedness for any eventuality as they go forth into the future.

This is why, when Alien Ness discusses how to b-boy in the rain, he could just as easily be talking about a b-boy's attitude toward life in general:

Steelo and me were judging the X Air Games in New Zealand, and it started raining, right? The linoleum started getting slippery, the host was about to stop it.

I told them, "Don't stop the battle." And I told Steelo, "Let's see who uses it to their advantage."

And all the b-boys was going out there trying to do their thing [and] sliding. And this one kid called Katsu...came out. Slid across the linoleum. Shhhhhh. Like Silver Surfer. Boom. Spun. Went down and did a whole run of body rolls and threads. *Used it to his advantage.* And I'm like, "*That's* what I'm talking about."

*You take whatever you got, and you work with it.* (Alien Ness, interview)

# 6

## "I Hate B-Boys—That's Why I Break"

### Battling

I'm the merciless God of everybody that enters my
universe and that cypher's my universe, and I ain't
got no time to like you. If you're not backing me up,
you're my enemy.
—Alien Ness (Mighty Zulu Kings)

Part of being a b-boy or b-girl is to be able to deal with any situation that may arise on the dance floor. This ability is developed, tested, and proven in battle. In fact, battling and b-boying created each other in their own image: battling is the best venue for b-boy style, and the best b-boy style is that which is most suited for battling. "I think it's the most important thing in b-boying," says B-Boy Phantom:

My whole approach to the dance is a battle, you know? I don't really have thoughts of loving my enemy when I dance. When I dance, I dance to let out aggression. I'm kind of upset when I dance....Number one, you're letting out that aggression in a positive manner.

And you can only get better from it. 'Cause if you battle somebody and he's better than you, then you gonna have to take a loss, go back to the laboratory, review your notes, get back on your p's and q's, [and] come back again....

It also teaches you a lot about yourself and a lot about other people....You could battle somebody and you can know everything there is to know about that guy. You see what I'm saying...it brings out parts of you. You're never gonna know a person fully until you battle them....If you fight somebody, you know the type of person he is: "he's gonna go for your eyes," "just be careful, this guy's gonna kick you in your nuts," you know what I'm saying? You know what type of character he is! It comes out in the battle. (B-Boy Phantom, interview)

As Phantom suggests, battling has numerous benefits, for both the individual dancer and the culture as a whole. These include using competition to push individuals toward greater achievement (which also improves b-boying in general); developing fighting strategies that can be used in other kinds of conflict;

developing strategies for positive self-presentation in difficult circumstances; building overall self-confidence; developing the ability to predict the behavior of others; learning to objectively rate one's own strengths and weaknesses; and learning to deal with setbacks in a productive way. In other words, it is the purest way to engage with the issues discussed in the previous chapters.

"I think that battling is very important," says Tiny Love:

> That's what made hip-hop what it is . . . it's like trying to reach the sky. And, you know, the sky is infinite. So basically, I'm gonna reach over here, and then somebody from behind is gonna start reaching further up. And that's how we're gonna go on. It's not like trying to kill each other. It's more like topping the next one and going to the next level. (Tiny Love, interview)

"It's just like sharing," adds b-boy Ru. "That person comes out and then all right, 'You know what? You did that? You shared that with me?' All right: boom. I'm gonna get down—boom boom boom—I'm gonna do what you did, and then what I'm gonna do is, I'm gonna reverse that and I'm gonna show you something that *you* need to respond to" (Ru, interview).

Battling provides a highly defined focus for this kind of development; any change that does not contribute to one's ability to win battles cannot be considered an improvement. Beyond physical abilities or particular dance moves, the ability to control the way one is perceived is also significant. In previous chapters, I have discussed the nature of the overall b-boy persona and how this influences—and is influenced by—the aesthetic of the dance. The battle is the context in which those interactions happen, and it guides both. In the context of battle, the b-boy attitude is not hostility as such, but more like resentment against others for their audacity in challenging your reputation.

"You know what? I *am* cocky! I *do* have a ego problem! I *do* got a big mouth!" proclaims Alien Ness:

> But it's part of the game. That's what keeps me grounded. That's what b-boying is about! Do you enter a battle to be diplomatic? Do you enter a battle to share energy and to express yourself? No! You enter a battle to win! I don't care what anybody says. Everybody's trying to water down and put panties on the game lately, you know what I'm saying? I'll keep it real: I enter battles to win. I live off my dancing. I battle for meat. If I don't win, I don't eat. It's that simple. And I talk a lotta crap. I'm gonna try to talk you out your game. I'm gonna try to talk the judges out your game. And don't *let* it be a crew battle. Don't let it be a crew battle. 'Cause if I got a tight unit? People will never even remember what our opponents are doing! You know, we doing routines on the sideline while *you're* breaking. I'm doing crazy stuff the whole battle. (Alien Ness, interview)

"A battle to me is when you have something on the line," agrees Waaak:

> I look at it like a fight: I'm out there to survive. If we get into an altercation when we leave this restaurant right now—somebody's there and we get into a fight—I'm

gonna fight to survive. I'm not gonna fight hoping the cops come and break it up. I'm gonna fight to survive. So in a battle, I'm gonna go out, I'm gonna battle you. I'm gonna do as much as I can to make sure I'm beating you until you give up. That's what a battle is to me: until *you* give up. (Waaak One, interview)

"That is the b-boy," says Anthony Colon. "The b-boy is not if you can do the moves. It doesn't matter if you can do 28,000 head spins. Who are you inside?...Do you have the fire? When you have that [attitude] where you be like, 'you know what? This is *me*. This is who I am. This is how I'm coming. And you wanna take what *I* got? Let's go. *To the death*'" (Anthony Colon, interview).

Alien Ness feels strongly that the way one presents oneself can have a profound effect on the outcome of a battle:

There's a lot of things you can do to lose a battle before the battle even starts, like shaking your opponent's hand. That is *dead*. I don't care. I've been booed by the crowd. I don't care. I'm not gonna give you that much energy. Never. And I'm not gonna clap for you either. The minute you start clapping for somebody, you giving them all your energy. (Alien Ness, interview)

B-girl KaoticBlaze, who is a perfectly nice person, adopts a similar approach: "Me, I get into a bitch's face," she acknowledges:

In the beginning, I give them love, because I don't want them to think I'ma fight them. I'm a positive person. I don't like negativity, but when it comes to a battle, obviously I'ma be in your face. I'ma get close, I'm not gonna touch you....But I'ma make it evident that I'm there to battle. And if she brings it the same way, more props to her, you know what I'm saying? (KaoticBlaze, interview)

Never one to mince words, Alien Ness follows this path to its logical conclusion. "I *hate* b-boys—that's why I break," he says:

You cannot get into that whole "love" thing....You know when I like b-boys? When I'm home and I'm watching somebody's video, you know what I mean? Or when I go to an event and I'm judging. You know what I mean? That's when I like b-boys. But when I walk into a cypher, man? *Everybody there is my enemy.* (Alien Ness, interview)

What b-boys and b-girls are really bragging about is not necessarily their aggressiveness, but their ability to be aggressive when the circumstances call for it and then to completely commit to their choice regardless of the consequences. The act of embodying an aggressive persona—or any persona—is a fundamental skill of b-boying. And it *is* a skill.

For those who are not naturally heated, becoming comfortable in the battle environment may take some effort. "I'm not, like, [a] mean person," says B-Girl Emiko. "When I battle, I still smile—I can't help it. I was like, smiling, and people [were] like, 'don't smile!' I can't help it!" (B-Girl Emiko, interview).

KaoticBlaze. Photo by author.

"We used our faces and our hands and our looks equal to the moves, back in the day," says Ken Swift:

> Because there were so [few] moves. So we had to try anything in our power to let you notice us and notice that we were clowning you or calling you out.... All that stuff was equal to the actual legwork. See, 'cause you could do legwork, but if you're clowning someone while you're doing it, that's a little bit extra. That's like, "Wow, this guy has personality." (Ken Swift, interview)

Again, this speaks to b-boying's ability to train its practitioners to deal with life. A strategy of setting clear boundaries with an opponent and then taking the most aggressive possible position *while staying within those boundaries,* would clearly be valuable outside the cypher as well. The ability to consciously control one's level of intensity is quite useful, as is the ability to create situations where one can have the maximum freedom to do so without inviting retaliation from those whom one is being antagonistic toward ("In the beginning, I give them love, because I don't want them to think I'ma fight them"). Moreover, the fact that one is taking responsibility for setting the ground rules in any given circumstance automatically puts that individual in a position of strength. Finally, battling allows dancers to practice and refine their skills in all of these areas.

The b-boy attitude can manifest itself in other ways besides generalized aggressiveness. The most common of these is verbal abuse. B-boys are quick to categorize the denigration of their opponents as a part of their strategic arsenal, with little or no personal significance. B-Boy Character sees a twofold strategic value in verbal abuse, in that it directly undercuts the opponent's confidence with pointed insults and indirectly saps their will to compete by turning the crowd against them:

> What you want to do is just laugh at him. Just play with his head. And just tease him. And kill him. Like, once you kill him in the head, and once the mentality is gone, that's it. . . .
>
> They could be the person with the illest moves, but if you start laughing at them and getting the crowd on your side: "Aah, he did that move like three times already," and "Oh, you're breathing too heavy! What's going on with you? You smoke too much!" You know, stuff like that, it gets you down, you know?
>
> A lot of times, I battle people and that's when my character comes out, when I talk shit. And I tell people, "you're fuckin' wack, bro," "you're a biter," or "how many times you did that move?" or "you want the paramedics? 'Cause it looks like you're breathing hard." (B-Boy Character, interview)

Although, in other circumstances, this might be considered poor sportsmanship, the practice is a recognized—and even celebrated—part of the culture of b-boying. "Man, I talk so much crap in a battle," confirms Alien Ness. "See, that's all part of the game, though. That's all part of the game: the mental aspect. The trash talking. All that is part of the game. Whoever says it ain't, don't know what this game is about" (Alien Ness, interview).

Creatively insulting one's opponent is a part of many competitive traditions across the African diaspora. "The integration of percussive music and verbally abusive song is a widespread phenomenon," writes Thomas A. Green:

> Powe [1994], in fact, describes songs containing challenge, boasting, and derision as pervasive aspects of African combat sports. As an example, at Huasa *dambe* matches the fights are preceded by drummers playing the boxers' *take-take* (signature drum call) and praise singers extolling the virtues of the combatants. The boxers shout boasts, insults, and taunts. (Green 2003b:135)

At the same time, precisely because the verbal abuse is understood to be part of the competition, b-boying can provide an opportunity to express real hostilities in a safe environment without inviting the kind of conflict that would likely result if those sentiments were expressed elsewhere. B-girl Seoulsonyk, who—as her name suggests—is Korean, felt deep nationalist sentiments emerging when she found herself battling two Japanese b-girls:

> That's when the Korea-Japan thing just came, like *fire*....It just flooded out of nowhere. And I remember just being so amped and so hyped, just talking *mad* shit to these girls, both in my head and out loud....
>
> In my mind, I was going off. I was like, "This is for all the fucking years of oppression that your country has put on my country. This is for taking away all of my country's cultures, and our fucking silver, our gold, our *rice*, our language, our customs, and oppressing my people and, like, forcing my grandmothers and grandfathers to speak Japanese." It was all of these stories that I had heard growing up in my life, and it just physically manifested at that moment.
>
> But out loud I was saying—you know, 'cause, like, one of the girls was smiling, and she was squatting after she had her throwdown—and I was like, "GET THE FUCK UP!" I was like, "THIS IS A FUCKING BATTLE!"...I was just, like, *stalking* the cypher, like stalking around in a circle before I got down and started dancing. I think I was just so amped that no one could have done anything to me at that point. (Seoulsonyk, interview)

B-girl Seoulsonyk. Photo © Martha Cooper.

The aesthetic values discussed in the previous chapter come into play here. How do b-boys and b-girls creatively integrate the attitude with the aesthetic? How can they use style to project aggressiveness and vice versa? The ideal, it seems, is to be aggrieved, yet simultaneously restrained enough that they can still execute the maneuvers perfectly, to the point that that itself becomes part of what they are bragging about. One should be furious and yet totally in control. "[When] Ken Swift, or any other old-school people, talks about battling, they always say toprock, footwork, and execution is like the biggest part," says Character:

> And I always stuck with the execution part, 'cause ever since Ken Swift told me that, I feel like people will go crazy and do, like, so many power moves. And it's ridiculous what they do, but they crash. And it looks like they hurt themselves real bad. And they think it's really worth that, "Oh, I did all of this, but I messed it up at the end." I think, to me, I'd rather do a basic go-down and finish clean, come out of it fresh. (B-Boy Character, interview)

For Character, wild emotionalism and elaborate acrobatics are meaningless in a battle if they cannot be performed in a controlled fashion. In fact, it is the control itself that is most important.

For Alien Ness, this is not only an aesthetic principle; it is the cornerstone of a strategy:

> **Alien Ness:** You know what else I like to do, man? And I tell people this and they think I'm crazy, and they don't believe me. But, in a big competition...you have the prelims, first round, second round, finals, right? A lot of b-boys like to hold back....like, you'll see b-boys lose competitions and not advance, and then you see them in the cyphers later and they going off. Me? I'm hittin' you my *best*, first round of the prelims. I'm comin' at you with everything I got.
>
> **Joe:** How can you afford to do that? 'Cause you have so much...or you change everything up—
>
> **Alien Ness:** It's not that; it's a mind game. It's a mind game. You see, if I attack you that hard right now, the crowd is feeling me. They're all like, "Whoa, the match just started, and this kid's blowin' up!" The judges already got an impression on 'em. They're like, "OK, I'm feeling this guy. He came here to win." Forget the guy you're battling; everybody else you're gonna battle later, that's their first impression.
>
> So now, we come to the next round, they call up you and Alien Ness. You got Alien Ness in front of you, you don't even see me. You seein' the first Alien Ness you saw. You saw that guy that came and blew up. And to make things even harder, I'm changing clothes every round!...
>
> You know, it's like you're battling the first impression. So now you saw me going off, *you're* gonna try to go off. And that's when Alien Ness takes it easy....

You're trying so hard to beat him, you're messing up. You don't even got control. And at that point, I don't gotta do nothin' impressive—all I gotta do is look neat. Eighty percent of the battles I've won, I've won because I looked neat. Not because I'm the best man in the room, not because I'm better than my opponent, not because I'm the best battler on the planet. Just because I can stay neat. If you're trying extra hard to beat me, chances are you're gonna mess up. And if you're messing up, all I gotta do is give you a flawless run. It doesn't have to be nothing incredible! Boom boom boom boom boom. You could have one judge go, "He didn't do nothin'!" He's like, "Yeah, but the other guy was falling on his face, he was trying so hard!" (Alien Ness, interview)

Self-control, then, is really the essence of the battle aesthetic, and the goal is to make your opponent lose his. "If you're breakdancing in a circle, you always have to have stamina, because once that person finishes, you gotta attack quick and come back out," emphasizes B-Boy Character:

And make that person come back out again and do something better than what you just did. And what they're gonna do is most likely start slowing down or start messing up on their moves. And what I talked about before, the execution, is very key. So once he goes down, messes up, you go out and you do something simple and you're clean? It doesn't matter—you're already winning. And you're eating him away. Eating him away. And you start talking and just bullshitting him. That's how you battle, to me. A lot of emotion and a lot of heart. (B-Boy Character, interview)

To achieve this goal, dancers use a variety of strategies, many of which are jealously guarded and handed down from teacher to student like secret martial arts techniques. "Richie [Santiago]...had taught us about battle techniques and battle strategies," reflects b-girl Seoulsonyk, "and one of his things was, 'you never squat [while your opponent is dancing],' 'cause that shows that you're tired and it shows that you're weak" (Seoulsonyk, interview).

Other battle tactics involve the strategic timing of moves. Since it is considered poor form to repeat a move, a dancer must weigh the benefit of using a particular move at any given time, knowing that it cannot be used again later in the battle. "If you repeated a move, then that's it," says Trac 2. "We know you ain't got no more" (Trac 2, interview). Given that expectation, b-boys and b-girls are faced with a constant dilemma. If they deploy their best moves too soon, their options will be severely limited later on. But if they avoid using their better moves, then they may be defeated early in the battle and never even get the chance to compete later.

Generally speaking, most b-boys and b-girls will try to gauge their opponents' skill level and then perform at a level that is slightly better—just good enough to beat them—but that does not require them to sacrifice too many of their signature moves. In response, b-boys will often try to lead others to underestimate them, then deploy more extravagant moves once it is too late for the opponent to respond.

These kinds of strategies come into play because, unlike other kinds of dance contests, a b-boy battle is not simply a matter of dancing better than one's opponent. B-boys and b-girls are expected to directly respond to each other's performances:

> It's like a fight: I can't prearrange the moves, you know? If I'm fighting you, how do I know you're gonna throw a jab, or a cross, or a side kick? So how am I gonna practice that prearranged move? I can practice a *kata*, which teaches you the movements.[1] Same thing with a [b-boy] routine. I could do routines to practice the routine. But in an actual fight, you have to fight.... So, same thing with breaking. (Anthony Colon, interview)

"It's all chess," Ken Swift adds:

> It's all strategy, and it's a poker game. You know, it's like, we all got similar moves. So then, it's like a boxer will study a boxer. You got b-boys that'll study your shit down to the T. But the issue is your mental strategy and your physical strategy. It's a combination of both.... Because nobody can tell what you're gonna throw. They probably know what you *have*, but if you throw it at a specific time... it's like, "yeah, I know he's got that fuckin' move, but... he hasn't done it yet, and I know he's gonna hit [me] with it any minute now." It's a poker game. (Ken Swift, interview)

This issue is considered so important that many b-boys and b-girls will even hide moves from their fellow crew members, just in case they should ever have a falling out and wind up battling each other. Trac 2 notes that this was the case with his partner Spy (a b-boy pioneer who is credited with creating many of b-boying's most foundational moves). "Even when we were partners, [Spy] would practice in one room and I would practice in the other," he recalls:

> Couldn't see each other. Because I always said to myself, "Well, you know, I don't trust him." You know, there's probably gonna be one day, gonna be on the basketball courts, and he's gonna challenge me. So I could never let him see my whole arsenal. And he would do the same thing. That kind of kept us at ease, to do that. You understand? 'Cause nobody knew what the other one had. (Trac 2, interview)

The battle aspect of b-boying has its immediate roots in teenagers' natural competitiveness. "During that time, in the summer, guys used to have their equipment. Bring it downstairs, in front of the projects, hook it up to the light poles, play some music," remembers Amigo Rock:

> When the music was getting good and the crowd was dancing, there was always some guy that wanted to outdo everybody else. And he'll do his moves. And then

another guy would come in—always—and challenge: "I can do better." Not really battling... but just doing footwork and dancing. And the crowd would decide by cheers and everything. (Amigo Rock, interview)

Over the years, this fairly commonplace, low-key practice—trying to out-dance your friends—became incrementally more formal. Being recognized as the best dancer at a party or nightclub went from being a momentary triumph to a long-term goal. Sometimes, rather than being spontaneous, dancers would agree in advance that they would battle at a particular jam. If a battle was arranged in advance, it could also be integrated into the advertising for that event. In addition to seeing deejays and emcees, audiences could look forward to seeing well-known dancers or crews battle each other.

At the same time, some jams also offered formal dance contests, a practice that of course predates hip-hop by decades (if not centuries). At least initially, these were two different things. Battles were personal, emotional, organized by the participants, often spontaneous, judged by peers or the dancers themselves, and frequently used to address conflicts that were only marginally dance-related. Dance contests were more objective, organized by third parties who often didn't know who would actually enter, arranged in advance, judged by designated and often paid judges who (presumably) had some kind of qualifications for the position. And most significantly, the contests existed for their own sake, not to resolve any particular conflict (though they often did do that). In event flyers that King Uprock showed me from Brooklyn hip-hop jams of the late '70s, the evenings often included dance contests for hustle, salsa, or funk dancing, usually with cash prizes and trophies.

Incidentally, one of the things that struck me about these flyers is that many of them not only specified the amount of cash to be won, they also noted the exact size of the trophy (e.g., "Thirty-Inch Trophy for Winners!"). The idea that a 30-inch plastic trophy would be that much more valuable than a 24-inch trophy shows how significant such mementos were to the participants. The stakes were higher than they may have appeared, and battles were taken extremely seriously. This is not to say that they always—or even usually—led to violence. But they became violent often enough that it was always a possibility. Battles were very much integrated into the social world of their participants and required the same kinds of negotiation that any other large-scale interaction would under those circumstances.

"I ended up battling a crew called Hot Feet Rockers one time," remembers Alien Ness:

And a lot of times [when] you battled Hot Feet Rockers—anybody from the old school will tell you—you'd end up getting beat up afterwards. Hot Feet Rockers was the hardcore roughneck squad, the realest street squad back in those days. Everybody was scared of Hot Feet. Even a battle. If you had to battle Hot Feet

Rockers, you came with a billion people, you know what I mean? (Alien Ness, interview)

The fact that Alien Ness would make such a statement so offhandedly, as if getting beaten up was just a standard part of the battle experience, says a lot about the personal nature of battles in that era.

Speaking in 2005, uprocker and graffiti writer Pedro "Pjay71" Martinez compared the modern era to the early days of b-boying, specifically referring to a battle we had attended in Queens the previous weekend:

The other day, we was at a jam.... the first kid that came out touched the other kid on the head... touched the kid right on the head! They don't understand that, back then, it would've been—yeah, it's beautiful that you can touch somebody today and you get forgiven right there. That's beautiful. I'm not saying there *should* be a fight. I'm not saying you *should* punch the kid for touching you. No. But that ruins the whole dance.... It's a dance. You're not dancing if you tryin' to touch the guy. If you're trying to be in his face, how you gonna dance? (Pedro Martinez, interview)

Eddie Luna makes a similar point. "The dance has no... *written* rules. You know, per se," he says. "But there *are* rules to it: you know, you don't get close to a dancer. You don't make too much of a statement disregarding the other dancer. You know, if he's in the midst of throwing his routine, [you don't interrupt]" (Eddie Luna, interview). To intentionally violate these expectations is to

Pedro "Pjay71" Martinez. Photo by author.

publicly disrespect your opponent. And to accept such disrespect from another dancer would be to compromise your own reputation. This is why Pjay suggests that the threat of violence—not violence *itself*, necessarily, but its potential—was an important factor in the origins of the art form. While Pjay formulates this equation rather narrowly—the threat of minor violence enforced the mutual respect which allowed the dancers to express themselves without inviting larger-scale violence—many people would actually go further than that.

In many ways, breaking was a form of allegorical fighting that came very close to actual fighting, not only in its physical movements, but in its social and symbolic dimensions as well. This relationship is most clearly found in b-boying's precursor, uprocking (see chapter 7), but it is also found in break-ing itself. In fact, when b-boys and b-girls talk about battling, it is sometimes hard to tell the difference between metaphor and reality. There is a noticeable semantic slippage between the concepts of "battling" and "fighting" in many of the quotes in this chapter, as in Phantom's earlier quote where he describes his attitude toward battling by drawing examples from actual physical fight-ing. Alien Ness takes a similar approach when discussing aspects of his battle strategy:

**Joe:** I noticed some of the times when I've seen you at places…you don't get down immediately. You watch for, like, 15, 20 minutes to see what other people are doing.

**Ness:** I see who's who. I like to see who's who. To me, everything is a war, all right? And you never run out on a battlefield blind. You don't go out on the battlefield shooting your gun like "pow, pow, pow," not knowing who's there, who's around you, what they got, you know. I'm walkin' in there, OK, I'm looking for the low-level thugs, I'm looking for snipers, I'm looking for the weapons of mass destruction. OK, I know where everything's at, now I know how to approach it. (Alien Ness, interview)

In "Surviving the Middle Passage: Traditional African Martial Arts in the Americas," Thomas A. Green discusses the general relationship between mar-tial arts and dance in the African diaspora. While this relationship is commonly accepted in specific cases, such as capoeira in Brazil or kalenda in Trinidad, Green attempts to synthesize these cases into a more general profile. He writes:

Whether armed or unarmed, African martial arts generally share at least three of the following characteristics:

- Association with festival or celebration
- Use of supernatural assistance
- Accompaniment by percussive music, leading to a blurring with dance and performance art
- Boasting, bragging, and similar agonistic behavior. (Green 2003b: 131)

The similarities to b-boying are clear: three of the four characteristics that Green cites are fundamental to the dance, and even the fourth (use of supernatural assistance) may come into play in certain circumstances. But what is truly striking is that the characteristics themselves were so common that Green could generalize about them in the first place. In other words, it is not so much that b-boying is similar to a particular African-derived martial art, but that b-boying is similar to *all* African-derived martial arts. That seems significant, and there are other subtleties that support this line of thinking, such as the parallels that b-boys and b-girls tend to draw between their training and martial arts training, the use of the circle, and the word *battle* itself. But perhaps the clearest connection is the widespread use of the term *throwing* to describe the performance of a particular move or type of move (e.g., Ken Swift above: "Nobody can tell what you're gonna throw"). The use of this term (as opposed to "doing" or "performing") is a clear tie to the fighting context, where one would refer to "throwing" a punch or kick.

The conflation of fighting and dancing is common in the African diaspora, an approach that clearly comes from Africa itself. In his landmark study of African martial arts traditions in the Atlantic world, T. J. Desch Obi cites numerous African and New World traditions that mix fighting, music, and dance in a manner that is strikingly similar to b-boying. In southern Angola, for example, he finds the *engolo*, a combat form in which the fighters begin by dancing aggressively against each other in a circle:

> In its ritual practice the engolo, like most African combat forms, was inseparable from music and dance. Language evidence indicates that the art's early history included inverted kicks, sweeps, and evasions.[2] However, our description of how these techniques played out in ritual practice must rely on twentieth-century ethnographic evidence. Neves e Sousa documented the ritual practice of engolo as taking place in a circle of singers/potential combatants, which was at times controlled by a kimbanda, or ritual specialist. The music began with clapping and the call-and-response songs that accompanied the practice circle. In some songs a rhythmic humming could take the place of a response of a chorus. Soon after the mantra-like song was fully established, a practitioner would enter the circle dancing and often shouting to accentuate the techniques he would begin to demonstrate. When a contender joined the challenger in the circle, the two would continue to dance to the music as they squared off while sizing each other up until one adept launched a kick or sweep at the other. (Obi 2008:36)

Igbo wrestling, found some 2,000 miles away in modern-day Nigeria, shows similar features:

> The community...formed a circle around the wrestlers, many of whom had their own drummers....Drums sounding special wrestling rhythms and then songs, often provided by female vocalists, charged the area. Then the ritual taunts and

challenges between the wrestlers began. Talbot [1969] noted that after a contender accepted a challenge the two would "bend down and touch the earth with their fingertips, apparently to beg for help from Mother Earth."[3] Then the two would square off dancing; each looking for the moment to engage in the actual grappling contest until one person was thrown. These ritual matches were community events in which all members of society participated. . . . Older males who had retired from wrestling acted as judges (*atamaja*), and even spectators participated by singing call-and-response songs to urge the wrestlers on.[4] (Obi 2008:65)

Again, we see a martial form that begins with the combatants dancing in a circle and even aiming ritual taunts at each other. Similar practices can be found among people of African descent in the the New World as well, most obviously in Brazilian capoeira, but also in other lesser-known forms, such as the *ladja* of Martinique:

[A]s with other combat arts, the ladja took place in a circle of singers/fighters known as the won. The main musical elements were the percussion provided by a drum called tanbou alendje, musical sticks (tibwa) that played on the backs of the drums, and soloists who led the chorus in call-and-response songs. The ritual began with the kouri lawon, in which the drums called a fighter to enter the circle in a stylized counterclockwise run.[5] The combatant began the monte tanbou, in which he danced to the drummer, saluted the instruments, drew energy from them, and tried to intimidate his adversary with the agility of this dance. After appraising the challenger's skill level, another adept would emerge from the circle to perform his own kouri won and monte tanbou. (Obi 2008:135)

Although the precise nature of the relationship between b-boying and African martial arts remains an open question, a relationship clearly does exist. In the absence of direct historical or ethnographic evidence, three general observations can still be made. First, given both the extensive similarities between the two sets of practices and the fact that the creators of both activities trace their origins to the same cultures, our default assumption should be that there *is* a historical relationship, even if we do not yet know exactly what it is. At the same time, given that we do not yet know the history of this relationship, we should exercise caution before speculating too extensively. Finally, we may note that, regardless of where it came from historically, b-boying does serve martial purposes. It teaches many abstract aspects of fighting, including balance, speed, physical discipline, judging and controlling spatial relationships, reading an opponent's emotional state, and anticipating his actions. On a more social level, b-boying also helps its devotees to practice the kinds of interactions that, if improperly handled, could lead to physical conflict, such as claiming one's own personal space and self-respect without violating that of others. And b-boying can serve as a kind of "prefight" interaction that can help to resolve conflict before it comes to physical violence. "Basically, it brings that dark energy that we all have inside us and . . . it filters all the violence out through [an] artistic point," says Tiny Love. "And that would save us from whatever [problems] we have" (Tiny Love, interview).

This, in turn, brings us back to a central function of b-boying (and hip-hop generally): using art to take problems to an abstract level, thereby giving practitioners a new perspective, a positive outlet for negative emotions, and the satisfaction of having created something artistic.

Eventually, the prearranged personal battle and the formal dance contest merged into a single event—the formal battle—which continues to be the primary environment for contemporary b-boying. These battles are arranged specifically as b-boy events: the music and space are designed to facilitate the dance, and virtually all in attendance are dancers. Generally speaking, the contests are open to any individual or crew who wishes to enter. In the formal battle, competitors take turns dancing within a circle of onlookers for a predetermined number of rounds, at the end of which designated judges decide the winner. Winners of each battle compete against other winners until a champion is decided. Champions are awarded a trophy and a cash prize, drawn from sponsorships or admission fees. In other words, the modern b-boy battle is essentially a dance contest that comprises a series of smaller battles. As a result, the modern battle combines elements derived from both of its parents.

"To me, a competition and a battle are two different things," says Waaak. "Competitions prepare you for battles, and battles prepare you for competitions" (Waaak One, interview). In the raw, street-battle style, dancers' moves are directed at their opponents and are designed to insult them. In a dance contest, the intended audience is not the opponent, but the judges and crowd, and the objective is to show superior technique. The contemporary b-boy battle combines both of these, which adds a certain amount of ambiguity, which in turn serves to energize the dance. Which is more important: demonstrating technical superiority for the judges or creatively demonstrating an aggressive attitude toward one's opponent? Opinions vary.

Battles take place in open spaces that hold several hundred people, usually gymnasiums, but also nightclubs, private spaces, and, in warmer months, outdoor venues with flat surfaces, such as basketball courts. A battle will usually last a total of about six hours, with a deejay playing appropriate music throughout. In fact, almost by definition, the event begins when the deejay starts playing records and ends when he or she stops. The battle proper usually accounts for only about a third of the event's running time, while the remainder is spent socializing, warming up, practicing, and dancing informally. While the formal battle is taking place, others will often take advantage of the music to develop their own informal circles on the periphery, which themselves sometimes evolve into heated battles. There are several reasons for this, the first of which is that everyone's there. If you want to battle a particular person, you are likely to see her at a large event. Also, these events feature two other battle-friendly features: music and witnesses.

Although almost everyone who attends such events is a b-boy or b-girl, not all will actually participate in the battle. Many are content to participate in the other activities. The vast majority of battles are held on weekends, as these tend to be times when people are willing and able to socialize for a whole afternoon or evening, and the venues—gymnasiums especially—are available for rental.

As I mentioned earlier, the deejays who play the recorded music for b-boy events usually also perform in nightclubs. Deejaying for b-boys, however, is viewed as a specific skill in the hip-hop deejay's toolkit, and it requires a wide array of abilities, resources, and specific contextual knowledge. These include having the right recordings at one's disposal, knowing how to structure the flow of an event, and knowing when to change records (a good deejay will usually keep the same record playing through both competitors' turns, so that one does not have the unfair advantage of dancing to a better song).

As with any competitive endeavor, it is important that battles are perceived to be run fairly, as suggestions of bias naturally devalue the accomplishments of the winners. In the case of b-boying, this tendency specifically works to deemphasize demographic issues, whether those are of age, ethnicity, geographic origin, or otherwise. To suggest that someone should be looked upon more favorably due to her cultural background, for example, would be taken to imply that she couldn't prevail on the basis of skill alone. Conversely, to suggest that opponents should be judged negatively due to their age, gender, or ethnicity would be viewed as an indirect—and somewhat pathetic—admission of one's own inferiority. To acknowledge such factors at all is to question the idea of b-boying as a meritocracy, one of its most foundational doctrines.

A striking example of this principle occurred at the Rock Steady Crew's 30th anniversary celebration in 2007 in New York City. One of the main events of the week-long festival was a crew battle held on Saturday afternoon. Among the many crews that had traveled from across the country, and beyond, to compete was one with the strange name of Curfew Breakers. When they were called up to battle, the name's meaning immediately became apparent: all of the members were children or young teens, including two girls. They battled—and defeated— the adult crew that had been chosen at random to be their opponents. After the win was announced, Crazy Legs, president of the Rock Steady Crew, took the microphone to explain the decision. The adult crew had lost, he said, because they had gone easy on the Curfew Breakers due to their young age. The lesson was that all b-boys and b-girls are to be taken seriously. Not to do so is actually worse than performing poorly, because it undermines the ideals of b-boying itself. This idea—that skills are more important than background—also influences the perception of gender in breaking. Several b-girls have expressed to me that, not only should b-girls be expected to be able to battle b-boys, but also that any man who did *not* expect this is, by virtue of his discriminatory expectations, not a real b-boy.

One of the main differences between formal and informal battles is the presence of designated judges. Even before assessing the judges' general preferences and sensibilities, competitors must take into account their physical location. "You have to put into consideration all the time where the judges are," says Alien Ness. "See, I have won battles and I've watched the footage, and I have said to myself, 'the only reason that person lost that round to me was because he was off in how he did it, and the judges really couldn't see the intricacy of his set.'"

"I have runs [that] I wanna do so bad in a battle, but I can't do it 'cause I could only do it one-sided, and if I do it to that one side, the judges won't see," he continues:

> And if I turn it around for the judges to see, I won't be facing [my opponent]. So, the minute I step up to the plate, I see where my judges are. I know everything I'm doing. Everything is gonna be aimed at this person, but all my intricate stuff that the judges are gonna be counting on? They're all gonna be facing the judges. You know what I'm saying? People don't put that into consideration. I've seen so many good b-boys lose rounds and even worse lose battles, because they don't know how to...project their moves. (Alien Ness, interview)

Once dancers make sure that their moves will be visible to the judges, participants must then be aware of the individual judge's value system. "I really have to think [about] who is judging, what they want," says B-Girl Emiko:

> So I will try to be flexible of the needs. If they say, "Oh, we are looking for power move," then of course I have to do power move to win the battle. It's really different....Like, last battle, [We] B*Girl[s] battle, I didn't know what Honey Rockwell and Rokafella were looking for, so I just did whatever I do for the battle. But if I knew what they wanted to have, I would have done it different way. (B-Girl Emiko, interview)

Alien Ness is even more explicit on this count: "You're not battling the opponent. In a organized battle, you're not battling your opponent. You're battling judges. If you really think about it. They just put the other guy in front of you, so the judges don't take the heat. Which is basically the truth, right? 'Cause who's making the decisions?" (Alien Ness, interview).

> **B-Girl Emiko:** I give props for the judge, too. 'Cause it's really hard to judge people, anyway. But they should be just...ready to be hated. Because that's the position they're getting in. They're getting money, so—
>
> **Joe:** That's what they're getting paid for? To be hated?
>
> **Emiko:** Exactly. To be hated. (B-Girl Emiko, interview)

The seriousness with which b-boys and b-girls take competition may be surprising to see at first. But when one begins to understand what is at stake, the reason for their dedication becomes clearer. Each aspect of dancers' battle strategy is meant to simultaneously express and defend a significant aspect of their identity: from their attitude, to their timing, to their place in their peer group.[6]

All of these things are consistent with battle practices in other elements of hip-hop, particularly those of deejays and emcees, who hold formal battles that are organized along similar lines. Both emcee and deejay battles developed from informal battles in an analogous process to that of b-boys and b-girls, both have the same general format, and both have the same general goals. "[I]f power is not available in the larger world," writes Mark Katz about deejay battles, "it is available in the battle world. DJs engage in symbolic and bloodless violence, and can make outrageous claims about themselves or others without, for the most part, seeming arrogant or hateful. DJs construct fantasy selves—they take on new names and identities in battle—and can vanquish foes and even claim world domination" (Katz 2004:131).

Like deejays, b-boys and b-girls are battling for that most elusive prize, a sense of self. They have developed sophisticated and nuanced strategies for achieving this goal, and they apply these strategies both inside and outside of the cypher. Battle tactics are at the foundation of hip-hop, and that is no accident. Battling trains its practitioners to, in Trac 2's words, "adapt, overcome, and excel." And this is why it remains so central to the hip-hop aesthetic. As Waaak puts it:

> To me, battling is very important for the growth of our culture. As a people, our dance and our culture is something that came from basically nothing. We took these things from different venues and different areas and created what we have: this music and this dance and this art form. And if we didn't have all those hardships and things in our way that inspired us to do this? We wouldn't have it. You know? So everything that it took for this art form to be created was a battle, in a sense. It was a fight. It was... very revolutionary times. And battling helps you maintain that.
>
> And you learn things from a battle, just like you would learn things from a fight. And it's definitely needed in today's society 'cause you have microwave everything. EZ-pass everything. You know, instant everything. And a lot of people are getting lazy and getting weak, as a people. And my personal belief is that the system does that to us: they want us to be weak. They want us to be sheep. So we must—we must—continue to battle. (Waaak One, interview)

# 7

# From Rocking to B-Boying

## History and Mystery

The early history of hip-hop, writes Johan Kugelberg,

> is a riddle wrapped inside an enigma stuffed inside a mystery hidden in a sock. The more you read, the more people you talk to, the more likely you are to run into contradictions. If you inquire about an event from two gentlemen who were there, each gentleman will remember the same event in completely different ways, and sometimes the same gentleman will remember the very same event in another four or five ways depending on his mood or who he speaks to. Not to mention those Grandmaster Caz refers to as the "lie-oneers" of hip hop: there are guys walking around uptown taking credit for what other people did. What are you going to do? It isn't all that unlike the Kennedy assassination conspiracy when you think about it. Zapruders and grassy knolls are all over the place in the history of early hip hop, and it sometimes seems as if the old-timer old-schoolers have pitched tents and called the grassy knoll their permanent conspiratorial home.[1] (Kugelberg 2007:140–141)

Of course, this phenomenon is not unique to hip-hop or b-boying, but b-boying in particular does exhibit two distinctive traits: a strong expectation that any historical claim should be supported with documentary evidence and an almost total lack of documentary evidence.

The early development of the dance took place among small groups of working-class black and Latino teenagers, many of whom did not even know about *each other* at the time. As New York City was abandoned by the federal government and working-class neighborhoods were abandoned by New York City, youth in those neighborhoods were, in turn, abandoned by traditional institutions that were supposed to care for them. As a forgotten minority of a forgotten minority of a forgotten minority, their culture was almost totally ignored. On top of that, as teenagers teaching themselves to dance, most innovators were far more concerned with the moves they were going to debut *next* Saturday night than archiving the previous Saturday night for posterity. (If you won a battle, everyone who needed to know already knew; why would you be concerned with what some stranger would think in 30 years?) Combine that with the economic and technological limitations of the era, and we are working with a profound lack of documentation. Virtually the only material support for any historical claims are the kinds of things teenagers have always kept: fading snapshots and flyers advertising events they attended.

But, as Trac 2 points out, even photographs may be hard to come by:

> People say, "Oh, why you don't got pictures?" Come on. Nobody had cameras. If you had a camera or a video recorder, you was rich! And you wasn't living in *my* neighborhood! Our photos was in Woolworth's, where you paid 25 cents and you'd get like six pictures. So you wanna take the first picture and throw in your friend real quick before the next picture came up. You know, it was that little booth that you put your quarter in.... That was our camera. Now how the hell you gonna be dancing in that little booth? (Trac 2, interview)

Even in cases where pictures have survived, they can have their own liabilities for researchers trying to reconstruct the history after the fact. Specifically, as BOM5 notes, when Latinos of African descent appear in photographs, they are often perceived as African Americans. "Puerto Ricans are dark-skinned, too. Blacker than black. That's why hip-hop gets a little confusing, too. A lot of people see the pictures and they go, 'Oh shit—this is black music only'" (BOM5, interview).

As a result of this state of affairs, innovations are often attributed to several different dancers, and dates for historical developments can vary by as much as 10 years. But even that would not necessarily be a problem. In certain cultural environments, there may be room for multiple interpretations, conflicting perspectives, and unprovable assertions. But b-boying is not one of those environments. B-boys and b-girls take their history extremely seriously, and this should not be surprising. In most cases, their place in history is all they have received in return for the years of time and energy they have invested. And a b-boy or b-girl's place in the history of the form is almost entirely based on being an innovator.

As a result, within b-boy culture, the most prominent scholars tend to be historians, such as PopMaster Fabel, Thomas "T-Bopper" Guzman-Sanchez, Alien Ness, Ken Swift, Trac 2, and Mr. Wiggles, who focus their efforts on documenting and critically evaluating claims about the origins of moves and styles (see Pabon 2006, 2007; Guzman-Sanchez 2008; Clemente 2007).[2] As dancers who were actually involved in many of the events they document, these researchers tend to be skeptical of broad historical analyses that flatten out the contributions of specific innovators and will almost always reject such narratives if they feel they are not doing justice to the individuals in question. In other words, their

PopMaster Fabel at VH1 Hip-Hop Honors, 2005. Photo by Joe Conzo.

scholarship is driven by a moral imperative—giving credit where credit is due—
that is often secondary to outside analysts. It is no accident that Fabel concludes
an essay on the origins of hip-hop culture with the words "Bound by honor and

loyalty, Jorge 'PopMaster Fabel' Pabon." He is, in essence, swearing an oath to the community to tell the truth about their lives (Pabon 2007:205).

This chapter, then, begins with an exploration of the ideologies and methodologies of b-boy history. How are the community's values reflected in the way it constructs its own history? Next, in order to get a sense of how the b-boy approach to history works in practice, I will explore a specific historical debate within the b-boy community: the relationship between uprocking and b-boying. At the same time, I also will try to integrate a more traditionally academic view of the same question as a point of comparison. Ultimately, I am suggesting that the academic world can and should more fully appreciate hip-hop's internal scholarship as a legitimate practice unto itself (this, of course, should go without saying; unfortunately, it does not).

B-boys' and b-girls' approach to history, I argue, is derived from their approach to the dance itself. Historical truth is established in the same way as dance superiority—through battling—and the same strategies, expectations, and standards apply. For instance, after obtaining a particularly significant piece of information, many b-boy researchers will actually hold it back until the moment when it can be deployed to greatest effect, much in the same way that they would wait until the right moment in a battle to throw a signature move.

Similarly, there is a great emphasis on creating objective standards by which an individual's credibility can be judged, not unlike the value that battle judges place on objectivity. One interesting example of this phenomenon is the tendency of hip-hop's internal scholars to objectify terms and titles that others may view as being subjective. The question of whether a b-boy is a "pioneer," whether a graffiti writer is "all-city" or a "king," or whether a deejay is a "grandmaster" is not a matter of opinion. They either are or they aren't. One of the major factors in b-boying's internal scholarship is the establishment of criteria for these and other terms, the evaluation of individuals according to those criteria, and the enforcement of those evaluations. "Technically speaking, is person X a b-boy pioneer?" is the kind of question that these scholars concern themselves with.

At first glance, this may seem like hairsplitting, but it is crucially important to the community because these titles, and the status they indicate, are an extremely important aspect of b-boys' and b-girls' individual identities, one that speaks directly to their credibility as sources of information. There are, similarly, accepted generational divisions for b-boys, and one's generational identity is an important aspect of how one is viewed historically. Alien Ness is emphatic about the fact that, having started b-boying later in life, he is technically a generation behind other b-boys of his age:

> Let me just make one thing clear: the only reason my name should be even in the same sentence as Kenny [Swift], [Frosty] Freeze, or [Crazy] Legs is because we're the same age. But you gotta remember, I'm a late bloomer. I'm way behind

them. . . . I'm a third-generation b-boy. I'm what we call the bandwagon clan. We jumped on the bandwagon when Rock Steady and New York City Breakers started blowing up. So that's what I consider my generation, the bandwagon clan.

This statement is interesting in two ways: first, that the generations are considered objective ("I'm a third-generation b-boy"), and, second, that he is concerned that someone might think he doesn't know where he belongs. To unjustly claim the mantle of an earlier generation would be a violation of the principles of b-boy history, and being seen as someone who does not respect b-boy ideologies would far outweigh any benefit he could get from making a manifestly false claim.

A related concern can be seen in what I refer to as the "meticulous list of names" phenomenon. When discussing any historical development in b-boying, it is typical for a dancer to carefully list every single b-boy or b-girl who was involved or could possibly be considered to have been involved. Again, this emphasizes the importance of historical memory in an oral culture. If you do not include someone in your list, you are effectively writing them out of history. And if they worked years to achieve their historical status, they would tend to take that very seriously.

Joe Austin has noted a similar phenomenon with regard to graffiti writers:

Although some writers gained skills from one or two primary teachers, most learned and borrowed from a long list that reads like the acknowledgments in a dissertation. Asked which writers influenced him, IZ THE WIZ came up with fifty-seven names "and a host of others." Responding to a similar question, FUZZ ONE listed twenty-four writers as influences. These two are in no way unusual among their peers, and the diversity of the names in these lists of influences is significant. (Austin 2001:171)

Although Austin sees this as an example of the breadth of graffiti writers' influences, it is equally an example of the extent to which writers are concerned about leaving someone off their lists. In other words, as with b-boying, the default assumption is that all writers who have influenced you at all should be included unless you have a specific rationale for *not* including them. And if they are not included, they are likely to want to know what that rationale is.

One result of the gravity with which history is treated is that most people in the community are extremely hesitant to make factual claims about events that they didn't personally witness and are distrustful of others who do so. If one is going to make a claim about history, one is necessarily giving credit to someone and—more important—taking it away from someone else. Such an act is considered very serious and requires appropriate proof. But, as I have noted, there is very little in the way of indisputable evidence for *any* historical position. So, "I was there; I saw it myself" becomes the standard against which all others are judged. When I asked Buz—one of the earliest uprockers—about the origins of one of the dance's characteristic moves, his response was instructive in this regard: "I don't think anyone could give you an answer.... Somebody must have just pulled it out.... *But I cannot say those guys did it if I didn't see them*. So, basically, you read what everyone writes and just kind of put two and two together" (Buz, interview).

This can create difficulties for younger dancers who are trying to understand the history for themselves. Although it would be considered disrespectful to question the assertions of any individual elder, the elders routinely contradict each other, thus putting the student in a fundamentally untenable position. Waaak, who is in his mid-20s, compares this process to the study of religion, not only due to the difficulty of obtaining accurate information, but also—presumably—for the sensitivities involved in doing so. "We pass on the knowledge as it's [given] to us," he says:

> And I don't take every single word I hear for the truth, either. I do my research. I try to talk with everybody. I'll write things down. I'll read them and try to see if it makes sense, you know? But unfortunately, a lot of times, you can't take the history for what it is. For the truth. It's like religion. Look at religion. Look at the bibles. Don't just read the first Testament. Don't just read one bible and think you know what's going on. Do your research. Don't only read it from the religious point of view, read it from the historians'. Read it from the scientists' as well.... Same thing with the b-boying: talk to your elders. Record the history. And research the history. (Waaak One, interview)

"It's hard," admits Trac 2. "And the reason it's hard right now is because by not being documented—because, again, we didn't have access to it—there's a lot of speculation and hearsay. That door's open for anybody to come in and say, 'Well, I was a part of this.' And, you know, unless you can prove that they wasn't, then guess what? It has a certain validity to it" (Trac 2, interview).

Thus, we have the story of b-boying: a tale whose details are crucially important to the individuals involved, but in which virtually nothing is verifiable. How did it come to be this way? Why do b-boys think about their history the way they do? And what have been the results? What kinds of historical questions do they prioritize, and which do they avoid? What, ultimately, is the goal of their histories?

Of course, b-boys' approach to their own history is rather different from that of academics, who are more concerned with general trends and the relationship of those trends to larger social and cultural developments. But even if one has different goals from those of hip-hop's internal scholars, it is certainly possible to investigate the kinds of questions that academics are interested in without violating the standards of the community. At the same time, such an approach does have its hurdles to overcome, the most obvious of which is b-boys' strong commitment to their particular version of history—and its social implications—

regardless of the extent to which it contradicts those of others. In my opinion, however, that contentiousness is not a weakness but a strength. It indicates that the power to define this community's history remains profoundly decentralized. B-boying has existed for almost four decades, and no central authority has yet emerged with the power to establish acceptable historical fact. That, to me, is a much more significant phenomenon than who was the first person to do a continuous back spin. There are those—including many within the b-boy community—who see this as a sign of disorganization, but to me it is a sign of respect for individual experience.

As I mentioned in the introduction, one way that I have attempted to merge the internal and external approaches is to base this work on my own individual experience in the New York b-boy community, while simultaneously maintaining an essentially academic outlook. The voices that have been quoted here are the voices of the people whom I met during the course of my research. They reflect the shape of my own experience as someone who was engaging with the community to learn about the dance, an experience which has run parallel to that of actual b-boys. But an unforeseen factor was soon introduced: in New York City, it is extraordinarily easy to meet legendary b-boys. They regularly attend events and, in most cases, are eager to be interviewed. At a certain point, however, this became a problem. I realized that I had interviewed a large enough number of historically significant b-boys that those whom I *didn't* interview would be conspicuous in their absence. To me, this is by far the most significant area in which my approach to representing the culture diverges from that of b-boys themselves. I am trying to understand the general conceptual approaches at work in the community, rather than proving a specific historical thesis. As a result, the credibility I seek in my consultants is based more on their being a part of a contemporary community than on their having witnessed or participated in specific historical events.

But one way that such an academic approach can productively interact with that of community scholarship is to categorize the different points of view in the community (as opposed to—or even in addition to—advocating one of them). As part of this process, we can note which facts are actually agreed upon and point out the extent to which individuals can represent different interpretations without actually contradicting each other. With that as my goal, I will spend the rest of this chapter looking at one such point of contention: the relationship between uprocking and b-boying.

All cultural practices have antecedents and precursors. But the question of where an old style ends and a new one begins is always subjective, political, and to some degree arbitrary. For those that love the old ways, new styles are merely superficial variations of existing practice. For those who love the new ways, the old styles were merely precursors to the true art. It is always a matter of interpretation, and what is at issue here is the nature of that interpretation. How can the same facts be stitched together in different ways to tell totally different stories?

In the late 1960s, Brooklyn Latinos combined African American and Latin dance styles with a confrontational attitude and a few insulting gestures to create "rocking" (also known as "uprocking"), the first modern battle dance of New York City. Sometimes, at the peak of the percussion-heavy funk records they favored, when the instruments cut out and the drums took over, dancers would even drop to the ground to perform a special class of moves called "downrock." A few years later, when black kids began throwing rebel street parties in the Bronx, DJ Kool Herc was inspired to repeat those same percussive breaks over and over again, and the dancers dropped to the ground to showcase their most devastating moves. Their dance was also called rocking, though it soon became known as b-boying, and later gained international acclaim under the name breakdancing. What I will explore in the following pages is how people think about this relationship today, why they choose certain interpretations over others, and how those choices affect their attitudes and behavior in the contemporary community. This is significant because the stakes are high. Depending on the position one takes, the issue has the potential to profoundly decenter our conception of hip-hop history. As one latter-day Brooklyn rocker told me, "If breaking comes out of uprock, then hip-hop didn't start in the Bronx."

In its simplest form, rocking is a battle dance in which two people—usually, but not always, men—square off and simultaneously taunt each other through movement.[3] Competitors make use of three general tactics: superior dance technique, insulting gestures, and mimed physical attacks. At its best, the dance actually becomes a form of sparring, in which dancers are expected to respond to each other in real time. This is an even more complicated process than it seems. Each dancer must decode the symbolic meaning of the attack, think of an appropriate response, and translate that idea into movement—all within a fraction of a second. For example, if one competitor imitates shooting a machine gun at the other, the victim must (1) understand the meaning of the gesture, (2) formulate a response (for example, catching the bullets and eating them one-by-one), and (3) actually do it without losing the flow of the dance.

Unlike b-boying, which is often performed to a medley of repeated percussion breaks, rocking is always performed to complete songs. Each record still must have a break, but in rocking, the break is only one of many parts of the musical form. Moreover, there is no time limit to a rock battle; the dancers are expected to dance through many songs, competing until one of the dancers becomes exhausted or is decisively defeated.

For most of each song, the dancers perform what is known as "freestyle" dancing, which is essentially solo dancing in the style of their choice. The goal at this point is to demonstrate stamina and to show off their personal style. This portion of the dance may use a variety of steps depending on the preference of the individual dancer; but given the dance's origins, it should not be surprising that Latin dance influences often predominate. As Pedro "Pjay71" Martinez notes, "There's a lot of those uprock songs that you could bust a Latin, total-straight-up salsa step to it, and it would work. You won't look stupid. It would totally work with it. On beat, on time, and everything" (Pedro Martinez, interview).

As the song moves forward, the dancers try to incorporate interesting song lyrics and musical figures into their body movements. Basically, to act out the words of the song. "Like in the song 'Yellow Sunshine'...if I make a motion that I'm...letting the rays of the sun shine on my face," Pjay71 explains:

> That's not a big-deal move. It's not a breakdance power move. But that's important in uprock. It's not the point if it's hard to do. You understand? Just doing it, that's the point. Knowing when it comes in the song, knowing to catch the lyric or catch that part of the song. That's, like, a big deal in uprock. (Pedro Martinez, interview)

Sometimes, during this part of the dance, rockers will use variations of that technique to openly insult their opponents, a process known as "burning." "The burns are where you, like, take the guy, cut him up, shoot him," explains Tiny Love. "You cut [off] his head, throw it up in the air, play ball with it. Play soccer with his head. Cut his guts out. There's a lot of violent movements, and those are called burns"[4] (Tiny Love, interview).

"In burning," King Uprock adds:

> we use the words. You know, if [the singer's] saying, "Huh! Hah!" you know, like you wanna maybe throw a punch, like "huh!"...What you're doing is, you're dancing, but you're looking at the audience and saying, "listen, how can I describe this music?"...By my way of dancing and showing the symbols and these gestures, you would think, "Oh, I know what he's doing: he's shooting the guy, he's got a gun." Or, "He took a guy, he stabbed him," or "He took the guy, he threw him on the floor, he's digging a hole, and he threw him in it, he covered it and he left." So that's what we do with uprocking. That's what makes a good burner. (King Uprock, interview)

As Harlem-based rocker Fabel emphasizes, the point is not simply to taunt your opponent, but to do it in a way that makes creative use of the music. "The songs in particular that have drum rolls...you can machine gun someone down on that part. Certain yells, you know, you could jump up and grab their head and pull it towards your crotch, or pretend you did. Those were the moves back then. The real sort of insulting burners, you know?" (Fabel, interview).

An essential part of being a good burner, then, is to know the songs by heart and in meticulous detail. Dancers do not know in advance which songs will be played, and a battle can easily be won by knowing a song that your opponent does not. This, in turn, provides a strong incentive to keep the repertoire very limited. When I asked Pjay how important it was that rocking be performed to certain well-known songs, his response was immediate: "It's those songs—those *are* the songs. The '60s, '70s funk songs, soul songs, those are the songs. There are no other songs" (Pedro Martinez, interview).

The songs he is referring to—"The Mexican" (Babe Ruth, 1972), "Give It Up or Turn It Loose" (James Brown, 1969), "Listen to Me" (Baby Huey, 1971), "It's Just Begun" (Jimmy Castor Bunch, 1972), "I Couldn't Believe What Happened Last Night" (Rare Earth, 1972), and a few others—have two major qualities in common: a clear mix of funk, rock, and Latin influences and percussion breaks. (It is also worth noting that most of these songs are also considered part of the b-boy canon discussed in the first chapter.) The break is particularly important, because when it comes in, the dance changes dramatically. The burns become more intense and energetic, and they are now accompanied by a movement that is known as a "jerk."

The jerk is difficult to describe, but it is essentially a four-count movement in which the dancer thrusts forward over the first two counts, then drops to a squatting position over the third and fourth. When a burn is thrown on the first or second count of a jerk (i.e., as part of the thrust), the two aspects combine to form a cycle of insult and punctuation that can be repeated indefinitely: the burn is thrown, the attacker drops to the ground as if to say "so *there*," then rises to attack again. The dropping portion of the jerk is also sometimes presented as a takedown, in the sense that it is used to suggest that the opponent is being thrown to the ground after being weakened by the burn. When two opponents do this simultaneously, the rhythm of the form is emphasized all the more. "In the middle of the song, there's usually the break," says Tiny Love. "That's when you do the jerk. You take it to the guy, and you break him down. Those are the parts most of the time when you wanna make fun of him, you know?" (Tiny Love, interview).

"The jerk in itself is supposed to set you up for your burn," explains Richard Santiago, before backtracking slightly. "But I don't wanna even say that it's *supposed* to be part of your burn, because your burn can happen at any time, even on your freestyle element. But usually in most cases, a person would definitely use the jerk and burn hand-in-hand, side-by-side" (Richard Santiago, interview).

Burns are usually thrown on the first or second count of the rhythmic cycle, drawing energy by rising from the jerk on the final beat of the previous cycle.

The crouching, in turn, is given momentum through double-time ("3–and") movements on the third beat. Not surprisingly, this is also the primary rhythm of virtually all songs that are used for uprocking. This is the same rhythm, essentially a cha-cha-cha, that is associated with b-boying and discussed in chapter 2. The association of these songs with this dance clearly serves to maintain the dance's existing rhythm and—by extension—the shape of its choreography. In other words, the rhythm of the dance is as follows:

| 1 | and | 2 | and | 3 | and | 4 | and |
|---|-----|---|-----|---|-----|---|-----|
| THROW | | | step | | step- | step | crouch |
| [burn] | | | | | [——— | jerk | ———] |

The relationship between the jerk and the break serves to maintain the relationship between the song and the dance. If there's no break, it is more difficult to jerk, and if it's more difficult to jerk, it's that much harder to uprock. "The jerk is what separates the freestyle of your song that you're listening to [from] the break portion of the song," notes Richard Santiago. "In rocking, you have your intro...the freestyle; your break, or where you execute the jerk; and back to your freestyle; and your outro" (Richard Santiago, interview).

"Where the jerk comes from, I don't know," says Buz from the crew Touch of Rock. "I look at jerks as a double stab [i.e., imitating squatting down and stabbing someone twice in rapid succession]. When they used to turn around and go down and 'ch-chu.' And it was almost like a double stab" (Buz, interview).

Santiago sees the jerk as a vestige of rocking's association with biker gangs (see below), pointing out its connection to the kind of posturing that often precedes a real fight, specifically the kind of sudden feints that are meant to intimidate an opponent:

> One thing that I gotta say about the jerks: the jerk in the rock dance is gonna be like the most vulgar, the most physical, part of the dance....The jerk is where you're actually gonna go and hit somebody. If I were to break down the jerk, it's about the point at which you're gonna actually fight against your opponent. If you look at it in the perspective of a...biker. 'Cause usually those hip movements or shoulders, those chest throw-outs, is when you're actually physically going after somebody, to hit....So that's the part that I wanna be able to see [through] the eye of a [biker]. [In] the sight of a dancer, there is no logic for that part. (Richard Santiago, interview)

The jerk is the centerpiece of the dance and is treated reverentially. There are names for different types of jerks (power jerks, soft jerks) and specific moves (bow jerk, etc.).[5] Good uprockers are expected to have a variety of different jerks in their repertoires. And the power of the movement is only multiplied when there are more than two opponents competing, which usually occurs in a formation known as the "Apache line."

The Apache line. Photo by author.

The Apache line is derived from a common gang initiation in which the candidate must run a gauntlet between two parallel rows of individuals trying to attack him, a process also known as being "jumped in." To make it to the end of the line is to pass the test. In his description of the initiation ritual of the Bronx-based Javelins, Jeff Chang describes the practice vividly: "In the middle of the wall was a graffitied genie, the symbol of passage, the end of the Apache line," he writes:

> Two rows of twenty guys stood in the way. If a kid could make it past the swinging fists and boots and chains and baseball bats to touch the genie, they could don the Javelins' colors: a denim jacket with a hand-painting of the green genie on the back, ready to be customized with letters and patches, iron crosses and swastikas, emblems of war. (Chang 2005:42)

Interestingly, according to the former president of the Bronx-based Ghetto Brothers, Benjy Melendez, a variation on this practice required the prospect to be beaten for the playing time of a 45-rpm record. "But it had to be the right record," he emphasizes, "so they would have the will to fight" (Benjy Melendez, interview). Given that gang clubhouses probably had a limited number of records on hand, it is likely that the same songs would tend to be used for both purposes, thus drawing subconscious connections between the two practices. As a result, music, dance, "the will to fight," loyalty, and personal pride could become associated with each other on several different levels. Not incidentally, the Apache line also had to be run when an individual wanted to leave the gang ("blood in, blood out," as the common saying has it). For many, this was an important step on the road from gangs to hip-hop.

In the context of rocking, there is no candidate; the two lines attack *each other*, though only symbolically. As Richard Santiago notes, participants will often change places with each other, so as to ultimately work their way through each opposing dancer before they finish, a practice that echoes the origins of the practice as an initiation rite. "The line in a gang environment is one individual walking down the line, having to defend himself against people hitting him," he says. "In the rocking line for dance, it's one dancer dancing against a whole membership clique" (Santiago, interview). It is not a coincidence that the same term, Apache line, refers to both activities. "There's so many different codes of ethics in the mythology of it, of why you're doing those things," he concludes, referring to the complex gang ideologies underlying the dance (Santiago, interview).

There is also a practical connection: opposing sides of Apache lines often represented opposing neighborhoods and thus, indirectly, actual gangs. As Buz remembers, this was a concern at the time:

Whenever you rocked against someone else, it was OK to change places but only when you were at your neighborhood or, as we say, "your house."...It was a safety issue thing! Because, back in the days, if you were in someone else's house, you needed to stay on your side because you always wanted your boys looking out for your back.

Knives were a big thing back in the days, and the art of stabbing was pretty popular. Anyway, I once saw these two guys going at it, rocking,...and one of the dancers got stabbed in the back while rocking...and no one saw that coming. After that, I kept [to] my side of the ground when I was rocking away from my neighborhood....But always kept my eyes open so when we also rocked and battled in our house, we would have a couple of our rock crew members stand on the opposite side so that they can be the eyes on the other side. (Buz, cited on www. freestylesession.com, April 5, 2007; edited by author with permission)

In the context of the Apache line, the moment when the break begins can be especially powerful. As the song builds to its peak, tensions rise as the dancers anticipate what they and their opponents will do. Suddenly, the music drops out and the drums come roaring forward. The dancers immediately interrupt their attacks to drop to a squat simultaneously on the beat, before leaping back to their feet and continuing their attacks on each other. The combination of strenuousness and rhythmic consistency represented by the jerks creates a powerful sense of organized chaos, which is precisely the point.

As wild as such moments can appear, they are in fact carefully controlled. An important part of rocking expertise, as in b-boying, is to know how to insult one's opponent without being perceived as disrespectful—a thin line, to be sure. One way to clearly cross that line is to actually touch another dancer in the heat of battle. Even coming too close would often be considered a personal affront. For this reason, as Amigo Rock recalls, rocking was actually more vicious between friends, since they could be expected to take burns in the proper spirit. "There was rocking that I saw, like in parties, where the guys used to try to really burn each other, when 'Just Begun' or whatever came on," he says. "But, you know, that was among friends, because you couldn't touch somebody's head or [come too close], because that would be disrespectful" (Amigo Rock, interview).

As Pedro "Pjay71" Martinez notes, failure to understand this principle is a major problem for those who are new to the style:

> [Beginning rockers] think they have to get to almost touching the person to uprock. Back in the days, that was—I'm telling you—that was a fight. Right there. You couldn't come that close to nobody.... They come this close, for real! Sometimes even touch! And then they just blow it off. No. It wouldn't have been blown off back then. It would have been a fight. It would have been an immediate fight. (Pedro Martinez, interview)

In this regard, rocking is the dancers' equivalent to verbal insult traditions like rap battles, mother jokes, and the dozens. The goal is to use creativity to get onlookers to laugh at your rival—without going so far that the opponent will turn to physical violence in response. "A battle back in the day was spontaneous," remembers Amigo Rock. "It was just guys bugging out.... It was hilarious. I mean, it was like a comedy show, you know? And that's how we burned" (Amigo Rock, interview). And, like the dozens, an important part of becoming an expert was developing the ability to judge exactly how far someone could be pushed before they would strike back.

In addition to its role as a source of entertainment, then, rocking encouraged the development of a variety of qualities that would be useful to its practitioners in other areas of their lives: general dance ability, knowledge of music, quick-wittedness, a sense of humor, creativity, the kind of coordination and reflexes necessary to be a good fighter, a highly refined feel for personal space, and the ability to control the boundaries of interpersonal conflict.

Rocking has antecedents in battle dances of the Spanish Caribbean, which is no surprise considering that it was created by first-generation Nuyoricans. B-boy Alien Ness (who is not a rocker, but has observed the dance for decades) specifically cites the Cuban dance tradition of rumba columbia as a precursor:

> **Alien Ness:** Rumba columbia...they messing with the drummer, and they go against each other, too. They battling the drummer. The drummer is trying to trip them up by—I don't know what it's called in English, but in Spanish, it's called *repetiando*. And *repetiando* is when you roll on the congas....The drummer is trying to trip the dancers up—

**Joe:** To make you think it's going to stop—

**Alien Ness:** Right. And the dancer's job is to keep up with that drum. And you see the dancers going at the drummer, like, "What! I *got* you beat." You know what I'm saying? They're uprocking! (Alien Ness, interview)

When one sees—or even reads descriptions of—rumba columbia, it is easy to see the parallels to rocking, particularly in its emphasis on spontaneously reacting to specific musical figures:

In [rumba] columbia the aim is perfection of form and style, interchange, bravado, and competition. As the fastest of the three types [of rumba], it displays virtuosity in rhythms, stylistic form, creativity, and musicality. It features the male dancer in all his glory and provides the forum for danced competition. Columbia is danced in a series that encourages each man to dance in virtuoso style and puts everyone in competition. The columbia dancer kinesthetically relates to the drums, especially the quinto (the highest-pitched drum) and tries to initiate rhythms or answer the riffs as if he were dancing with the drum as a partner. (Daniel 1995:69)

BOM5 feels that the dance has its roots in the mixture of African and native cultures in Puerto Rico:

It was like Indians back in the day, when they did a war dance. They would go in the circle....I felt like that's where this was coming from.... 'Cause you gotta understand almost every people, especially the Puerto Ricans, are Indians, too, you know? Not American Indians, but Indians from their own country. Our own island. And a lot of that is already inspired through music, making music. And, like they say, in Africa they had that. And so when the Africans came over to be slaves in Puerto Rico, we picked it up, too. (BOM5, interview)

According to rockers I spoke with in Brooklyn, the specific rock dance was developed in Bushwick, Brooklyn, in 1968, by two Nuyorican dancers, Rubberband and Apache. As King Uprock recalls, it began when Rubberband developed a new approach to Latin street dance and then shifted that dance from the context of neighborhood percussion jams to recorded funk music:

Rubberband used to be a great salsa dancer. So when we used to play handball in Knickerbocker Park, people used to bring their percussion instruments out. And they used to play. And when they used to play,...Rubberband, he used to do gestures. And, you know, do things where it's like salsa: if you're dancing with a girl old-school salsa,...once you let her go, she would take off! It was like she was doing her solo, and then you would do your solo. So what he used to do is to do the same thing.

He used to be like a comedian guy. Like, he used to always rank—used to joke—on you or whatever and make people laugh. So he took that same thing: what he said with his mouth, and he did it with his hands.

Like, he would describe something like…he found a rock and he shot you with a slingshot…and you kind of, like, shaked-up and you passed out or something. So he was doing it to the funk and soul music, and that's how it started getting to uprocking.

People liked what he did, and he used to go like, "Yo, I'll rock you, man, what!" "I'll burn you, what!" And that was the word: I'll *burn* you, I'll *rock* you. (King Uprock, interview)

Richard Santiago, a rocker who grew up in Williamsburg, Brooklyn, has a slightly different perspective. According to him, Apache and Rubberband refined uprock from an earlier battle dance that was done exclusively by bikers, which was much closer to actual fighting:

The whole…dance evolved from the M.C. [motorcycle club, i.e., biker] cliques.…Those were the first rockers. Now those rockers were full contact. No holds barred. "Let's rock." Boom boom boom. Down and dirty.…Full contact. I'm gonna raise my hand, hit you on the shoulder. Boom. Your turn. Boom. We're gonna go up, gonna go catch the chest. Boom.

Now, mind you, when you have all that jeans and the leather, it's not gonna hurt as much. But yet it is full contact. It wasn't [until] the development of…two individuals, Apache and Rubberband, *which are M.C. guys,* adapting to "let's make it a little bit more controlled" and [adding] the other dance influences. That's when you start having the footwork, jerks, some freestyle sections, some mambo, salsa, or disco or lindy hop added to it. That's the break-off of making this rock dance

Richard "Breakeasy" Santiago. Photo © Martha Cooper.

from a full-contact, dirty, grungy thing to a new development. To its next level. (Santiago, interview; emphasis in original)

It is not difficult to reconcile these perspectives: uprock was created at the nexus of Latin dancing, rock music, and biker horseplay by people who were deeply involved in all three. Nevertheless, the issue of rocking's origins remains controversial At a 2008 discussion of rocking sponsored by Ken Swift Productions and the Seven Gems Rock Division, for example, seven panelists—all rockers from the '70s—were each asked who invented the dance. One panelist said that, while he had no firsthand knowledge on the issue, he had heard from older dancers that it had been invented by Rubberband. The other six panelists essentially declined to answer the question.

Within the community, the significance of such questions is determined not only by the answers, but by when and where they are asked, when and where they are answered, by whom, and in what context. In addition to the problems I raised at the outset—lack of documentation, personal investment in claims of origin, conflicting loyalties, and so forth—there is also a definitional question related specifically to rocking. "What they call uprocking now is because they added something to...a freestyle dance that was created in [the] late '60s to early '70s," says Bronx b-boy Trac 2. "OK, Brooklyn started doing what's called the burns and jerks. So what they did was, by adding these two styles, [they] changed the looks of the jam"[6] (Trac 2, interview). In other words, from the Bronx perspective, Brooklyn's rock dance—the potential ancestor of Bronx b-boying—was *itself* a new version of an earlier dance which had been widely practiced across the city, including in the Bronx. So, was rocking a new dance? Or merely a distinctively Brooklyn way of doing an old dance? The answers will be purely subjective.

In any case, once in Brooklyn, the dance developed in the context of an urban Latino environment, as one of the many activities that operated in public space alongside handball, informal percussion jams, other forms of dancing, hanging out, and making fun of people. As Buz puts it, "It was basically all a Spanish neighborhood-type thing" (Buz, interview). "Most uprockers were Puerto Ricans," agrees King Uprock. "We had black people who uprocked, though. [But] most of the uprockers, 80 percent, were Puerto Ricans. Blacks, wasn't too many. Not too many. They were doing other things" (King Uprock, interview).

As Pjay notes, the physical environment of Brooklyn neighborhoods like Bushwick and East New York also contributed significantly to the way that uprocking was able to develop:

**Pjay:** You saw the older guys do it, like on corners, hanging out in front of your porch. 'Cause East New York has a lot of houses with front porches, backyards. You know, people think it's houses that don't look like ghetto houses, but they are. It was the ghetto. It was hardcore. But you had yards. You had front yards. Backyards. And so...guys would hang, you know. More opportunity to bring out your radio. You had more property than you have in other urban areas. You have guys dancing, chilling out. A lot of deejays bringing out the equipment by the window. Playing, and the people and the kids in the street would get down and start rocking, whatever. With the boomboxes. So you would see it....

Matter of fact, I was talking to my neighbors, who are bikers—outlaws—and they would play right on this corner....And they would have a live band out there and play to the wee hours of the morning.

**Joe:** You mean, back in the day.

**Pjay:** Back in the day, yeah, when there was no "quality of life"! [laughs] Ain't nobody gave a fuck! Especially down here! (Pedro Martinez, interview)

Pjay's reminiscences raise several important points about the relationship of uprock to social space. Before the so-called quality-of-life initiatives of Mayor Rudolph Giuliani's era (1994–2001) began to limit street noise in New York City, people were freer to dance publicly into the night. At the same time, Pjay is making a kind of play on words with the phrase *quality of life*. On one level, he means that there was no enforcement of quality-of-life ordinances, but at the same time he is also saying that there was no quality of life for Puerto Ricans in New York, that nobody in a position of power cared about the quality of Puerto Ricans' lives (in this case, whether they were awakened at four in the morning by bikers dancing outside their window). Rocking often featured large groups of outlaws performing a violent dance on the street in the middle of the night. This would simply not have been allowed to happen in communities with a more consistent law enforcement presence. It is an uncomfortable truth, but one that lies at the heart of many aspects of hip-hop's history: it was precisely the city's neglect of the community that allowed the dance to flourish.

Neighborhoods knew that they were responsible for their own well-being, and this inevitably drew each block closer together as a social unit. It is not surprising, then, that some of this neighborhood identity would be manifested in the culture of rocking: "It was almost like how we used to play stickball," recalls Buz, "blocks against blocks" (Buz, interview). Over 30 years later, Buz still identifies rocking crews by the blocks they were associated with:

Dynasty Rockers were from Knickerbocker and also Irving Avenue, and Touch of Rock were from Bleecker Street and Central Avenue....Disco Rockers were from Stockholm Avenue and Central Avenue....MTC [Music To Communicate] were from Evergreen Avenue and Grove Street, and Lil Dave Rockers were from Cooper Street and Knickerbocker Avenue...and Dynamic Spinners were from

Central Avenue and Troutman....So basically it was kind of representing our neighborhood. (Buz, interview)

"Back in those days, boy, there was no way you were gonna learn how to uprock or anything if you didn't know somebody," remembers Amigo Rock. "And it was very closely knit crews, man, you know? From neighborhoods. You were from 92nd, you could not join a crew from 100th Street. No matter how good you were. It was just, it was like, if you're a Mets fan, *you cannot be a Yankee*" (Amigo Rock, interview). These kinds of tensions could affect the dance on many levels. For instance, when BOM5 learned to b-boy, he couldn't tell his teachers that he already knew how to rock, because they would want to know how he had learned. He would then have had to tell them that he learned as a member of the Savage Skulls. If the teachers had ties to other street organizations or neighborhoods, this could have presented a serious problem (BOM5, interview).

Neighborhood loyalties were so strong that each area developed its own distinct style of uprocking. "When I rock, I rock for my particular segment of Williamsburg, my piece of Brooklyn, or my piece of the rock, as I like to say it," explains Richard Santiago. "My piece of the rock has always been for Williamsburg. So that's how come I favor more of a rock style or freestyle. As opposed to the jerks and burns...which is Bushwick. Here, I love style. If I can burn your style, I'll take that. I like to be smooth" (Richard Santiago, interview).

Pjay tells the story of a friend from Bushwick who started rocking at a party in East New York, only to realize that his dance style had been identified by fellow partygoers as that of a rival neighborhood. Although he immediately adjusted his movements, he was chased from the party anyway. "You know, neighborhoods used to go to neighborhoods to dance," he concludes, "but that doesn't mean they were welcome, you know what I'm saying? 'Cause in different neighborhoods, you still had the gangs. And if you won in a certain neighborhood, you would have problems. You'd have problems afterwards." One way to avoid such problems, if the situation became too dire, was to intentionally lose the battle. Another was to travel in large groups, but that approach could cause problems of its own. "If you came with a lot of people," he points out, "then they probably wouldn't even have a dance; you'd probably have a fight. Like, 'Why you comin' with all these people?'" (Pedro Martinez, interview).

In retrospect, it is not surprising that street parties and other musical events would become the venues for block-on-block conflict. Recalling his days as a gang member—before he took up dancing—Buz points out that the connection was mainly a practical one: if you had an issue with someone in a particular neighborhood but you didn't know exactly where he lived, he could usually be found at his neighborhood's parties. "Basically the reason we went to where there was music was to start trouble with people that we wanted to start trouble," he remembers, "'*cause that was where everybody was at.* And whoever we were looking for would be there.... So if... a block party would be at that turf, we would come down here ... to start with that gang. That's basically what that was" (Buz, interview).

If strength in numbers was a requirement for day-to-day living, it was a small step to formalize that group into a gang. The formality of official gang membership could actually serve to deescalate violence in many cases. It provided a leadership structure that could negotiate and make treaties between neighborhoods, it could establish standards for membership in order to bring stability and responsibility to the group itself, and it could punish its own members for misbehavior. These concepts, along with the general power of the gang, were represented through an elaborate symbolism of initiation rituals, gang vests, patches, and street protocol. And the more these things could be addressed in the symbolic arena, the less they needed to be dealt with through physical action. The rock dance, with its extensive and often violent symbolic vocabulary, was well suited to this purpose, and it quickly spread to gang members across Brooklyn and the other boroughs of New York.

As Amigo Rock recalls, "Some of my cousins that were down with [the gangs], they used to tell me that when they used to rock—gang-related rock—they used [to] do it to show the guy what they was gonna do to him. 'I'ma chop your head off.' 'I'm gonna hit you with a bat.' So that was their style" (Amigo Rock, interview). In some cases, rocking was even used like a coin toss before gang wars: the warlords of each gang would rock against each other, and the winner would then have the right to dictate the rules of the ensuing fight (Del Barco 2002).

Buz, however, disagrees with the idea of rocking as being primarily a gang dance:

> [Rocking] was what got me *away* from the gang. People say it was something related to gangs, but I didn't experience that.... I see it so different. Like, I can't see a guy who would beat the crap out of somebody with a bat and then take time to go rock. You understand? That's what I'm saying: when *I* was in gangs, you know. I don't how *they* mixed it up or whatever. But not in my time. (Buz, interview)

In its earliest years, as I have noted, the dance was simply called "rocking" or "the rock dance." As King Uprock noted, the term partially came from street terminology: to "rock" something was to demonstrate creative control over it; one could rock a microphone, rock fresh clothing, or even rock other people by dominating them in some way. "The idea of style, and competing for the best style, is the key to all forms of rocking," states a voiceover in the groundbreaking 1983 graffiti documentary *Style Wars*, which has since become a mission statement for hip-hop purists, "For the rap MC, it's rocking the mic. For the b-boys, it's rocking your body in breakdancing. Or for writers, rocking the city with your name on a train" (*Style Wars*). Buz, however, gives an alternative explanation for the term:

> The biggest question is, "well, why did we call it 'rock'?"...It's all about *bori-quas*—Puerto Rican guys—and you guys named it "rock." Why didn't you guys name it *timbales* or something, you know?...
>
> And it's very simple: the reason why they named it rock, it was because...all of the artists of all the music that we danced to...were rockers. They were all rock. (Buz, interview)

More than anything else, this explanation represents a generational rift within the Puerto Rican community in New York in the '60s and '70s. It suggests that younger Puerto Ricans, in addition to listening to the mambo and salsa of their parents, were also gravitating to the rock music that could be heard on the radio and in various public spaces. In fact, to name their dance "rock" really only makes sense if they were trying to distinguish it from something else that was *not* rock—in this case, more conventional forms of Latin music and dance. As Trac 2 notes, "Mostly Puerto Ricans did that freestyle [rock] dance. Again, because of the interpretation to the music, through their heritage, Puerto Ricans had that salsa-, mambo-type dancing, and they incorporated more or less an aggression on top. And it was called rocking because they danced to rock music" (Trac 2, interview). People who were operating entirely within a rock culture wouldn't call their dance "rock" because the term would be too general. Young Latinos, by contrast, used the term *rock* to refer to a new cultural fusion that they had created, one which combined elements of their parents' culture with those of African Americans, bikers, and white rock fans to represent the complexity of their own New York experience.

Richard Santiago, for example, recalls the musical tensions he encountered on his block in Brooklyn during the '70s:

> Here on this block, you had Puerto Ricans, you had Peruvians,[7] you had Cubans, right? You had a Latino-based group. Then you also had the *young* Cuban, Peruvian, you know? But these were Americanized. So now you had a clash between the real hardcore *bomba*, *plenero* listeners, and you had the children now, which were somewhat rebels, which we—and I—was....
>
> So now we had this clash by where the family would come in and have a barbecue and be out there [sings mambo melody]. And yet on the other side, you have someone that wants to listen to the old-school rap. You know, listening to Billy Squier, which was a rock, punk band. ESG and stuff, you know? Listening to Santana. Listening to Led Zeppelin and stuff. All this other stuff.[8] (Santiago, interview)

As the dance spread, confusion between the Latino rock dance and rock music as the culture of middle-class rebellion and hedonism was one of the reasons for the emergence of the more precise term *uprock*. Specifically, flyers for rock events tended to draw individuals expecting a rock concert rather than a dance battle. "Yeah, like heavy metal and stuff like that," confirms King Uprock. "'Cause right a couple blocks from Bushwick [Brooklyn], it becomes Queens. So in Queens, they have a lot of guys that were into rock music. And they were thinking like, 'Oh wow, they're gonna have, like, a rock band.' Meanwhile, we were talking about uprock music. They didn't understand it" (King Uprock, interview).

Buz, however, has a different explanation for the change from "rock" to "uprock," noting that the dance was also known as "Brooklyn rock" or sometimes even just "Brooklyn":

> It's just…very clear that nobody from the Bronx is gonna say, "Yo, c'mon, let's go: let's do some Brooklyn!" It's just like Brooklyn turning around and saying, "Yo, I wanna go over there and get me some nice clothes so I can look like them guys from the Bronx." No. You'd never buy that. It just don't happen. (Buz, interview)

Finally, it is clear that the term *uprock* was also intended to distinguish the upright aspects of the dance from "downrock" moves, in which the dancer stayed closer to the ground. "We did floor work, which we called downrocking," recalls King Uprock, going on to specify several moves that were later absorbed into b-boying. "The only thing we didn't do was spins. You know, we did helicopters, we did freezes" (King Uprock, interview).

The change of terminology from rock to uprock, then, represents an important moment in the life of the dance form. If a new term was needed to distinguish this dance of Brooklyn Latinos from those of proud Bronx residents, Queens rock 'n' roll fans, and people who dropped to the floor when they danced, it could only mean that the rock dance was expanding, pushing up against its boundaries. The question is, what happened next? Did uprock explode across the city in its natural form? Did it dissipate and die, to remain only as a faint echo in the style of new dances like b-boying? Or did it change itself to suit its new environment?

In principle, uprock differs from b-boying in three respects. First, uprockers dance simultaneously, while b-boys dance in alternating turns. Second, uprock is performed to whole songs while b-boys dance primarily to the breaks.[9] Finally, uprockers mainly dance "on top," in an upright position, while b-boys dance "on the bottom," in a more horizontal position.

So the question is essentially the following: in each of these three areas, are there links that would suggest a direct evolution from one to the other? If not, it would suggest that b-boying was conceived as a separate dance that later integrated some aspects of rocking into its style. If, on the other hand, there *are* connections to be found in these three realms, then it may be more useful to think in terms of a continuous history.

The first issue is complex: uprock competitors dance simultaneously, while b-boys dance in alternating turns. As Pedro "Pjay71" Martinez notes, to change from one format to the other would require overcoming significant practical obstacles, particularly when you have groups, rather than individuals, battling. "They can't be mixed," he notes, "because the rules are different.... It's a whole different ballgame" (Pedro Martinez, interview). A group uprock battle, he notes, occurs in the Apache line, a format that is designed to connect simultaneous individual battles into a larger contest. The two groups line up to face each other, and each crew member battles his counterpart on the other side until they run out of energy or are decisively defeated. At that point, the winner can rest, or substitute for one of his fellow crew members in his battle (which is occurring at the same time). Eventually, this process whittles the crews down to a single one-on-one battle, and the outcome of that contest then determines which crew wins.

A group b-boy battle, however, works totally differently. Crews face each other and send members out one at a time for solo performances directed at the entire opposing crew. After an individual performance (or set) is concluded, the opposing crew sends out a member to respond. Occasionally, a crew will substitute a choreographed routine for an individual set. In any case, performances are alternated until both crews have sent out all of their members, at which point the round is considered over. In formal competition, battles usually last for a predetermined number of rounds, while in informal situations, a battle will usually continue in this fashion until one side gives up or the crowd declares a winner. The two formats, in other words, are so different that it is difficult to see how one could evolve into the other.

In a one-on-one situation, however, the issue is murkier, and—as I just mentioned—all uprock battles eventually become one-on-one situations. When surrounded by excited onlookers, the audience for a one-on-one uprock battle can easily transform itself from an Apache line to a cypher, without even intending to. BOM5, for example, specifies that the Savage Skulls used to rock in an Apache line "in the clubhouse, one group on one side. But also, after a while when the girls start jumping in, everybody wants to watch, so it becomes a circle" (BOM5, interview).

Moreover, Buz notes that one of his uprock tactics in such situations was to actually stop dancing, in order to put pressure on his opponent:

> What I did there was that, on purpose, I would turn around and say, "If you're
> really that good, show the crowd." So the guy would dance...and I would just

stop going, I would pull out. And then he would do his stuff.... Now, I'll come in and do my stuff, and I come out. Then he'll come out for a little bit, then I'll come out different, then come back out. And he would stand there waiting. And if he doesn't come out [to dance], he's telling you, "Yo, I can't hang with you." (Buz, interview)

In other words, Buz would actually stop rocking as a show of disdain for his opponent, as a way of saying that the opponent wasn't even worthy of his competition. That such a tactic could slowly change from a one-time insult to a regular practice is not difficult to imagine.

When Amigo Rock describes his own early experiences dancing in Manhattan in 1975, the dance he describes is called uprock and focuses on burns, but is performed by dancers who alternate turns and do not do jerks. "It wasn't Brooklyn-style uprocking," he says. "[Manhattan] uprocking back in those days was just, you know, guys getting in a circle and doing burn moves. You know, grab your head, go 'uhh.' Go like this or that. No jerks involved. No jerks at all. It was mostly burn moves" (Amigo Rock, interview).

Amigo Rock demonstrates an important, though subtle, intellectual distinction here. In referring to "Brooklyn-style uprocking," he is implying that there are also legitimate non-Brooklyn styles of uprocking. This is a contention that would not have been accepted by Brooklyn uprockers at the time (there are many who *still* do not accept it). From their perspective, the non-Brooklyn styles of uprocking are not styles at all, but simply examples of people doing the dance incorrectly. This, in turn, would create a different climate when it comes to innovation. A new move is much more likely to be accepted by people who see it as an example of a new style of rocking than it is by people who see it as a mistake. Since, by definition, the former were located in the Bronx and Upper Manhattan and the latter in Brooklyn, it simply stands to reason that uptown dancers would be more open to change.

The second and third questions must be addressed together: uprockers dance primarily on top to whole songs, while b-boys dance primarily on the floor to repeated breaks. The transition from whole songs to repeated breaks—universally credited to the Bronx's DJ Kool Herc—is considered to be the birth of hip-hop. Kool Herc, in turn, attributes his innovation to dancers' preferences. "The moment when the dancers really got wild was in a song's short instrumental break, when the band would drop out and the rhythm section would get elemental," writes Jeff Chang in his groundbreaking history *Can't Stop, Won't Stop*: "Forget melody, chorus, songs—it was all about the groove, building it, keeping it going. Like a string theorist, Herc zeroed in on the fundamental vibrating loop at the heart of the record, the break" (Chang 2005:79). Noticing the dancers' attraction to the rhythm breaks of the songs he was playing, Herc decided to play two copies of the same record, in order to repeat that section for their edification.

But what exactly was it that Herc was responding to? What were the dancers actually doing on those breaks that was powerful enough to force their deejay to create a whole new culture? Herc gives a clue in the 2002 b-boy documentary *The Freshest Kids*: when discussing his decision to focus on the breaks, Herc notes that he, too, was a b-boy in the early 1970s. He then illustrates this by executing a Brooklyn-style jerk. Similarly, when Michael Holman described the history of b-boying in 1984, he began with a description of dancers he saw in Central Park in 1975 performing a move that also sounds very much like the jerk. "Their drop move was crazy fresh!" he remembers:

> I'd never seen it before. First they hopped, then stepped, then abruptly dropped to a squat with backs straight, on the snare drum note and popped back up into standing leg steps on the bass beats. Each guy had unique leg steps in between the drops, like Ali shuffles, spins, hops with one leg up then dropping down in a squat and coming up fast, all on the beat and with serious finesse. (Holman 2004:32)

So when "the dancers really got wild" in the Bronx, were they (as most academic hip-hop historians have assumed) disco dancers executing crazy moves? Or were they uprockers downrocking on the break? The more likely answer would seem to be the latter.

But let's take a step back. The transition from playing whole songs to breakbeats—from funk and disco to hip-hop—was not instantaneous. Even after Kool Herc's innovation, repeating breakbeats was usually only one of the tricks of the deejays' trade. Throughout most of the city, it was employed sparingly.

> Before, the deejays were all just playing whole songs. You know, like all those old classics like "Melting Pot" [Booker T. & the MGs, 1971] and "Expansions" [Lonnie Liston Smith, 1974] and a lot of old disco songs. In the beginning, just to get the crowd. When it was time to get jumping, when the people were hyped and into it, that's when they started bringing in the breakbeats. When the deejay said, "Oh, I got the crowd, now I'm gonna take over." You know, 'cause once you peak…you got the crowd in the palm of your hand, after that. You could do no wrong. So they would peak for four records and then bring it down again, you know? Put a slow jam like "Heartbeat" [Taana Gardner, 1981]. You know, so the crowd could take a breather, start mellowing out. And then he would start all over again. (Amigo Rock, interview)

In the '70s, a New York street deejay had to be responsive to a variety of needs. Some people wanted to uprock, while others wanted to dance with partners or socially in small groups. Some just wanted to talk. Uprocking had to fit in, and it did. As King Uprock notes:

> It was a disco era. Disco, you had funk, R&B—not R&B like now, but more the soul music. And then you had Latin music. Deejays played a little bit of

everything....Deejays would play everything for everybody. Because, you know, there was girls there, and you wanted to dance with girls. And after you dance with different girls, you want to show your talent—you went and uprocked. (King Uprock, interview)

According to Pedro "Pjay71" Martinez, some people even did both at the same time, although this was largely limited to moments when the deejay played a song that was suitable for both, such as the previously mentioned "Expansions." "I also know that you could dance with a girl and do jerks," he says:

> If a girl knew what was going on, knew about rocking, she wouldn't be offended by it. She would go with it. You could be dancing with her, like for instance, you could be dancing with her any song, let's say, what's a good song? Let's say, "Expansions." "Expansions" is like a song that, it's not hardcore. So then you could be dancing with her, then all of a sudden come with some jerks, and she'll be like, "Oh, OK," and she'll go with it. Then you can resume to dancing like you would with a girl. (Pedro Martinez, interview)

Fabel reports similar expectations in Spanish Harlem. "Even some of those breakbeat songs, we would dance with the girls until the break came," he remembers. "Well, we'll start getting away from them, 'cause we knew it was coming. A lot of us knew, when it sort of built up to a crescendo.... And they knew it, too. The girls knew when the breaks came on, what was gonna happen" (Fabel, interview).

It seems clear, then, that uprocking could operate as part of a broader social dance scene:

> **Pjay71:** A lot of uprockers were ladies' men. And uprocking brang the ladies, you understand what I'm saying? That's why, when b-boying came, a lot of them didn't want to go to the floor. Because...ladies were not attracted to that. They were attracted to the sexual freestyle dance. Like, hustle, if you look at the hustle, that's why they made a movie about it. 'Cause it's [a] very sexual, attractive-looking dance. It's like the tango. The tango is a very sexual, romantic dance.
>
> **Joe:** Plus you wouldn't mess up your clothes.
>
> **Pjay71:** Right! Of course. Yeah, because you could dress fly, look good, uprock. You know, you could do all that. (Pedro Martinez, interview)

"You could be dressed in a *tuxedo* and go off," points out King Uprock, "and the only thing you're gonna do is sweat. But you ain't gonna get dirty" (King Uprock, interview).

In retrospect, we may see certain aspects of the deejays' performance—such as the inevitable breaks medley—as being more significant than others, but the opinions of future scholars were not a motivating factor for any deejay at that time. As Amigo Rock points out, the deejay's goal was to balance the desires of the different factions of his audience in the moment, so that the crowd *as a whole* would be entertained:

> If you kept it too much toward the breaks, people would get bored and leave the park. "Man, I'm tired of this shit, man." Even though *we* would have loved it, it's not all about us.... The deejays were very hip. They tried to please everybody....
>
> Then, a couple of years later, that's when the hip-hop came in. The same scenario, guys putting up the equipment, except now they were strictly doing breakbeats. And what kept the crowd entertained now, instead of them lowering the beats, were the emcees. 'Cause back in those days, the deejay was the master; the emcee was his subordinate.... The emcee would keep the crowd entertained. Which was good, because it kept the [b-boy] circle going, with those high-energy beats. If not, they would have to bring the music down and bring the crowd back in. (Amigo Rock, interview)

The dancers' excitement over the breaks led the deejays to accentuate those sections of the songs. This new focus on breaks provided emcees with an isolated rhythm that they could rhyme over, which gave them the opportunity to develop longer and more complex rhymes. These rhymes, in turn, made the breakbeat section interesting for people who weren't dancing. The nondancers' increased interest in the breakbeat section then gave the deejay license to play more breaks, which led to more rhymes as the cycle continued. But soon this exploding breakbeat section presented the dancers themselves with an unforeseen challenge: how are you supposed to dance to a really, really long break?

For uprockers, the initial answer would have been obvious: as always, you were supposed to perform jerks. But, while dropping to the ground and immediately popping up again may be an impressive feat to perform three or four times during a 30-second break, what do you do during a *20-minute* break? It would be physically impossible for even the most aerobically fit uprocker to perform this movement repeatedly for such an extended period of time. But *not* to do it—that is, to revert to the freestyle section of the dance—would almost be an admission of defeat. So how do you dance in a way that honors the *concept* of the jerk, but which can be sustained for longer periods of time?

*You stay down.*

Uprockers looked into their repertoire to find moves that fit the bill. "We have steps that we did on the floor," notes Buz. "It was just floor moves that we would just throw once in a while, just for highlights. But that was just a highlight...on the break" (Buz, interview). But as the break got longer, these break-exclusive highlights naturally became more central to the dance. The earliest b-boys, such as Beaver, Robbie Rob, Spy, and Trac 2, focused their energy similarly:

> **Joe:** When they went down [to the floor], did they wait for the break to go down? Or did they just go down at any point?
>
> **BOM5:** Yeah, they waited for the break. (BOM5, interview)

"We would listen to the record," confirms Trac 2:

Then [a dancer] would go off on his top; then, if the beat dropped—bingo! He would go down. Right? Then we would stop it right there. After we would go down, we didn't want to toprock no more. You know, 'cause the [break] was very short. We would get up, and then we would put the needle back for the next guy. And then, on top of that, and listening to it, we'll try to incorporate something real quick before the beat ends. So that's where you get little freezes happening. (Trac 2, interview)

A transformation was occurring. In the beginning, there was the traditional uprock battle dance in which the dancer would dance freestyle to the majority of the song and then briefly engage in jerks or downrocks on the break. Then, as the breaks began to be repeated, the jerk and downrock section became longer, and the freestyle section became correspondingly shorter. Finally, when the transition was complete and the music consisted primarily of breaks, the dance would consist primarily of downrocks, framed by a brief transitional section of upright dancing at the beginning and end. Which, for all intents and purposes, is b-boying.

But extending the downrock part of the rock dance is no less revolutionary than extending the break of a record. If we consider hip-hop to be a new form of music, and not merely a new style of playing funk records, why shouldn't we consider b-boying—whose origins are, after all, directly analogous—to be a new form of dance? In other words, if we recognize that Kool Herc's innovations were more conceptual than sonic, should we not extend the same courtesy to the earliest b-boys? Simply stated, I am arguing that b-boying evolved out of uprocking in exactly the same way that hip-hop evolved out of funk. In fact, these evolutions were mutually dependent. And, just as hip-hop's emergence was based on a new way of thinking about funk records, b-boying's emergence was based on a new way of thinking about uprocking. And that new way of thinking developed in the Bronx.

"The rock being the father to the b-boy is the way I see it," says Richard Santiago:

And Bronx was blessed enough to take the intricacies of what the rock dance was doing on top and add a lot more intricate footwork on the floor. For the break. 'Cause that's what they're all about: they're about going off on the break of the record. Where the rocker would go on the jerk, the b-boy goes off on the footwork. And that's where the Bronx has mastered that. (Richard Santiago, interview)

At this point, it would seem that not only are the historical questions surrounding the origins of uprocking and its influence on b-boying almost insurmountably complex, but even the few answers that can be found are thoroughly distorted by ideology, point of view, and the vagaries of memory (we are, after all, asking

40-year-olds to remember the details of something that they did in their teens). A closer look, however, leads to a startling conclusion: the facts are not significantly in dispute.

Sometime in the late '60s, Latinos across New York began dancing to rock and soul music as if they were mambo, and they called it rocking. In Brooklyn, rockers added burns and jerks to create Brooklyn rocking, or uprock. This new, more aggressive style then spread back across the city via the gangs. As the economic and social conditions of the early '70s led Latinos into closer contact with African Americans, uprocking merged with African American dance styles. Finally, when the break was extended and hip-hop was born, uprocking transformed into b-boying. In other words, there were three basic stages to the development of the dance: the early rock dance of the '60s, which was Latino and citywide; Brooklyn rocking or uprocking, which was Latino and Brooklyn-based; and b-boying, which is black *and* Latino and Bronx-based. Within this basic framework, it is not difficult to see how three constituencies—Brooklyn Latinos, Bronx Latinos, and African Americans—could have three totally different perspectives on the history.

From the Brooklyn Latino perspective, the early citywide rocking style was merely a transitional style between mambo dancing and uprocking, and was not significant for its own sake. Uprocking, defined by the jerks and burns, was invented in—or at least primarily associated with—Brooklyn. This style then spread across the city, merged with black dance styles, and gave birth to b-boying. Thus, b-boying traces its roots to Brooklyn Latinos.

From the Bronx Latino perspective, the early citywide rocking style was the root dance that gave birth to all the others. Although it made a brief detour to Brooklyn, its home was always the Bronx, where it merged with black dance styles and evolved into b-boying. Thus, b-boying traces its roots to Bronx Latinos.

From the African American perspective, b-boying represents a confluence of Latino and African American traditions in an environment that—due to geographic, generational, social, economic, and musical forces—was predisposed to such a fusion. But did African Americans join a Latino tradition? Or did Latinos join an African American tradition? The answer depends on one's point of view. If one chooses the latter interpretation, then b-boying is a style of black dance that was influenced by uprocking. Thus, b-boying traces its roots to African Americans in the Bronx.

What I would like to emphasize here is that *all three* versions of the story are consistent with the historical facts as they are commonly understood. The points of contention have more to do with definitions, boundaries, and emphases than with factual disputes. Does uprocking begin when Latinos begin dancing to rock music, or when they add the jerks and burns? Does b-boying begin when rockers first drop to the floor, or when they stay there? Does a new dance happen when the style changes, or when a word is invented to describe a change that has long been established? Ultimately, as Buz puts it, "*No one* can give you the real history of the rock dance, because no one can tell where it blends" (Buz, interview).

The uprock debate embodies the benefits and liabilities of the b-boy approach to history. Full of mystery and apparent contradictions, it was never meant to be comprehensive. Each person has his or her own perspective, and each perspective is an important part of the overall fabric of urban dance history. If these stories resist being assimilated and smoothed over, perhaps that itself is where the significance lies. I would argue that b-boy history, like b-boying itself, *has* to be contentious. Any history that pleases everybody would—by that fact alone—lack important elements of b-boying: competition, ego, self-aggrandizement, battling. The goal of b-boy histories, like the goal of b-boying itself, is to represent yourself and your community. Is the Bronx more significant than Brooklyn? Are African Americans more important than Latinos? Is uprocking a gang dance or an anti-gang dance? It depends on where you stand, and it should.

# 8

## Conclusions

> You know why it's never gonna die, right? It's because
> it's in your essence. It's your heartbeat. It's percussion.
> That shit's natural. That's spiritual. As long as the
> spiritual side is there, this shit could die and be reborn
> again in another 20 years. A whole new generation
> who don't know the history, but they have that natural
> instinct. They have that heartbeat, and that's what's
> gonna make it survive. It's natural.
>
> So b-boying is gonna be one of our last true forms
> of hip-hop.
> —Waaak One (Breaks Kru)

B-boying developed when dancers from across the African diaspora found
themselves living together in New York City and created a new form based on
their shared sensibilities. Like twins separated at birth who have an instant relationship when they meet as adults, the descendants of enslaved Africans raised
in Puerto Rico, Jamaica, the South Bronx, and elsewhere created b-boying from
the common roots that they recognized in each other's cultures. Knowing this,
it should not be surprising that b-boying would have profound ties to the social,
cultural, spiritual, and martial traditions that preceded it. It is equally predict-
able that, almost 40 years after its birth, such a cultural practice would have
developed deep traditions of its own. So, considering that b-boying is one of
the fundamental elements of hip-hop, why do these propositions seem so radical when applied to hip-hop generally? Why—to put an even finer point on
it—does the idea of hip-hop as a deep cultural tradition seem almost laughably
pretentious? The fault is largely our own. When the images of hip-hop found in
the media are almost universally those of a pop-culture trifle, it is not enough
to simply *say* that hip-hop is a complex and sophisticated cultural tradition. We
must demonstrate it.

The idea of tradition is often floated as part of a project that seeks to invest the
apparently mundane practices of hip-hop with a legitimizing veneer of cultural
value. In many cases, however, this approach ends up detracting from hip-hop's

power due to the kind of relativism that its defenders almost always engage in. They may overreach by imputing cultural intentions that do not actually exist, or they may hedge their bets by arguing that hip-hop is valuable by virtue of being part of a larger "real" culture. But those of us who believe that hip-hop culture has value on its own terms have to demonstrate why, and that is what I have tried to do here. B-boys and b-girls are not simply people who like to spin on their heads, nor does the value of their activity derive from a postmodernist analysis of head spinning in the age of mechanical reproduction. B-boys and b-girls are people who are attracted to a practice that *they* view as complex and powerful and sophisticated and spiritual.

The music of b-boying—what I have called the b-boy canon—is also the foundation of hip-hop as a musical form. The mechanical isolation of the breaks for dance purposes created a whole new mentality about musical production. Choosing short sections of popular songs for their ability to create a danceable rhythmic pattern when repeated became the fundamental intellectual gesture of hip-hop deejaying and, eventually, the foundation of hip-hop music to the present day. In b-boying, this is viewed as a way of maintaining the social, cultural, and kinesthetic traditions of the b-boy community and, thus, the community itself. As I detailed in my previous book, a similar process is at work in hip-hop production—and is equally overlooked. The samples that form the foundation of hip-hop music draw on this same mentality and often on the same recordings. Even when samples are not used, the mentality that they have created is still central. Yet hip-hop is viewed as traditional in only the broadest possible terms and even then only in terms of its connection to other, more universally recognized cultures.

Similarly, the way b-boys preserve and transmit their culture is consistent with what can be found in other cultural traditions around the world. The concept of foundation as a core set of traditional ideas that must be mastered by individual practitioners so that they can then improvise a personal vision that is consistent with the values of the larger community is found in everything from karate to South Indian classical music. Again, this is an example of the way many elements of hip-hop culture are formally taught according to a specific philosophical scheme. And, again, we must ask why someone would expect that that *wasn't* the case.

The complexity of the b-boy aesthetic, and the amount of intellectual energy that b-boys and b-girls expend in philosophical discussion about it, is not surprising either. The fact that people in difficult circumstances would design a form of expression that allows them to make abstract statements about things that are important to them is consistent with the vast majority of artistic expression in the world. Again, why should we assume that hip-hop would be an exception? When this approach is applied to physical and conceptual space, the same holds true. The practice of battling represents a trial by fire of the b-boys' and b-girls' assumptions about themselves and their art. The attitude that b-boys exhibit toward their history is the intellectualization of this physical battle.

Ultimately, what b-boying offers is an increased consciousness of one's life options and a set of techniques for mastering them. The promise of b-boying is that, through a study of the discipline, b-boys and b-girls can exercise control over the meaning, value, and direction of their lives. This, too, is the promise of hip-hop culture: that artistic power can be ideological power and that ideological power can be the key to creating a place in the world for themselves and their community.

To return to the question I raised at the outset, this is how hip-hop critiques itself. Any form of expression that either fails to achieve this goal or—even worse—achieves it and wastes it is arguably at odds with the principles of hip-hop culture. If hip-hop reduces your options, if it pressures you to be something you're not, if it asks you to reject your own history, if it expects you to judge yourself by someone else's standards, it is violating its own most fundamental principles. The fact that b-boying not only lives by these principles but also continuously tests itself on them is the reason that so many identify so deeply with it. It is the reason that so many b-boys and b-girls view the dance as a discipline to be mastered, a history to be preserved, and a legacy to be treasured. It is the reason that Alien Ness says the following words, and the reason that I know, beyond a shadow of a doubt, that he means them:

> Man, competitive dance is *it*. It's been around for ages. B-boying is in our genes. It is in our blood. It is in our system. It has been part of our religions. Things have just been wiped out and stuff like that. But that's my religion. That's my culture. I'm a b-boy. (Alien Ness, interview)

# Notes

## Chapter 1

1. As pioneering hip-hop promoter Michael Holman observes in the b-boy documentary *The Freshest Kids*, "Rap had product. It had something they could sell. It had music, it had CDs, it had records. It had something that one could take home. [You] can't take a breaker home with you."

2. Forty-ounce bottles of malt liquor.

3. One slightly odd aspect of my fieldwork experience has been that, for the majority of the time I was conducting the research that led to this book, the traditional dynamic between the academic world and the field was reversed. I lived in New York, in "the field," and commuted to Boston to teach each week. In other words, to enter the academic world each week required a physical and emotional journey, while returning to the field was coming home. My possessions, friends, and social life were in the field, while entering the academic world required effort, planning, and an increased consciousness of the social mores of my environment. I imagine that this experience is actually quite a bit more common than is generally supposed, but it is often obscured by the fact that the vast majority of the work that's been done in this area is written to be read in the academic world, thus rendering it invisible. But I suspect, just to take one example, that almost all ethnographers feel more comfortable—more "themselves"—in the clothing that they wear in the field than in the clothing they wear at university functions.

## Chapter 2

1. Oddly, Ned Sublette quotes this exact same paragraph in his excellent discussion of the influence of Cuban music on American popular music (Sublette 2007). Sublette also points out that it was Graham—who was raised in the Bronx in the '40s and '50s and went on to become the most influential concert promoter in northern California and, later, arguably in all of rock music—who encouraged the Mexican-born blues musician Carlos

Santana to experiment with Afro-Cuban rhythms. I would add that this contributed to the popularization of the Latin rock sound that, in turn, influenced many of the musicians who created the breakbeats that became favorites of a new generation of Bronx youth, thus completing the cycle.

2. A dance circle (see chapter 5 for a more extensive discussion of the cypher).

3. Standards also serve as a measuring device for comparing soloists' abilities to those of other musicians. This is another clear similarity to b-boying.

4. Founded from the ashes of the Black Spades street gang in November 1973 by DJ Afrika Bambaataa, the Universal Zulu Nation has become the preeminent cultural organization in hip-hop, maintaining chapters around the world to the present day. Its b-boy division, the Zulu Kings, was a pioneer in b-boy style and technique and also played a central role in defining b-boying's relationship to other elements of hip-hop. For more information, see www.zulunation.com and Chang 2005.

5. Though he is best known as an emcee with the Cold Crush Brothers and as an uncredited ghostwriter of the Sugar Hill Gang's "Rappers' Delight," Grandmaster Caz is also a deejay.

6. To "go down," or shift from an upright position into one in which one's hands (or back or head) can contact the floor, is the defining act of b-boying. To go down is to formally commence a given act of b-boying.

7. Technically, this was actually a partial exception to my point. The song was a modern hip-hop song: "Made You Look" by Nas (2002). It is worth noting, however, that the song was accepted into the b-boy culture primarily because its rhythm track samples from the b-boy anthem "Apache."

8. Of course, sometimes this can be taken too far. "Honestly, sometimes it's so tiring," says b-girl KaoticBlaze:

> Because every time we go to a club, let's say, or a spot that maybe not a lot of breakers go to, but they see a breaker so the deejay will automatically think, "Boom! Put on Jimmy Castor Bunch," or whatever, "put 'Apache.'" And then, you know, you're feeling the beat, 'cause that's like a classic. "Apache," "Just Begun"—those are classic beats. But after a while, it's just like, hearing the same beats over and over again, like, for practicing, it doesn't even get you amped any more. (KaoticBlaze, interview)

9. DJ Kool Herc, a Jamaican immigrant to the United States, introduced the sound system aesthetic to the Bronx in the early 1970s, and he developed technical innovations that gave rise to hip-hop (see Hager 1984; Rose 1994; Fricke and Ahearn 2002; Chang 2005).

### Chapter 3

1. As I complete this manuscript (in 2008), hip-hop dance competitions are becoming the focus of a new wave of reality television programming. Whether this will produce significant economic opportunities for b-boys and b-girls remains to be seen.

2. The Bronx River Houses is a housing project in the Soundview neighborhood of the Bronx. It was the home of Afrika Bambaataa and the Universal Zulu Nation, which presented the jam that BOM5 speaks of.

3. In some cases, usually those in which there is a family relationship or the mentor's style is particularly prominent, the student will take on a name that is an overt tribute to the teacher, usually by taking the teacher's name and adding "Kid" or "Lil" in front.

4. This television show may well be the single most significant unacknowledged influence on New York hip-hop culture. Films like *Five Deadly Venoms* (1978), which I personally remember seeing on *Drive-In Movie*, became touchstones for future generations of hip-hop artists, in terms of attitude, physical movement, social organization, and—particularly in the case of Wu-Tang Clan—lyrical references. In my opinion, virtually every kung fu reference made by artists who grew up in the New York metropolitan area is to a large degree an expression of nostalgia for youthful Saturday afternoons spent watching these movies on television (see http://dvddrive-in.com/TV%20Guide/drivein-movie5.htm, accessed December 7, 2007).

5. The term *cypher* is an evocative one for b-boys and is discussed extensively in chapter 5. While it literally refers to the circle in which b-boys and b-girls dance, Ru is using it in a more abstract sense here, to mean, essentially, an area of expertise.

6. Not all parents were so supportive, as Alien Ness points out. "I tried it one time and almost got my ass whupped," he remembers. "'Cause we grew up poor. So for your mother to see you rolling around the floor in clothes that she spent good money—that she didn't have—on, was a problem" (Alien Ness, interview).

7. Since the '80s, many of electric boogie's most respected figures have disavowed the form entirely, arguing that, in essence, no such dance ever existed. Electric boogie, they say, was not a legitimate style but simply West Coast boogaloo-style popping performed incorrectly. The fact that people would make such a strong criticism of *their own* dance style says a lot about dancers' commitment to maintaining the authenticity of their traditions and to the communities that those traditions represent.

8. In our interview, Holman proposed a three-part distinction in which the uninitiated would refer to the dance as "breakdancing," younger dancers who were more concerned with history and culture would use the term "b-boying," but the *real* insiders would call it "breakdancing" again.

9. Section 8 refers to federal housing assistance for low-income families.

## Chapter 4

1. *Toy* is a somewhat pejorative graffiti term for a beginner.

2. After reading this section, BOM5 asked (by email, January 29, 2008) that I also include the following:

> I used to put the gang name and my name up all around the city...but not with spray paint and not as a graffiti writer....I used to tag it up with a brush and a can of paint I would steal from the super of a building, or steal it from Korvette's department store and Martin Paints. I would steal quarts and brushes...and walk around hitting up my gang....So some people used to say, "BOM was not writing graffiti then ('72)"...but I said,..."I never said I was a graffiti writer then." I didn't care about that then....I wanted to be a gangbanger like my cousin and Hollywood....I wanted to be tuff, macho, and fearless...with the deadpan look!

3. *Wildstyle* is an approach to graffiti that values style over readability. In referring to it in this way—"my wildstyle"—BOM5 is suggesting that each writer is supposed to have his or her own version of this approach, not unlike the way other visual artists may work in different media or styles. So, just as other artists may express themselves differently in charcoal or oils, a graffiti writer could have many separate styles.

4. Apparently, this was not always the case. Speaking of the early days of b-boying, Trac 2 points out:

> Back then, in order for you to determine who was a good b-boy, you would look at his sneakers. If you have [a] brand-new pair of 69 Pro-Keds or Chuck Taylor Converse, the canvas part would be ripped on the side from the concrete. The sneaker would look new at the bottom, [but] the sides of it would be torn up from the concrete. Now if somebody challenged you, you looked at his sneakers and [if] they look like he just bought 'em? Not a b-boy. Those sneakers look too freakin' new. (Trac 2, interview)

5. It is worth noting that even Buz—a strong opponent of the connection between uprocking and gangs—was himself both a gang member *and* an uprocker, though at different points in his life. Which is only to say that, at a minimum, uprocking had to fit into a social world that was dominated by gang culture, a negotiation that required a significant amount of intellectual, social, and sometimes physical energy:

> **Joe:** I think a lot of people in those situations don't get the credit for making their lives work, you know what I mean, in terms of dealing with all the different situations with the gangs and all that kind of stuff and it's . . . very strategic. To me, as someone coming in from the outside, it's very well thought out. It makes a lot of sense, and it seems like it works as a system.
>
> **Buz:** You gotta make it work, though. You gotta really dedicate yourself to making it work. I mean, when . . . I said I wanted a crew, I knew exactly [that] when I was coming in, I was gonna come in to the fact that you had to deal with the little crews that, "Oh, they think they're gonna take over the neighborhood," and stuff like that.
>
> **Joe:** So was there already a gang in the neighborhood that you had to deal with on that level?
>
> **Buz:** Yeah! Well, there was the Young Rebels . . . the Devil's Rebels was there, the Spanish Kings was there. You had the Young Kings, the Baby Kings. I was one of the Young Kings. From the Young Kings, I went into dancing. (Buz, interview)

6. Chang (2005:102) notes that street gangs—and, later, the Universal Zulu Nation, which is not a gang—"kept private 'Gestapos,' inner-core cliques of their fiercest warriors who would act as elite intelligence and battle units."

7. This reflects another area in which the dance crews modeled themselves on gangs. Most gangs, in addition to their fully initiated membership and "prospects" (probationary members), also had "junior" (approximately 12–15 years old) and "baby" (9–12 years old) divisions that were often made up of the younger siblings of members and other neighborhood youths. This gave the older members an opportunity to observe and educate prospective members before having to make a decision about whether to put them up for initiation. Junior and baby members also served important functions as spies and often carried the gang's weapons, as their youth was felt to insulate them from prosecution should they be

caught by law enforcement. What Buz indicates here is that, in addition to Touch of Rock and Another Touch of Rock, there was also a Junior Touch of Rock, consisting of younger dancers. By presenting it in this way—"we had juniors"—he is presuming that the social structures associated with gangs are transferrable to other areas of life and that anyone who would be interviewing him on this subject would understand that.

8. Occasionally, a modern b-boy will even choose to dress in old-school style: a mock-turtleneck shirt (universally referred to as a "mock neck"), Lee jeans, and canvas Chuck Taylor hightops, often capped with a Kangol hat and Cazal sunglasses. Unlike the rest of hip-hop (or American culture generally) where such a choice would be understood as ironic, b-boys accept the notion of an individual dressing up in '70s fashion as a sincere tribute to the era.

9. After our interview, Colon asked me to remove the profanity from his quotes, but since the word in question was so integral to his thought here, we agreed that it could not be removed without altering the sense of the quote, thus the striking of certain letters.

10. Following Ken Swift, many b-boys and b-girls refer to this narrative as "b-boy text." The quality of a dancer's b-boy text—or its absence altogether—is one aspect of how that dancer is to be judged. Since the dance is improvised, the text doesn't refer to specific choreography, but to the overall flow of the narrative in the moment. So the term *original b-boy text*, for example, does not refer to a specific series of traditional moves, but rather to a dancer's ability to use movement to evoke the *emotional content* of the traditional b-boy style. And each part of the form has a role to play in achieving these goals. Strangely, there is another common term, "b-boy techs," which refers to transitional moves in footwork. Since both sound extremely similar when pronounced aloud (tex' versus techs), it is often difficult to distinguish which term is being used, and they may actually blend into each other.

## Chapter 6

1. *Kata* is a Japanese martial arts term that refers to a choreographed sequence of movements designed to train the student to integrate attacks and defenses into a larger flow.

2. Obi reports that, in addition to their immediate combat value, the inverted maneuvers were significant for spiritual reasons as well. Practitioners believed in a spirit world, or *kalunga*, that was coterminous with the mundane world, but inverted relative to it. By turning upside-down, a fighter could "mirror" the spirit world, thus bringing the power of that world to bear against his opponent (Obi 2008:40).

3. This practice, common in capoeira, is also sometimes performed by b-boys and b-girls.

4. Many songs of the b-boy canon (discussed in chapter 2) also contain call-and-response sections, though this may simply be a result of the fact that they have been drawn from the African American tradition, which emphasizes that form in general. One practice that is notable, however, often occurs when James Brown's "Give It Up or Turnit a Loose" is played at b-boy events. During the break section of the song, Brown repeatedly chants,

"Clap your hands, huh! [pause] / Stomp your feet, hah! [pause]." After each command, the crowd as a whole will clap or stomp accordingly. I don't recall ever learning to do this; it's just something everyone seems to know.

5. It is interesting to note that counterclockwise motion is specified here, as that is also the conventional direction for many other circular rituals of the African diaspora, such as the ring shout. Most b-boys and b-girls tend to emphasize a counterclockwise orientation as well, although that may be the result of a more practical consideration: for most moves, this would tend to favor the right leg.

6. B-boys' and b-girls' motives are not entirely idealistic; there is also money at stake here. A prize of $2,000 is not uncommon for a major battle, and—even split five ways—this can be a substantial sum for individuals in their late teens.

### Chapter 7

1. In reference to this phenomenon, BOM5 jokes that the title of his autobiography is going to be *BOM5: More Lies*. "That way, I can continue all the lies that everybody's been talking about in hip-hop" (BOM5, interview).

2. Many b-boys and b-girls do historical research for their own interest. I am referring here to people who have both engaged in research beyond their own personal experience and produced scholarship that is accessible to the general public or at least to other b-boys and b-girls.

3. Whether this is done seriously or in jest depends on the relationship between the dancers.

4. Conventionally, when uprockers talk about burning, they speak as if the mimed attacks are real, which can be somewhat disconcerting to those unfamiliar with the convention.

5. According to Buz from Touch of Rock, this word is properly spelled as "yerk," although it is still pronounced as if it is spelled with a *j*. Initially, I assumed that this reflected the fact that the early rockers were bilingual in Spanish and English, and thus disagreed about which language's pronunciation rules should apply. A trip to the *Oxford English Dictionary*, however, revealed that not only did such a word exist, but that in addition to its primary meaning ("to draw stitches tight, to twitch, as a shoemaker in sewing"), it carried the following secondary meanings: "to pull, push, or throw with a sudden movement; to jerk," "to move (some part of the body) with a jerk or twitch; *esp.* to lash out with (the legs), as a horse," "to engage eagerly in some proceeding, to 'pitch *into*,'" and, most intriguingly, "to spring or rise suddenly." The earliest of these definitions dates to 1565. How this word made its way into the lexicon of Puerto Rican teenagers in Brooklyn without touching the rest of American society is a mystery I have yet to unravel (see http://ezproxy.library.nyu.edu:2088/cgi/entry/50289396?query_ type=word&queryword=yerk&first=1&max_to_show=10&sort_type=alpha&result_ place=2&search_id=6UUL-EhQrFK-4098&hilite=50289396).

6. Demonstrating the contentiousness of the issue, Trac 2 goes on to dispute the Brooklyn origins of the burns and jerks: "and it's crazy because Brooklyn lay claims to the burns and the jerks, and it's not even a Brooklyn style—it's a Manhattan style."

7. It is likely that Santiago mentions Peruvians because he is partially of Peruvian descent, rather than because they made up a significant portion of the Latino population of Brooklyn in the '70s.

8. The extent to which hip-hoppers drew from rock music in creating their art form is one of the great untold stories of hip-hop scholarship and points up one of the most glaringly false assumptions of many academic hip-hop scholars: that early hip-hop participants were only familiar with African American music. What are we to make of this assertion from Bronx b-boy pioneer Trac 2? "I had guys dancing to Kiss records. To *a lot* of Kiss records. You know, we used to dance to [sings "Shout It Out Loud," from Kiss's 1976 album, *Destroyer*]. You know? And we would rock to it, you know? We would rock to it because it was a rock dance. A lot of the rock groups had beats that moved us" (Trac 2, interview).

9. In thinking about whether or not there is a connection here, it is worth noting that b-boying and uprocking are performed for the most part to the same repertoire of songs; it is just that b-boying focuses on the break portion, while uprock uses the entire song.

# Bibliography

## Published Works

Allah, Father Clarence 13X. *Supreme Lessons of the Gods and Earths*, ed. God Supreme Knowledge. African American Bookstore Publications, 1993.

Almeida, Bira. *Capoeira*. Berkeley, CA: North Atlantic, 1986.

Alter, Robert. *Canon and Creativity*. New Haven, CT: Yale University Press, 2000.

Austin, Joe. *Taking the Train: How Graffiti Art Became an Urban Crisis in New York City*. New York: Columbia University Press, 2001.

Becker, Howard. *Art Worlds*. Berkeley: University of California Press, 1982.

Berliner, Paul F. *Thinking in Jazz*. Chicago: University of Chicago Press, 1994.

Bohlman, Philip V. "Epilogue: Musics and Canons." In *Disciplining Music: Musicology and Its Canons*. Edited by Katherine Bergeron and Philip V. Bohlman. Chicago: University of Chicago Press, 1992.

Browning, Barbara. *Samba: Resistance in Motion*. Bloomington: Indiana University Press, 1995.

Bourdieu, Pierre. *Outline of a Theory of Practice*. Translated by Richard Nice. Cambridge: Cambridge University Press, 1977.

Castleman, Craig. *Getting Up: Subway Graffiti in New York*. Cambridge, MA: MIT Press, 1982.

Chang, Jeff. *Can't Stop, Won't Stop*. New York: St. Martin's, 2005.

Chasteen, John Charles. *National Rhythms, African Roots*. Albuquerque: University of New Mexico Press, 2004.

Clemente, Steffan. "Misconceptions." http://www.mrwiggles.biz/misconseptions.htm, accessed November 6, 2007.

Cooper, Mabusha "Push." *Push Hip-Hop History*, vol. 1: *The Brooklyn Scene*. New York: Mabusha Cooper, 2003.

Cooper, Martha, and Henry Chalfant. *Subway Art*. New York: Holt, 1984.

Daniel, Yvonne. *Rumba*. Bloomington: Indiana University Press, 1995.

Dawson, Daniel. Comments at conference titled "Contesting Cultures: Battling Genres in the African Diaspora," Baruch College, New York, NY, May 2, 2008.

Del Barco, Mandalit. "Breakdancing." Broadcast October 14, 2002. http://www.npr.org/programs/morning/features/patc/breakdancing.

Douglas, Deborah. "Hip-hop Attitude Leads to Mayor's Downfall." http://www.sun-times.com/news/douglas/865969,CST-EDT-douglas28.article. Originally published, *Chicago Sun-Times*, March 28, 2008.

Edgar, Andrew, and Peter Sedgwick, eds. *Key Concepts in Cultural Theory*. New York: Routledge, 1999.

Elfman, Bradley. *Breakdancing*. New York: Avon, 1984.

Ellingson, Ter. "Music: Music and Religion." In *The Encyclopedia of Religion*, vol. 10. Edited by Mircea Eliade. New York: Macmillan, 1987.

Emery, Lynne Fauley. *Black Dance from 1619 to Today*. Princeton, NJ: Princeton Book Company, 1988.

Epstein, Dena J. *Sinful Tunes and Spirituals*. Chicago: University of Illinois Press, 1977.

Erskine, Noel Leo. "Rap, Reggae, and Religion: Sounds of Cultural Dissonance." In *Noise and Spirit: The Religious and Spiritual Sensibilities of Rap Music*. Edited by Anthony B. Pinn. New York: New York University Press, 2003.

Forman, Murray. *The 'Hood Comes First: Race, Space, and Place in Rap and Hip-Hop*. Hanover, NH: Wesleyan University Press, 2002.

*The Freshest Kids*. Dir. Israel. Image Entertainment, 2002, DVD.

Fricke, Jim, and Charlie Ahearn. *Yes Yes Y'all*. Cambridge, MA: Da Capo, 2002.

*From Mambo to Hip-Hop: A South Bronx Story*. Dir. Henry Chalfant. 2006, DVD.

Gabbert, Kenny [Ken Swift], and Jorge Pabon [Fabel]. "To B-Boy or Not to B-Boy." *Source* 44 (May 1993): 6.

Garcia, Bobbito. "Breakin' in the Boys' Bathroom." *Rap Pages* (September 1996).

Gaunt, Kyra Danielle. *The Games Black Girls Play: Learning the Ropes from Double Dutch to Hip-Hop*. New York: New York University Press, 2006.

George, Nelson. *Buppies, B-Boys, Baps, & Bohos: Notes on Post-Soul Black Culture*. New York: HarperCollins, 1993.

———. *Hip-Hop America*. New York: Viking, 1998.

Glasser, Ruth. *My Music Is My Flag*. Berkeley: University of California Press, 1995.

Gottschild, Brenda Dixon. "Crossroads, Continuities, and Contradictions: The Afro-Euro- Caribbean Triangle." In *Caribbean Dance from Abakua to Zouk*. Edited by Susanna Sloat. Gainesville: University Press of Florida, 2002.

Graham, Bill, and Robert Greenfield. *Bill Graham Presents: My Life Inside Rock and Out*. New York: Bantam Doubleday Dell, 1992.

Grandmaster Caz. *Throwback Breaks and Beats*. Mix CD, 2004.

Green, Thomas A. "Freeing the Afrikan Mind: The Role of Martial Arts in Contemporary African American Cultural Nationalism." In *Martial Arts in the Modern World*. Edited by Thomas A. Green and Joseph R. Svinth. Westport, CT: Praeger, 2003a.

———. "Surviving the Middle Passage: Traditional African Martial Arts in the Americas." In *Martial Arts in the Modern World*. Edited by Thomas A. Green and Joseph R. Svinth. Westport, CT: Praeger, 2003b.

Guillory, John. "Canon." In *Critical Terms for Literary Study*. Edited by Frank Lentricchia and Thomas McLaughlin. Chicago: University of Chicago Press, 1990.

———. *Cultural Capital*. Chicago: University of Chicago Press, 1993.

Hager, Steven. *Hip-Hop*. New York: St. Martin's, 1984.

Hoch, Danny. "Toward a Hip-Hop Aesthetic: A Manifesto for the Hip-Hop Arts Movement." In *Total Chaos: The Art and Aesthetics of Hip-Hop*. Edited by Jeff Chang. New York: Basic Civitas Books, 2006.

Holman, Michael. "Breaking: The History." In *That's the Joint! The Hip-Hop Studies Reader*. Edited by Murray Forman and Mark Anthony Neal. New York: Routledge, 2004.

Jenkins, Sacha, Elliott Wilson, Chairman Mao, Gabriel Alvarez, and Brent Rollins. *Ego Trip's Book of Rap Lists*. New York: St. Martin's Griffin, 1999.

Katz, Mark. *Capturing Sound: How Technology Has Changed Music*. Berkeley: University of California Press, 2004.

Keil, Charles. "The Theory of Participatory Discrepancies: A Progress Report." *Ethnomusicology* 39:1 (1995).

Keil, Charles, and Steven Feld. *Music Grooves*. Chicago: University of Chicago Press, 1994.

Keyes, Cheryl L. "At the Crossroads: Rap Music and Its African Nexus." *Ethnomusicology* 40:2 (1996).

———. *Rap Music and Street Consciousness*. Chicago: University of Illinois Press, 2004.

Kitwana, Bakari. *The Hip Hop Generation: Young Blacks and the Crisis in African-American Culture*. New York: Basic Civitas, 2002.

Krims, Adam. *Rap Music and the Poetics of Identity*. New York: Cambridge University Press, 2000.

Kugelberg, Johan. "The Humble Beginnings of Hip Hop on Wax." In *Born in the Bronx*. Edited by Johan Kugelberg. New York: Rizzoli, 2007.

Lipsitz, George. *Dangerous Crossroads*. New York: Verso, 1994.

Mezzrow, Mezz, and Bernard Wolfe. *Really the Blues*. New York: Citadel Underground, 1946/1990.

Miller, Ivor L. *Aerosol Kingdom: Subway Painters of New York City*. Jackson: University of Mississippi Press, 2002.

Miyakawa, Felicia. *Five Percenter Rap: God Hop's Music, Message, and Black Muslim Mission*. Bloomington: Indiana University Press, 2005.

Monson, Ingrid. *Saying Something: Jazz Improvisation and Interaction*. Chicago: University of Chicago Press, 1996.

Morgan, Robert P. "Rethinking Musical Culture: Canonic Reformulations in a Post-Tonal Age." In *Disciplining Music: Musicology and Its Canons*. Edited by Katherine Bergeron and Philip V. Bohlman. Chicago: University of Chicago Press, 1992.

Obi, T. J. Desch. *Fighting for Honor: The History of African Martial Art Traditions in the Atlantic World*. Columbia: University of South Carolina Press, 2008.

Pabon, Jorge "PopMaster Fabel." "Physical Graffiti: The History of Hip-Hop Dance." In *Total Chaos*. Edited by Jeff Chang. Cambridge, MA: Basic Civitas, 2006.

———. "A Picture Is Worth a Thousand Moves." In *Born in the Bronx*. Edited by Johan Kugelberg. New York: Rizzoli, 2007.

Perry, Imani. *Prophets of the Hood: Politics and Poetics in Hip Hop*. Durham, NC: Duke University Press, 2004.

Poggiali, Chris. "Drive-In Movie on Metromedia WNEW Channel 5." http://www. dvddrive-in.com/TV%20Guide/driveinmovie5.htm, accessed December 11, 2007.

Potter, Russell A. *Spectacular Vernaculars: Hip-Hop and the Politics of Postmodernism*. Albany: State University of New York Press, 1995.

Poulson-Bryant, Scott, and Smokey D. Fontaine. *What's Your Hi-Fi Q? From Prince to Puff Daddy, 30 Years of Black Music Trivia*. New York: Fireside, 2002.

Powe, Edward L. *Black Martial Arts*. Vol. 1: *Combat Games of Northern Nigeria*. Madison, WI: Dan Aiki Publications, 1994.

*Power Moves*. Breakdance.com, 2004, DVD.

Raven, Lavie. "Lesson 4: Instructions on the Effective Use of the Spray-Can." In *The Hip-Hop Education Guidebook*, vol. 1. Edited by Marcella Runell and Martha Diaz. New York: Hip-Hop Association, 2007.

Richie, Donald A. *Doing Oral History*. New York: Oxford University Press, 2003.

Rivera, Raquel Z. *New York Ricans from the Hip Hop Zone*. New York: Palgrave Macmillan, 2003.

Rose, Tricia. *Black Noise*. Hanover, NH: Wesleyan University Press, 1994.

Schloss, Joseph G. *Making Beats: The Art of Sample-Based Hip-Hop*. Hanover, NH: Wesleyan University Press, 2004.

Spradley, James R. *The Ethnographic Interview*. Fort Worth, TX: Holt, Rinehart & Winston, 1979.

Stolzoff, Norman. *Wake the Town and Tell the People*. Durham, NC: Duke University Press, 2000.

Straw, Will. "Sizing Up Record Collections: Gender and Connoisseurship in Rock Music Culture." In *Sexing the Groove*. Edited by Sheila Whitley. New York: Routledge, 1997.

*Style Wars*. Dir. Tony Silver and Henry Chalfant. Plexigroup, 1983/2003, DVD.

Sublette, Ned. "The Kingsmen and the Cha-Cha-Cha." In *Listen Again: A Momentary History of Pop Music*. Edited by Eric Weisbard. Durham, NC: Duke University Press, 2007.

Sullivan, C. J. "There's Hope for the Bronx." In *New York Calling: From Blackout to Bloomberg*. Edited by Marshall Berman and Brian Berger. London: Reaktion, 2007.

Sullivan, Jim, and Lori Calicott. *Breakdancing*. Skokie, IL: Publications International, 1984.

Swift, Ken. Interview available at http://koreanroc.com/zboard/zboard.php?id=document &page=1&page_num=10&select_arrange=headnum&desc=&sn=off&ss=on&sc=on &keyword=&no=72&category=1%3Cbr%3E, accessed March 4, 2007.

Talbot, Percy Amaury. *The People of Southern Nigeria: A Sketch of Their History, Ethnology and Languages, with an Abstract of the 1921 Census*. London: F. Cass, 1969.

Thompson, Robert Farris. *African Art in Motion*. Los Angeles: University of California Press, 1979.

———. "Hip Hop 101." In *Droppin' Science*. Edited by William Eric Perkins. Philadelphia: Temple University Press, 1996.

*Underground Dance Masters: Final History of a Forgotten Era.* Dir. Thomas "T-Bopper" Guzman-Sanchez. 2008.

Walser, Robert. "Rhythm, Rhyme and Rhetoric in the Music of Public Enemy." *Ethnomusicology* 39:2 (1995).

Watkins, William H., and Eric N. Franklin. *Breakdance!* Chicago: Contemporary, 1984.

Whitlock, Jason. "NFL Buffoons Leaving Terrible Legacy." Available at http://msn.fox-sports.com/nfl/story/7343980, accessed October 19, 2007.

## Interviews by the Author

Alien Ness aka Luis Martinez. Interview by author. Tape recording. New York, February 21, 2005.

Amigo Rock aka Ed Mercado. Interview by author. Tape recording. New York, September 3, 2006.

B-Boy Character. Interview by author. Tape recording. New York, March 25, 2005.

B-Boy Phantom. Interview by author. Tape recording. Queens, NY, January 19, 2006.

Betancourt, Robert. Interview by author. Tape recording. Queens, NY, May 18, 2005.

B-Girl Emiko aka Emiko Sugiyama. Interview by author. Tape recording. New York, March 26, 2005.

BOM5. Interview by author. New York, January 23, 2008.

Buz. Interview by author. Tape recording. Undisclosed location. January 17, 2007.

Colon, Anthony. Interview by author. Tape recording. East New York, Brooklyn, NY, December 9, 2007.

DJ DV-One. Telephone interview by author. Tape recording. Seattle, WA, September 5, 2000.

DJ E-Rok. Telephone interview by author. Tape recording. Seattle, WA, August 3, 2000.

GeoMatrix. Interview by author. Tape recording. New York, September 19, 2003.

Holman, Michael. Interview by author. Tape recording. New York, August 16, 2006.

KaoticBlaze aka Margie Flecha. Interview by author. Tape recording. New York, March 25, 2005.

Kevski. Interview by author. Tape recording. New York, January 11, 2008.

King Uprock aka Ralph Casanova. Interview by author. Tape recording. Bushwick, Brooklyn, NY, April 2, 2005.

Luna, Eddie. Interview by author. Tape recording. Queens, NY, May 18, 2005.

Martinez, Pedro, aka Pjay71. Interview by author. Tape recording. Brooklyn, NY, May 12, 2005.

Melendez, Benjamin. Telephone conversation with author, February 7, 2008.

Mr. Supreme. Telephone interview by author. Tape recording. Seattle, WA, September 30, 2000.

PopMaster Fabel aka Jorge Pabon. Telephone interview. Tape recording. New York, January 15, 2004.

Ru. Interview by author. Tape recording. New York, January 11, 2008.

Santiago, Richard, aka Breakeasy. Interview by author. Tape recording. Brooklyn, NY, January 20, 2007.

Seoulsonyk aka MiRi Park. Interview by author. Digital recording. Harlem, NY, October 2, 2007.

Swift, Ken. Interview by author. Tape recording. Brooklyn, NY, August 9, 2005.

Tiny Love. Interview by author. Tape recording. Brooklyn, NY, December 5, 2005.

Trac 2. Telephone interview by author. Tape recording, West Hartford, CT, June 18, 2008.

Waaak One. Interview by author. Tape recording. New York, June 12, 2008.

# Index

Page numbers in italics indicate pictures.